THE COUNSELLING AND PSYCHOTHERAPY RESEARCH HANDBOOK

THE COUNSELLING AND PSYCHOTHERAPY RESEARCH HANDBOOK

EDITED BY ANDREAS VOSSLER AND NAOMI MOLLER

Los Angeles | London | New Delhi
Singapore | Washington DC

Los Angeles | London | New Delhi
Singapore | Washington DC

SAGE Publications Ltd
1 Oliver's Yard
55 City Road
London EC1Y 1SP

SAGE Publications Inc.
2455 Teller Road
Thousand Oaks, California 91320

SAGE Publications India Pvt Ltd
B 1/I 1 Mohan Cooperative Industrial Area
Mathura Road
New Delhi 110 044

SAGE Publications Asia-Pacific Pte Ltd
3 Church Street
#10-04 Samsung Hub
Singapore 049483

Editor: Kate Wharton
Assistant editor: Laura Walmsley
Production editor: Rachel Burrows
Copyeditor: Sarah Bury
Proofreader: Anna Gilding
Indexer: David Rudeforth
Marketing manager: Camille Richmond
Cover design: Lisa Harper
Typeset by: C&M Digitals (P) Ltd, Chennai, India
Printed in Great Britain by Ashford Colour Press Ltd

First published 2015

Library of Congress Control Number: 2014936022

British Library Cataloguing in Publication data

A catalogue record for this book is available from the British Library

ISBN 978-1-4462-5526-1
ISBN 978-1-4462-5527-8 (pbk)

Contents

About the editors and contributors

Andreas Vossler is Director of the Foundation Degree in Counselling and Lecturer in Psychology at The Open University. He is also a Chartered Psychologist and systemic trained couple and family psychotherapist practising in relationship counselling. He is co-editor of *Understanding Counselling and Psychotherapy* (2010, Sage), and author of two German textbooks on educational and family counselling. He has published various sole- and co-authored journal articles and chapters in edited books within the areas of psychotherapy research, health psychology, psychiatry and education. He is a reviewer for several counselling and psychotherapy journals and member of the BACP Research Committee. Andreas is committed to the value of research as a means of enhancing practice.

Naomi Moller is a Lecturer in Psychology at the Open University. Previously Associate Head of Department in the Department of Social Science at the University of the West of England, Bristol, Naomi is a counselling psychologist by training. Her primary research interests are in the areas of psychotherapy research and training, with a special interest in diversity and attachment. She has published various journal articles, is a reviewer for several psychotherapy journals and is a member of the Editorial board of BACP's *Counselling and Psychotherapy Research* journal. Naomi has a deep belief in the value of research for counselling and psychotherapy practice.

Meg Barker is a Senior Lecturer in Psychology at The Open University and a practising sex and relationship therapist. Meg is the co-editor of the books *Understanding Counselling and Psychotherapy*, *Understanding Non-monogamies*, and *Safe, Sane and Consensual*. Meg also co-edits the journal *Psychology & Sexuality* with Taylor and Francis and co-organises the Critical Sexology seminar series and BiUK. Meg's research on sexualities and relationships has been published in several journals and books, culminating recently in a general audience book *Rewriting the Rules* (www.rewriting-the-rules.com). In 2013 Meg published a co-authored book on gender and sexuality for practitioners and a single-authored book on mindful therapy. Email: meg.barker@open.ac.uk

Tim Bond is an Emeritus Professor of the University of Bristol and Adjunct Professor to the University of Malta. His extensive research and publications about professional ethics include *Standards and Ethics for Counsellors in Action* (Sage). He is currently a consultant to the British Association for Counselling and Psychotherapy on professional ethics and standards and a member of the Ethics Committee for the British Psychological Society.

Virginia Braun is an Associate Professor in the School of Psychology at The University of Auckland. A feminist and critical psychologist whose research explores the intersecting areas of gender, bodies, sex/sexuality and health, her projects have included heterosex, sexual health, women's genital meanings and experiences, and female genital cosmetic surgery. Currently, she is involved in a project related to the intersections of art, scholarship and social engagement/change around pornography (with Nicola Gavey & Linda Tyler, The University of Auckland). She has an ongoing interest in qualitative research; with Victoria Clarke, she developed a theoretically-flexible approach to thematic analysis, and has recently published *Successful Qualitative Research: A practical guide for beginners* (2013, Sage). www.psych.auckland.ac.nz/uoa/virginia-braun/.

Victoria Clarke is an Associate Professor in Sexuality Studies in the Department of Psychology at the University of the West of England, Bristol, UK. Her research has focused on lesbian and gay parenting, same-sex and heterosexual relationships, sexual practices, sexualities and appearance, sexualities and higher education, and qualitative research methods. She has conducted ESRC and British Academy funded research on same-sex relationships and civil partnership. Her books include *Out in Psychology: Lesbian, gay, bisexual, trans and queer perspectives* (Wiley) with Elizabeth Peel, *LGBTQ Psychology: An introduction* (Cambridge University Press), with Sonja Ellis, Elizabeth Peel and Damien Riggs, and *Successful Qualitative Research: A practical guide for beginners* (2013, Sage), with Virginia Braun. She has developed a theoretically flexible approach to thematic analysis with Virginia Braun. Her current research interests include visible differences/disfigurements and the story completion method.

Mick Cooper is a Professor of Counselling Psychology at the University of Roehampton, London, and a practising counselling psychologist and existential psychotherapist. Mick is author and editor of a wide range of texts on person-centred, existential, and relational approaches to therapy, including *Existential Therapies* (2003, Sage), *Working at Relational Depth in Counselling and Psychotherapy* (2005, Sage, with Dave Mearns), *Pluralistic Counselling and Psychotherapy* (2011, Sage, with John McLeod), and *The Handbook of Person-centred Psychotherapy and Counselling* (2003, Palgrave, with Maureen O'Hara, Art Bohart and Peter Schmid). Mick has also led a range of research studies exploring the process and outcomes of humanistic counselling with young people, and is author of *Essential Research Findings in Counselling and Psychotherapy: The facts are friendly* (2008, Sage). Mick lives in Brighton on the south coast of England, with his partner and four children.

Mark Donati is Course Leader and Principal Lecturer on the Professional Doctorate in Counselling Psychology at London Metropolitan University and Lead Counsellor for the Brent Counselling Service. He has held a number of positions within the NHS and has extensive experience of providing research supervision to counselling psychology trainees at Masters and Doctoral level. In his clinical and training roles, he is a staunch supporter of the potential for research to enhance the therapeutic work, and the need to develop more holistic and sophisticated ways of conceptualising evidence-based practice. He has a long-standing interest in professional training and development in the psychotherapeutic professions, with a particular focus on the therapist's use of the self and reflective practice.

Linda Finlay is a practising existential integrative psychotherapist (UKCP registered) and she teaches both psychology and qualitative research methodology at The Open University. She also teaches, supervises and mentors psychotherapy students in training in institutions across Europe, including at the Scarborough Psychotherapy Institute and the New School of Psychotherapy and Counselling in the UK. She has acted as a visiting Professor for a number of universities, including contributing to the Masters of Psychotherapy course in Novi Sad, Serbia. Her particular research interest is in applying hermeneutic phenomenological, relational and reflexive approaches to exploring the lived experience of disability and trauma. She has published widely, being best known for her textbooks on psychosocial occupational therapy and qualitative research. Her two most recent books are published by Wiley and are research oriented: *Phenomenology for Therapists: Researching the lived world* and *Relational-centred Research for Psychotherapists* (co-authored with Ken Evans).

Sharon Finmark studied art and illustration at St Martins School of art in London. She worked as an illustrator for *The Guardian* and several magazines before going solo as a painter, fronting several exhibitions. She has taught at City Lit and privately, and is the author of several books on methods and techniques of drawing and painting. Sharon has been back-stage artist at the National Theatre and artist in residence for the BBC Radio 4 *Today* programme. Currently, Sharon has returned to illustration through an enthusiasm for contemporary graphic narrative and is now working on her own graphic stories.

Charles Frost is in his second year of a Doctorate in Counselling Psychology. Charles gained his BSc in Psychology in 1996 and has spent 18 years working with ChildLine, the telephone and online counselling service for children and young people. During this time he has also taught multidisciplinary teams how to use listening skills to assist with safeguarding children and families. Charles has published work on the conflict between humanism and the medical model and his Doctoral research explores the perception of the scientist-practitioner model within counselling psychology.

Elena Gil-Rodriguez is a British Psychological Society (BPS) Chartered Psychologist and a Health and Care Professions Council (HCPC) registered Counselling Psychologist. Elena is a Lecturer in Counselling at Goldsmiths College, University of London, and works in private practice. She is also a director of London IPA Training, an organisation that provides training in the qualitative methodology of Interpretative Phenomenological Analysis (IPA). Elena has spent her time since qualifying primarily working on counselling psychology Doctoral training programmes in London and is committed to the value of research as a means of enhancing practice.

Terry Hanley is the Programme Director for the Doctorate in Counselling Psychology at the University of Manchester. He is Editor of the British Psychological Society's *Counselling Psychology Review*, the lead author of *Introducing Counselling and Psychotherapy Research* (Sage) and the lead Editor of *Adolescent Counselling Psychology* (Routledge).

Clodagh Jordan is a Doctoral Counselling Psychologist in training at Trinity College, Dublin. Her clinical work includes working within the Health Service Executive, Primary Care and Child Psychology service and at the Women's Therapy Centre, Dublin, which specialises in domestic abuse. It also includes working in Adult Mental Health in a hospital setting, and within the Irish Prison Service. Her clinical and research interests include adoption, attachment, relationships, children in care and domestic abuse.

Elaine Kasket is the Research Lead for the British Psychological Society's Division of Counselling Psychology. She is a guest lecturer on the Professional Doctorate in Counselling Psychology at London Metropolitan University and a part-time visiting lecturer at Regent's College School of Psychotherapy and Counselling Psychology. Her primary research interests are topics at the interfaces between death/dying/bereavement, the digital age, and psychotherapeutic practice. She has published two articles and a book chapter on doing research in counselling psychology, and she supervises numerous students in their Masters- and Doctoral-level research projects.

John McLeod holds professorial positions at the University of Abertay, Scotland, and the University of Oslo, Norway. He has published widely in the field of counselling and psychotherapy, and is the author of *Case Study Research in Counselling and Psychotherapy* (2010, Sage), *An Introduction to Counselling* (5th edn, 2013, Open University Press) and *An Introduction to Research in Counselling and Psychotherapy* (2013, Sage).

Julia McLeod is a Lecturer in Counselling at the University of Abertay. She is interested in the role of counselling in enabling people to come to terms with long-term health conditions, the process and outcome of training in integrative therapy, and the development of methods of systematic case study inquiry. She is co-author, with John McLeod, of *Counselling Skills* (2011, Open University Press), and *Personal Development: A practical guide for counsellors, psychotherapists and mental health practitioners* (2013, Open University Press).

Nicola Rance is a postgraduate student in the final stages of completing a Professional Doctorate in Counselling Psychology. She has publications in eating disorders, fibromyalgia and personal development groups, and her thesis explores female eating disorder clients' beliefs about a female therapist's weight/shape, relationship with food and with their own body. As a relational psychologist she works integratively with adults, couples, families and groups, seeking at all times to develop meaningful relationships which empower her clients.

Paul Redford is a Chartered Psychologist and Senior Lecturer at the University of the West of England in Bristol, UK. He has taught research methods and statistics for more than ten years at both undergraduate and postgraduate levels, specialising in quantitative analysis and psychometrics. He is the Associate Editor for methods for *The Psychologist* magazine. He also specialises in teaching work psychology. His research has covered a wide range of areas, including teaching and learning, cross-cultural psychology and psychological measurement within organisations.

Andrew Reeves is a BACP Senior Accredited Counsellor/Psychotherapist and a freelance trainer, consultant and writer. He is co-editor, with Windy Dryden, of *Key Issues for Counselling in Action* (2nd edition, 2008, Sage); author of *Counselling Suicidal Clients* (2010, Sage), *An Introduction to Counselling and Psychotherapy: From theory to practice* (2013, Sage), and *Challenges in Counselling: Self-harm* (2013, Hodder Education); and co-editor, with Windy Dryden, of the forthcoming 6th edition of *Handbook of Individual Therapy*. He has published widely on suicide and self-harm. He recently stepped down as Editor of BACP's *Counselling and Psychotherapy Research* journal.

Harriet Smith is in the final year of her Doctorate in Counselling Psychology. She combines study with work as a High Intensity Therapist and freelance writer. Harriet has a Masters in Science Communication from Imperial College London and has worked in the media for over ten years before re-training as a Counselling Psychologist. She is passionate about understanding and communicating the multifaceted nature of relationships, from social media to family stories. Her research focuses on the process of change in family therapy seen from the perspective of both clients and therapists.

Brian Sreenan is in his final year of his Doctorate in Counselling Psychology. He has enjoyed a brief career as a secondary school teacher in Ireland before switching his attention to psychology. For the last two years Brian has been the Training Route representative on the Division of Counselling Psychology BPS committee. His final-year research project is a mixed method study looking at the importance of the therapeutic relationship in Increasing Access to Psychological Therapies (IAPT) services.

Peter Stratton is Emeritus Professor of Family Therapy at the University of Leeds and Chair of the Research Faculty of the United Kingdom Council for Psychotherapy (UKCP). He is also Joint Editor of *Human Systems*, Chair of the European Family Therapy Association Research Committee, Academic and Research Development Officer for the Association for Family Therapy, and Managing Director of The Psychology Business. Peter enjoys engaging with statutory processes that affect the provision of psychotherapy and offers workshops on research to improve therapy practice; humour and creativity in therapy; measuring and improving outcomes; active reflective learning in training. His research activities include the Systemic Clinical Outcome and Routine Evaluation (SCORE) outcome measure for families in therapy; attributional analyses of family causal beliefs and blaming; attitudes to terrorism; and fostering practitioner research networks.

Mhairi Thurston is a Lecturer in Counselling at University of Abertay Dundee. She is interested in the social and emotional effects of sight loss. She is a member of the Scottish Vision Strategy Advisory Group, the Scottish Cross Party Advisory Group on Vision Impairment and she is Chair of the Vision Impairment Network for Counselling and Emotional Support (VINCE). Mhairi is currently part of a team working on developing a practice model of counselling for people whose lives have been affected by sight loss, using systematic case study research.

Ladislav Timulak is an Associate Professor in Counselling Psychology at Trinity College Dublin. He is Course Director of the TCD's Doctorate in Counselling Psychology. Ladislav is involved in the training of counselling psychologists and various psychotherapy trainings as well. Laco is both an academic and practitioner. Apart from studying and working in his native Slovakia, he has also international research experience at academic clinical psychology departments in Belgium and the United States. His main research interest is psychotherapy research, particularly the development of emotion-focused therapy. He is currently developing this form of therapy for generalised anxiety disorder. He has written four books, over 60 peer-reviewed papers and chapters in both his native language, Slovak, and in English. His most recent books include *Research in Psychotherapy and Counselling* (2008, Sage) and *Developing Your Counselling and Psychotherapy Skills and Practice* (2011, Sage). He serves on various editorial boards and is Co-Editor-in-Chief of *Counselling Psychology Quarterly*. He maintains a part-time private practice.

Elspeth Twigg started her research career at the Psychological Therapies Research Centre at the University of Leeds, initially working on the Leeds Depression Project before moving across to work on the newly-developed CORE System. Elspeth remained at PTRC for almost ten years, until it closed in 2008. Following the Centre's closure she spent two years working as a freelance Research Consultant, specialising in data analysis and statistics and working on various research projects, before being employed as Research Lead at CORE Information Management Systems (CORE IMS), where she worked until early 2014. Currently, Elspeth is working once again as an Independent Research Consultant and Data Analyst. Elspeth's particular area of interest is outcome measurement and she has worked with both CORE System data and other outcome measures. Elspeth was responsible for the development of the YP-CORE outcome measure as part of her MSc in Applied Statistics and continues to be involved in work relating to the measure, which is widely used both within the UK and internationally. Alongside her academic publications she has produced in-house 'occasional papers' on data analysis and interpretation, sector-specific benchmarks on KPIs for CORE data and case studies on best practice in outcome measurement. Elspeth has also worked on large-scale data analysis and reporting for services nationally and internationally.

Kasia Wilk is a trainee Counselling Psychologist undergoing Professional Doctorate training at the University of Manchester. Her clinical work includes working in a private therapy centre with adults and within the NHS Primary Care Trust. She is currently creating a specialised counselling service for international students in partnership with the University of Manchester Counselling Service and the International Society. Her research interests include cultural and diversity issues within counselling psychology, implementation of cross-cultural understanding among diverse populations, integration of spirituality in therapy, and the pluralistic philosophy.

Preface

Hello and welcome to *The Counselling and Psychotherapy Research Handbook*!

We are Hope and Harry, both counselling and psychotherapy trainees, and this is our dog, Toto. As you can see, we are ready to start our big research journey – why don't you come with us?

We are both planning to do a research project – a prospect we are curious and excited as well as a bit scared about. We can't wait to see everything that we will discover together, all the adventures we will have on the way, but we are also kind of hoping that our journey into 'The Counselling and Psychotherapy Research World' will not be too frightening or tiring. We are also rather hoping we don't get lost along the way. Luckily we have this *Handbook* to bring along with us.

The *Handbook* will be our travel guide on our research journey, just as we are hoping it will be yours. It has been edited by Andreas Vossler and Naomi Moller, both of whom have a deep belief in the value of research for counselling and psychotherapy practice. Andreas and Naomi have brought together a group of leading and experienced 'research travellers' to share their knowledge and expertise on the different stages and aspects of a research endeavour. Oh, and they have also asked Sharon Finmark to draw pictures of our adventures and discoveries in each episode of our voyage into the research world – so you can see and follow us on our research journey in every chapter of the book!

The *Handbook* provides you with a comprehensive introduction to research process and methods within counselling and psychotherapy. It is designed as a

'Hello and welcome to our research journey!'

one-stop-shop for trainees and practitioners with little or no prior training in the area, but should still be of value if you are already a bit more familiar with research and research methods. The book takes you step by step through the research process, providing you with enough applied knowledge on selected methodologies to help you to understand research, and to support you with your own research projects. It is organised in four parts:

Part I ('**Introduction**') sets the scene at the beginning of our research journey, highlighting the increasing emphasis on research in counselling and psychotherapy (Chapter 1) alongside the often ambivalent attitudes to and meanings associated with research within counselling and psychotherapy (Chapter 2). This part will also help you to understand why it is necessary and beneficial for counsellors and psychotherapists to engage with research about their practice.

Part II ('Beginning the research journey') covers the different stages in the first part of a research journey in very practical terms. Starting with a chapter that guides you through the process of forming a researchable question (Chapter 3), this part includes chapters on how to read and understand research (Chapter 4) and how to do a review of the research literature (Chapter 5). Chapter 6 introduces different research paradigms and gives an overview of quantitative and qualitative research methodologies. Chapter 7 illustrates how knowledge about methodologies and methods helps to guide decisions about the best design, method and sampling strategy for a research project. Chapter 8 discusses ethical issues relevant in doing counselling and psychotherapy research, and the last chapter of this part (Chapter 9) gives guidance on how to write and put together a proposal for a research project.

Part III ('Methodologies and methods for doing research') provides a more detailed overview of psychological research methodologies (quantitative and qualitative) together with an introduction to the quantitative and qualitative research methods most relevant for research in counselling and psychotherapy. The section begins with a chapter on quantitative methods (Chapter 10), the methods that most shape funding and hence access to counselling and psychotherapy. The chapter on qualitative methods (Chapter 12) introduces the main qualitative approaches and argues for increased methodological sophistication in the field. Chapter 14 covers case studies methodologies, the oldest method used to explore therapy, allowing trainees and practitioners to use an empirical lens to explore their own practice. Part 3 also includes three hands-on 'how-to-do' chapters with detailed instruction on how to do t-tests (Chapter 11), thematic analysis (Chapter 13) and adjudicated single case studies (Chapter 15) – all eminently practical guides designed to help trainees and practitioners to embark on analysis of their own data.

Part IV ('Completing the research journey') covers the writing up and presentation of the results of research (Chapter 16), while the next chapter (Chapter 17) has 'top tips' from a group of trainees about what they found helped them to successfully navigate a research journey. The last chapter (Chapter 18) discusses the next steps – how to use and build upon research in a professional context.

To help you to get the most out of it, this 'research travel guide' is written in an accessible and engaging style, with lots of activities for you to try things out yourself and 'pauses for reflection' to encourage you to ponder the material before moving on. Every chapter ends with signposts to further relevant readings and materials so that you can further extend your understanding. We encourage you to engage with the material in the book, because the more you do, the more you will learn about research and research methods and the more beneficial it will be for your own research journey.

Oh, and before we forget, Andreas and Naomi have asked us to say a heartfelt 'thank you' to all the people who have helped to put this book together. Kate Wharton and Laura Walmsley at Sage have been both supportive and very patient with them. All of the chapter authors are owed a huge debt of gratitude – it is because of you we find our way out of the mist, do not drown, and avoid becoming tiger chow. We also personally want to thank Thierry Chessum for encouraging Andreas and Naomi to think about having a graphic narrative in the book (this means us and Toto!) and for making the contact with Sharon. And of course, many thanks to the real Hope and Harry (Naomi's niece and nephew) who lent us their names – very kind of them.

So now, please put on your rucksacks, lace your walking boots, brace your shoulders... and let's get cracking on our journey into the world of counselling and psychotherapy research!

PART I
Introduction

ONE

Setting the scene: Why research matters

Dr Andreas Vossler (Open University),
Dr Naomi Moller (Open University) &
Prof. Mick Cooper (University of Roehampton)

Introduction – towards a more research-oriented profession

At the beginning of this book you might wonder why there is a need for a whole handbook on research in counselling and psychotherapy, or more generally, why research matters so much in a field full of engaged and skilled trainees and practitioners focused on their work with clients in the therapy room. Both can be seen and understood in the context of a remarkable shift towards a more research-oriented profession in the field of counselling and psychotherapy in recent years (see, for example, Rowan, 2001), with a dramatic rise in the importance attributed to research evidence. Where once this was a relatively neglected backwater of the field, research findings are now an increasingly important factor in decisions about which forms of counselling and psychotherapy, as well as which services and practitioners, get funded (Cooper, 2010). For example, therapists who work within the Improving Access to Psychological Therapies (IAPT) programme in the UK are required to offer *only* those psychological therapies for clients with depression and anxiety that are empirically supported and endorsed by the guidelines of the National Institute for Health and Clinical Excellence (NICE). NICE provides guidance based on the best available evidence, not only for counselling and psychotherapy, but also for other health and social care professionals (there are, for example, NICE treatment guidelines for physical ailments such as diabetes).

However, it is not enough today for practitioners to be able to cite research evidence that the approach they are taking with their clients is effective. Within the National Health Service (NHS) and other professional settings practitioners are now under growing pressure to demonstrate *both* research awareness and competence. They are expected to be aware of a range of research methodologies, and to be able to evaluate research and other evidence to inform their own practice. In other words, there is an increasing assumption that counsellors and psychotherapists will be both consumers and producers of research (Stratton, 2007). As such, the move towards a more research-oriented profession has led to mounting pressure on counsellor and psychotherapy training programmes to incorporate research competencies and skills into their curricula, with the future of the profession seen as depending on the successful education of research-savvy practitioners (Wheeler & Elliott, 2008). The United Kingdom Council for Psychotherapy (UKCP), the main accreditation agency for psychotherapists, released new Standards of Education and Training in 2012. These standards require trainees to develop an ability to critically evaluate research reports and findings, and to understand basic research techniques to investigate and evaluate psychotherapeutic interventions (UKCP, 2012). Correspondingly, the British Association for Counselling and Psychotherapy (BACP), as the chief accreditation body nationally for counsellors, has also made research a required component of training ('Gold Book', released in 2009). BACP training standards require training programmes to be research-informed and students not only to develop a broad critical understanding of research findings, but also basic competencies in small-scale research projects (BACP, 2009).

In this introductory chapter we will explore the reasons behind the increased emphasis placed on research and the corresponding move towards a more research-oriented profession. We will discuss why counsellors and psychotherapists should engage with research about what they are doing, and we will help you to understand why research really matters in counselling and psychotherapy. The chapter will set the scene for this book – and we hope it will infect you with enthusiasm for the journey through both the book and your own research.

Activity 1.1   Reasons for being engaged with research

Why should counsellors and psychotherapists engage with research? Spend 10 minutes writing a list of reasons why you think it is important for trainees and practitioners either to be informed about research or to be doing research themselves.

Comment

It will be helpful to revisit and update your list of reasons throughout the book. This will help you see if you can identify other/different motivations to engage with research, and develop a feeling for your personal objectives in relation to research.

Evidence-based practice and practice-based evidence

The increasing influence of science in all areas of our life over the last century (see also Chapter 2) is undoubtedly a major driving force behind the push for empirical proof of the value of counselling and psychotherapy. In our days, it is not enough anymore for counsellors and psychotherapists to say to policy-makers, commissioning agencies and clients, 'Oh, we know that what we are doing is helpful for our clients, so please give us your money for our service'. And you will probably agree that it shouldn't be enough, given that a snake-oil salesman in the Wild West would have said exactly the same when praising the health-promoting effects of his fraudulent goods.

'I know he SAYS he can do all that stuff but where is the PROOF?'

Today, funding bodies – from government agencies, health providers, employers to private individuals – are more like critical consumers. To justify their expenditures they want to see concrete evidence for the service they are buying into. In this 'evidence-based' world (Cooper, 2011), practitioners and service providers are now required to prove the beneficial effects of their work with reliable evidence derived from rigorously conducted research. In this context, there are fears that those therapeutic approaches and modalities without supporting empirical evidence 'may soon find themselves permanently outside the health care system' (Wheeler & Elliott, 2008, p. 133).

When critically considering what is seen as evidence that a particular therapeutic approach 'works', it is useful to understand something about the historical development of the current perspective on 'evidence-based practice' (EBP). The EBP movement emerged in the 1980s and has since been strongly promoted in the NHS context in the UK. It originated in the practice of medicine and can, in theory, be applied to almost any aspect of health care (Bower, 2003). As defined by the American Psychological Association, evidence-based psychological practice is concerned with the 'integration of the best available research with clinical expertise in the context of patient characteristics, culture, and preferences' (APA, 2006, p. 273). In evidence-based practice in counselling and psychotherapy, all therapeutic work should be informed by and based on empirical evidence produced by rigorous scientific studies. As a treatment is only considered as effective if there is sound evidence from multiple, reliable sources, the EBP framework has been the driving force for numerous research studies, which aim to establish an evidence base for psychological therapies (Barkham & Mellor-Clark, 2003).

It is important to be aware that the medical understanding implicit in the EBP model means that certain types of research are seen as 'better' than others. The research design that is prioritised within the EBP movement is the randomised controlled trial (RCT), often seen as the 'gold standard' method to investigate the efficacy of a treatment or intervention in outcome research ('Does a treatment work?'). RCTs are credited with the ability to identify the 'potency of an intervention, as assessed under highly controlled conditions' (efficacy) (Bower, 2003, p. 320) in an objective and reliable manner (National Collaborating Centre for Mental Health, 2009). This is the reason why clinical guideline groups, such as NICE and SIGN (Scottish Intercollegiate Guidelines Network), tend to base their clinical recommendations on RCT evidence rather than on alternative sources of information, such as other types of research design, routine outcome data or clinical experience (Grimes & Schulz, 2002). Basically, an RCT is a research experiment in which participants are allocated to two or more different groups or 'conditions' – usually a particular treatment (e.g. cognitive behavioural therapy) versus another treatment (e.g. humanistic therapy) and/or a no treatment group (waiting list, placebo). Information box 1.1 provides more details on this kind of research design adopted from medical and pharmaceutical science as it is typically operationalised in counselling and psychotherapy research.

Information box 1.1   Randomised controlled trials

You have a client who you believe has benefitted from therapy – your evidence is the difference in some measure of client functioning before and after therapy. However, with only pre- and post-therapy measures it is not possible to prove that any improvement in symptom levels and other outcome criteria are due to the received treatment. For instance, it might be that the psychological problems simply improved over time, entirely without any impact from the counselling you provided (Eysenck (1957) referred to this as 'spontaneous remission'). Alternatively, other factors outside therapy might have been responsible for the changes measured (e.g. the client got a new job or fell in love). In fact, if you want to show that counselling or psychotherapy is responsible for a desired effect (in other words, that the intervention is 'efficacious'), what you need to do is to compare changes in two clients groups: clients who have undergone therapy (the treatment group) with individuals who have not undergone therapy (a 'control group'). If you find more change in the treatment group compared to the control group at the end of the intervention, then you can be fairly certain that it is the treatment they have received that is responsible for the changes, and not any other factors. The data that goes into the statistical analysis in this kind of quantitative research is typically client ratings of their symptomology before and after treatment.

There are some basic principles in planning and conducting RCTs aimed at minimising or controlling possible influences on client improvement other than the therapeutic intervention(s) being studied. This is to ensure that any outcome differences between the conditions can be attributed to the therapy effect only.

Randomisation

If you are comparing groups in an RCT, it is important that they are as similar as possible (e.g. on average, equally depressed) so that any difference you find is due to the intervention (treatment/no treatment) and not to group differences. Hence, in RCTs, participants are allocated randomly to the different conditions. While it is acknowledged that some differences will inevitably exist between the groups, randomisation is still seen as the best method in ensuring that these differences between the groups are minimal.

(Continued)

(Continued)

Homogenisation of samples

RCTs are usually highly selective in recruiting their participants. Potential participants are screened to maximise homogeneity of diagnosis (e.g. only unipolar depression) and minimise co-occurring (comorbid) conditions (e.g. depression and anxiety) that could increase variability of the response to the treatment (Westen, Novotny & Thompson-Brenner, 2004).

Manualisation of treatment

The involved practitioners are supposed to deliver the counselling or psychotherapy intervention following a particular 'manual' of practice (i.e. a therapy manual with specific prescriptions or general practice guidelines). Sessions are usually recorded and assessed for 'adherence' to ensure that the therapy is delivered according to the manual. All this is done to avoid, as much as possible, variation between therapists so that all participants in a particular group receive exactly the same intervention/treatment. It also makes it less likely that any differences are due to the therapists rather than the treatment being studied.

PAUSE FOR REFLECTION

How do you feel about RCTs and the evidence they produce? Is this a suitable research methodology for something as complex as counselling and psychotherapy? What do you think are potential pros and cons of RCTs in this context?

Evidence-based practice and research with the RCT methodology has certainly helped to build a body of practice that promotes the adaption of proven interventions in everyday practice (Bower & Gilbody, 2010), giving a clear statement of all scientific evidence to date in different clinical areas. However, one thing to keep in mind when reading this book and going on your own research journey is that every research methodology has its weaknesses and limitations, and RCTs are no different in this respect. In fact, due to the reification of RCTs as the 'gold standard' in counselling and psychotherapy research, there has been rigorous debate about their positives and negatives (see, for example, Cooper, 2011; Rawlins, 2008; Schmitt Freire, 2006; Westen et al., 2004). There is not space here to rehearse all of the arguments made, but the main problem associated with the application of RCT methodology is that the kind of therapy carried out in these studies can bear little relationship to the real world of therapeutic practice (e.g. McLeod, 2013). For example, due to strict inclusion criteria (e.g. if the research is focused on depression, researchers will exclude clients with comorbid conditions such as anxiety), the client samples used in these studies are often not representative of clients seen in real-world settings. The closely controlled design, with its adherence to a treatment manual, also undervalues factors which have been shown to influence therapy outcome in practice settings, such as the personality and competence of the therapist (Baldwin & Imel, 2013), client motivation (Bohart & Greaves Wade, 2013) and the strength of the therapeutic relationship (Norcross, 2011). In addition, the symptom-focused outcome measures that are used in RCT research are not able to capture some perspectives on therapy outcome relevant in real-world settings, such as client experiences and satisfaction (e.g. Elliott & Williams, 2003). It is therefore no surprise that many practitioners are sceptical about this kind of research; they feel that manualised therapy in a controlled, experimental RCT setting is not mirroring the 'messiness' of their everyday therapeutic practice, and they are generally reluctant to engage with RCT methods (e.g. Rogers, Maidman & House, 2011; Storr, 2011). Another problem is that conducting an RCT is quite expensive and time-consuming, making it impossible to finance this kind of study on all potential treatments and client groups (McLeod, 2013).

In reaction to the weaknesses and limitations associated with the EBP paradigm, an alternative yet complementary programme of research has emerged in the last two decades – the 'practice-based evidence' movement (PBE). This also mainly quantitative approach is rooted in practice settings (e.g. UK primary care setting) and aims to collect data by implementing routine data collection procedures with standardised measurement and evaluation systems – in other words, systematically collecting data from all clients in a setting so as to enable research into the effectiveness of the counselling conducted in that setting. An UK example of such a measurement system is the Clinical Outcomes in Routine Evaluation – Outcome Measure (CORE-OM) (Mellor-Clark, Connell, Barkham & Cummins, 2001). Data can be collected before and after counselling, at intervals through the therapy or session-by-session, and there is usually no control over sample or service provision (all clients and practitioners are included and no particular treatment model is prescribed). Data from various sites can be pooled together to build an evidence-base on the provision of counselling and psychotherapy in routine practice (Barkham, Hardy & Mellor-Clark, 2010). Large, practice-based data sets were, for example, collected in the context of both the CORE (National Dataset) and IAPT initiatives, and the analysis of this data found substantial pre-treatment to post-treatment improvements independent of the treatment approach (Stiles, Barkham, Mellor-Clark & Connell, 2008). This type of research is clearly important politically as it potentially allows some therapeutic approaches which do not have strong evidence from RCTs to demonstrate that they are effective in actual practice.

The aspiration with the PBE movement is to integrate research with practice and 'reprivilege the role of the practitioner as a central focus and participant in research activity' (Castonguay, Barkham, Lutz & McAleavey, 2013, p. 98). For this reason the PBE approach is very relevant for this book and more information on the PBE approach and the methods and procedures to collect practice-based evidence from real-life settings can be found in Chapter 10 on 'Quantitative Methods' and Chapter 18, 'Next Steps'.

Despite the tensions between the paradigms of evidence-based practice and practice-based evidence (Nathan, Stuart & Dolan, 2000), both types of research have the potential to complement each other (Barkham & Mellor-Clark, 2000). EBP takes a 'top-down' approach in researching the *efficacy* of an intervention under 'ideal' controlled conditions, and findings from these studies inform national treatment guidelines for practitioners. PBE follows a 'bottom-up' approach in monitoring the *effectiveness* of counselling and psychotherapy in everyday practice and routine, clinical contexts. Neither paradigm alone is sufficient to build a robust knowledge base for the counselling and psychotherapy profession (Barkham & Margison, 2007). As well as knowing what difference therapy *can* make (its efficacy), it is also important to establish what *actual* difference it makes (its effectiveness). Hence, both types of research are needed to enhance and develop the practice of counsellors and psychotherapists and to demonstrate the value of their work.

Beyond outcome research

Both traditions of research discussed thus far focus on the *outcome* of therapy. However, an important strand of counselling and psychotherapy research concerns *process* research, research that focuses on *how* therapy works rather than whether or not it does (McLeod, 2010a). Furthermore, both EBP and PBE typically use quantitative data and involve statistical analysis to draw their conclusions. But there is a growing and important body of qualitative research in the counselling and psychotherapy field (McLeod, 2013). In addition, the focus of quantitative research is *nomothetic*, which generalises from groups of individuals to the broader population, as opposed to *idiographic*, which is focused on understanding the particularities of individual experience. Yet there is also a long-standing tradition of psychotherapy research that focuses on understanding individual clients. Thus, while this chapter stresses the political and economic importance of PBE and EBP research, we do not want to give the impression that these are the only types of research that matter for the field. Actually, in times of financial hardship it can become more and more difficult to find external funding for large-scale RCTs undertaken by specialist researchers. Consideration of these restraints has led McLeod (2013, p. xii) to suggest that 'in the future, sustainable programmes of inquiry will be based in grassroots projects in which research data are generated as a by-product of routine practice'.

When investigating therapy practice, and here especially the lived experiences of both clients and practitioners, researchers can choose from a range of research methodologies. With the chapters on qualitative methods (Chapter 12 and 13) and case study methodologies (Chapter 14 and 15) we will introduce the main alternatives to the quantitative research paradigm. Being appropriately equipped to engage in different kinds of practitioner research can be seen as one motive for counsellors and psychotherapists to learn about research in the field. In the following, we will have a closer look at this and other important reasons to be or become research-savvy.

Reasons to engage with research

So what exactly are the reasons why research matters for the profession, and why should trainees and practitioners become research-knowledgeable and active? A whole variety of motives have been put forward in the debate around a stronger research-orientation (e.g. Barkham & Barker, 2010; Cooper, 2008; McLeod, 2013). We have clustered some of the most salient arguments into three thematic groups, starting with the moral argument that counsellors and psychotherapists really need to make sure that their clients are not harmed or damaged by their work.

Moral argument: Research provides insight into the client perspective and helps to prevent counselling from damaging clients

Based on their knowledge of theory and their own perception of their work with their clients, many trainees or practising therapists may feel that they already have a good insight into their clients' experiences, and that their clients benefit from their work. However, there is evidence that counsellors and therapists are in fact not always good at judging their work, or how clients experience it. This poor practitioner judgement almost certainly contributes to the 20% of clients who state problematic or harmful experiences in therapy (Levy et al., 1996), and the 5–10% who deteriorate during counselling or psychotherapy (Cooper, 2008).

- Walfish, McAlister, O'Donnell and Lambert (2012) looked at a sample of 129 privately-practising psychotherapists and asked them to rate their own skill and performance level relative to others in their profession. 25% of the sample felt their skills placed them in the top-performing 10% compared with their peers, and none viewed themselves as below average. This self-assessment bias is consistently found in the literature.

- There is only a moderate agreement between therapists' and clients' ratings of the quality of the therapeutic relationship (e.g. Gurman, 1977; Tyron, Blackwell & Hammel, 2007), which suggests that often therapists and clients are not in sync in their view of the therapeutic alliance.
- Therapists tend to underestimate the importance of relational, as opposed to technical, aspects of therapy. In addition, they only agree with clients in 30–40% of instances on what was most significant in therapy sessions (Timulak, 2008a), suggesting a lack of client and therapist agreement on what is or is not working in counselling.
- Michael Lambert's recent research (2010; Lambert & Ogles, 2004) shows that therapists are often not very good at predicting the outcomes of therapy (i.e. they do not reliably know when it is going well or badly). Lambert was also able to demonstrate that systematically giving therapists client feedback on the therapy process helps to improve outcomes.

In the face of this evidence, counsellors and psychotherapists have a moral duty to make sure that what they think is doing good actually is doing good. While in many situations trainees and practitioners are well advised to trust their own intuitive sense of what clients are experiencing, they should be aware that they are not immune from misperceptions and misjudgements. Research can help in this context to see counselling and psychotherapy from the clients' perspective and to understand what they are really going through. Brief research tools and questionnaires can be used to collect feedback on the progress of therapy, not only for research projects but also in routine practice. This information can be utilised by practitioners to review the therapy process and make sure they are on track with their work (McLeod, 2013; see also Chapter 10). Such a practice is in line with the increased focus on the importance of the service user's perspectives and experiences to improve treatment quality in the NHS context (National Collaborating Centre for Mental Health, 2011).

Financial argument: Research can prove the value of counselling and psychotherapy

As described above, practitioners feel more and more pressure to demonstrate the quality and benefits of their service as they are held accountable to clients and funding bodies. Knowing what the research says about the efficacy of the service provided can help counsellors, psychotherapists and service providers to communicate and promote their work, and help consumers understand the value of what it is that they do.

This financial argument has been highlighted in the UK by the high-profile Depression Report (Layard, 2006), which analysed the extent of anxiety, depression and other 'mental health problems' in the population and their impact on incapacity benefits. While mental health services may be 'Cinderella services' (under-funded and under-valued) that are likely to be under threat in difficult economic times, Lord Layard's report provided the government with a clear and convincing economic case for investing millions into the provision of evidence-based psychotherapy to reduce the benefit bill for the state. Layard's report and the resulting Improving Access to Psychological Therapies (IAPT) programme (DH, 2007; www.iapt.nhs.uk/) can be seen as an example of how research findings can be used to evidence the value of counselling and psychotherapy services and get the government investing in this area.

Professional argument: Research can improve the therapeutic work and help trainees and practitioners grow professionally

Research findings can provide trainees and practitioners with useful orientation and guidance in situations when they are not sure how to proceed. Similarly, trained practitioners who struggle in their work with a particular client group or presented problem can turn to research findings to learn more about client needs or the best ways of working with certain problems (e.g. the default therapeutic stance for a problem). Research findings can also help to avoid practices and approaches which are actually harmful (Barkham & Barker, 2010). In sum, research provides guidance in the absence of or in addition to other information (such as experience, intuition and theoretical concepts).

Research can also be valuable in challenging implicit assumptions and preconceptions about therapeutic work. Some study findings have the potential to push counsellors and psychotherapists to reconsider the way they think about their clients and the best way to work with them. The Information box below provides you with a personal example of how the belief system of one of the chapter authors was shaken by a research report, helping him to be more responsive to the actual client in front of him.

**Information box 1.2   Research can challenge assumptions
(from Cooper, 2008, p. 3)**

Mick:

'As someone trained in existential psychotherapy [...], my tendency in initial sessions had always been to warn clients of the limits of therapeutic effectiveness [...]. I did tend to adopt a rather dour stance, emphasising to clients that therapy was not a magic pill and highlighting the challenges that it was likely to involve. Then I came across a research chapter by Snyder and colleagues (1999) which showed, fairly conclusively, that the more clients hoped and believed that their therapy would work the more helpful it tended to be.

(Continued)

(Continued)

How did I react? Well, initially I discounted; but once I had a chance to digest it and consider it in the light of some supervisory and client feedback, I came to the conclusion that, perhaps, beginning an episode of therapy with all the things that might not help was possibly not the best starting point for clients. So what do I do now? Well, I don't tell clients everything is going to be fine the moment they walk through the door; but I definitely spend less time taking them through all the limitations of the therapeutic enterprise; and if I think that therapy can help a client, I make sure that I tell them that.'

Mick's example nicely illustrates how research can stimulate and encourage self-reflection and help to improve therapeutic work – if we are open and willing to consider its messages. And more than that, trainees and practitioners can carry out their own research to find answers for the 'burning questions' (McLeod, 2013, p. 5) that have emerged from their professional practice, or their professional journey. Engaging with research and getting answers to these questions can contribute to personal and professional development and help to consolidate our professional identity (as illustrated below, with the two personal examples from the editors of this book).

Information box 1.3   Engagement with research

Andreas:

In my practice as a family therapist, the integration of children and young people in the therapy sessions seemed to be a particular challenge. Some children displayed turbulent, fidgety and unruly behaviour during the therapy sessions so that it was at times quite hard to work with them in this setting. Others were afraid of the unfamiliar, adult-dominated family counselling situation, making it difficult to establish a working relationship with them. And many teenagers were initially unwilling to participate in a counselling process with their parents, sometimes trying to boycott the conversation in the counselling room.

These kinds of experiences led me to question the way children and adolescents may feel in counselling sessions: are their needs and interests considered appropriately by us professionals? These considerations constituted my motivation to investigate young people's experiences in child guidance and family counselling with a qualitative study (Vossler, 2004).

Naomi:

As a tutor on courses which utilise personal development groups, I was struck by the sometimes very negative reactions expressed by some students to the groups. I think I was surprised by this in part as a result of having had group therapy for about two years, which I found very helpful. Group therapy taught me things that I had not learned in years of personal therapy, mostly about how I relate in and to groups, and how my experience in my family growing up continues to play out. As a result of my own positive group experience, I had not questioned the idea that having personal development groups as part of training might be useful, nor had I really thought about the theoretical arguments for their use. I began by talking with my colleagues on the courses – why did they think personal development (PD) groups were important? – and went on to read theory on personal development broadly in counselling and psychotherapy and on PD groups in particular. After that I went looking for research and found that there was not much. So I decided, with a student, to do some research. What we found helped me decide that the theoretical rationale for PD groups in training is still under-developed and that trainers needed to be more aware of the potential negatives as well as the potential positives of these groups (Moller & Rance, 2013).

Conclusion – let the research journey begin

The aim of this chapter was to introduce the current field of research in counselling and psychotherapy and help you to understand why research matters for the practical work with clients, and for the profession more generally. We also hope that we were able to encourage you to engage with research and start your own research journey. If you want to keep up to date with the latest findings in the counselling and psychotherapy field, look at some of the suggestions we make in Chapter 18.

Going forward

This book is designed as a 'travel guide' for your own research journey. It will provide you with a comprehensive introduction to research methods and process within counselling and psychotherapy. It will take you step by step through the different stages of a research process, providing you with enough applied knowledge on selected methodologies to support you with your own research projects. In doing so, the book will focus on the common questions and concerns of practitioners and trainees around research.

PAUSE FOR REFLECTION   LOOKING FORWARD

Looking at the book content, do you feel prepared for your journey through the book and your own research? Which chapters do you think will be particularly helpful and which are you unsure about? Is this all new for you or do you already have some research knowledge and experience which you can consider as you read the chapters?

Ambivalences and uncertainties towards research can be a stumbling block at the beginning of the research journey. The next chapter will therefore focus on these concerns and suspicions, and encourage you to reflect on the images and fantasies you have about research.

Suggestions for further reading

Cooper, M. (2008). *Essential Research Findings in Counselling and Psychotherapy: The facts are friendly*. London: Sage.

    Comprehensive introduction to research findings in the field of counselling and psychotherapy.

McLeod, J. (2013). *An Introduction to Research in Counselling and Psychotherapy*. London: Sage.

    Accessible starter text introducing the basic principles of research theory and practice.

Timulak, L. (2008b). *Research in Counselling and Psychotherapy*. London: Sage.

    This book provides a presentation of counselling and psychotherapy research genres.

TWO

Attitudes to and perceptions of research

Dr Andreas Vossler (Open University) &
Dr Naomi Moller (Open University)

Introduction

As we have seen in Chapter 1, the importance attributed to research in counselling and psychotherapy has increased dramatically in recent years, indicated, for example, by the fact that decisions about the commissioning of psychological therapy services are now often based on research evidence. There is a growing awareness and understanding that research really matters for the profession, with leading figures and professional bodies continuing to stress the benefits for counsellors and psychotherapists of engaging with research about what they are doing with their clients (see Chapter 1). It is therefore no surprise that research awareness and skills are being increasingly required in practitioner training and continuing professional development (CPD) of counsellors and psychotherapists (Cooper, 2010).

Yet, trainees and practitioners often harbour negative or ambivalent feelings towards the growing research emphasis and new research related training requirements (Moran, 2011; Widdowson, 2012a). While they recognise the importance of research, they often experience a clash of cultures between what counsellors and psychotherapists characterise as the 'subjective' nature of their work (the focus on individuals, subjective experience, reflexivity) (Daniel & McLeod, 2006) and the values and practices in mainstream research involving quantitative data collection and analysis (positivist science, objectivity, generalisability). The underlying concern is that an increased focus and reliance on this kind of research can lead away from the engagement with the clients' individuality and uniqueness and create a greater dehumanisation of the therapeutic work (Cooper, 2007, 2010).

In this chapter we will encourage you to reflect on your own images and fantasies about research and explore the nature of the most common concerns and suspicions towards research held by trainees and practitioners. We will look at the underlying reasons for the 'research–practice gap' and discuss the role of research in our culture and society and in the field of counselling and psycho-therapy more specifically. We will also explore the range of social, personal and professional meanings that are associated with research, and investigate the experiences of research participants (clients, therapists) when asked to partici-pate in research. The chapter concludes with approaches to de-mystify research and integrate it into practice, highlighting the commonalities between counsel-ling and psychotherapy practice and research (such as, for example, curiosity and systematic inquiry). We hope that this chapter will both encourage you to engage in research and reassure you that any concerns or anxieties you might have are surmountable.

Exploring the gap – attitudes to research

Activity 2.1   Your attitudes and feelings to research?

Spend 15 minutes coming up with all the attitudes and feelings you hold in rela-tion to research and inquiry. To aid your reflection, try completing the statement 'Research is...', using your own ideas and meanings to make a list of completed statements.

Comment

Hold on to your list while you go through the book so that you can check for potential changes in your attitudes towards research.

By the way, the method used for this activity is a 'sentence completion task' (SCT), a semi-structured projective technique often used in psychology and other disciplines for the assessment of attitudes, beliefs and personality (Holaday, Smith & Sherry, 2000). SCT respondents are usually provided with a statement or beginning of a sentence, or 'stems' (just as in the activity above), and then asked to complete that sentence in a way that makes sense to them. The answers can be analysed quantitatively (e.g. categorising and counting answer types) or quali-tatively (e.g. looking at underlying motivations in the answers given).

Alternatively, we could have also asked you to complete a questionnaire about your attitudes to and interest in research, such as the 'Attitudes Towards Research Scale' (Papanastasiou, 2005), the 'Interest in Research Questionnaire' (IRQ) (Bishop & Bieschke, 1998) or 'Past Attitudes toward Research' scale (PATR) (Royalty, Gelso, Mallinckrodt & Garrett, 1986). These scales present a number of statements (e.g. 'Research makes me anxious' or 'Research is useful to every professional'), and respondents answer by circling a score (usually from 1 to 5 or 1 to 7) indicating how much they agree or disagree with each statement. While attitudes towards research can be assessed more broadly with a SCT

(because this is a free-response questionnaire), the advantage of employing a scale with fixed items is that answers can be quantified and compared. Closed versus open responses is one of the main differences between quantitative and qualitative research methodologies that you will hear more about in Chapter 6.

The lack of engagement with research by counselling and psychotherapy trainees and practitioners and their low interest in research findings is a phenomenon that is well known in counselling and psychotherapy. This 'science–practice' or 'research–practice' gap was first identified in the 1980s in a now classic study by Morrow-Bradley and Elliott (1986). This survey of the utilisation of psychotherapy research by practising psychotherapists in the USA showed that the majority of respondents did not consider research papers to be a useful source of information for their practice, and that they were not engaged in doing or participating in research in their field. Since then research has become far more important for counselling and psychotherapy practice internationally (as portrayed in the previous chapter), and with growing demands for professional accountability and evidence-based practice many trainees and practitioners now do not have a choice about taking account of research (Midgley, 2012). However, this does not necessarily mean that the gulf between the research and practice worlds and discourses has now been bridged. Ogilvie, Abreu and Safran (2005) found that psychotherapists reported that experience with clients, and supervision and consultation with others are still more useful sources of information for their clinical practice than research. Looking at the literature on current practitioner–research engagement, McDonnell, Stratton, Butler and Cape (2012) come to the conclusion that research has still only a small impact on counselling and psychotherapy practice.

So what are the reasons for the continuing gap between research and practice at a period when it becomes increasingly important for the profession to engage with research? A number of different explanations are discussed in the literature (Morrow-Bradley & Elliott, 1986; Ogilvie et al., 2005; Stewart, Stirman & Chambless, 2012), such as:

- Research topics, measures and samples in studies are not relevant and don't capture the complexity of clinical practice;
- Methods used in studies are not well described and are too statistics-heavy;
- Research findings are not communicated in an accessible way; the language employed in research publications is unfamiliar and alienating for many practitioners;
- Practitioners experience logistical barriers like lack of time or money and specific training to understand or engage with research.

In combination with these explanations, attitudes to and perceptions of research held by trainees and practitioners can be considered to play a key role in their relationship and engagement with research. The information we have about practitioners' attitudes and beliefs about research derive mainly from practitioner surveys in an US context (Cook, Biyanova & Coyne, 2009; Morrow-Bradley & Elliott, 1986; Pagoto et al., 2007; Riley et al., 2007). However, more recently, two UK studies have investigated research-related attitudes and perceptions of trainees in counselling and psychotherapy programmes using focus groups (Moran, 2011; Widdowson, 2012a), and you will see in Chapter 17 ('Student top tips') that in preparation for this book we have conducted our own focus group study on trainees' experiences with research. Results from these three studies, as summarised below, show that trainees hold ambivalent feelings about research, both recognising the importance of research while also fearing research (the study findings are presented as 'Research is...' statements so that you can compare them easily with your own attitudes and images as collected in Activity 2.1):

1. Negative attitudes and perceptions of research: Research is...

   o ...intimidating and anxiety-provoking (especially statistics and big numbers).
   o ...boring and time consuming.
   o ...complex, difficult to understand and frustrating.
   o ...degrading of the uniqueness and human aspect of therapy.
   o ...irrelevant to practice and far removed from the realities of the consulting room.
   o ...open to misuse to suit political ends.
   o ...an ethically dubious activity with the potential for exploitation of clients.
   o ...separate from and difficult to integrate into clinical work.

Interestingly, these negative attitudes often go along with trainee self-perceptions that they lack knowledge of both practical research skills and counselling and psychotherapy research findings.

PAUSE FOR REFLECTION

Do you think anxiety about and distaste for research could be a defence against anxiety about 'not being good enough' to do research?

The picture is not all bad. The following positive attitudes and perceptions of research are less evident among trainees than negative attitudes but they are more frequently expressed by those who are at a more advanced stage in their training.

2. Positive attitudes and perceptions of research: Research is...

   o ...interesting, creative, exciting and satisfying.
   o ...valuable in terms of building knowledge and establishing a foundation for practice.
   o ...useful in understanding how counselling and psychotherapy works and what interventions and approaches are effective.

- o ...an ethical requirement because when practice is evidence-based clients are protected from cowboy practitioners.
- o ...important in promoting the wider acceptance of counselling and psychotherapy.
- o ...useful in influencing policy-makers and funders.

In the next section we will have a closer look at the different meanings research can have on a personal, professional and social level as these will influence the personal attitudes and beliefs held about research.

Many first time researchers are scared by the idea of doing research

Different meanings of research

The images, fantasies and assumptions people hold about research are formed by – and can tell us a lot about – personal and professional experiences with research and the ways in which the role of research is portrayed and understood in our culture and society. Negative experiences and myths about research can act as a hindrance and prevent us from becoming interested and engaged with research, and so it is useful to look closer at some of the personal, professional and cultural meanings of research.

Personal meanings

McLeod (2013) argues that we are all 'intuitive' scientists as we constantly ask questions and look for evidence to confirm or change the 'models' and 'theories' we have about ourselves, others and the world around us (e.g. feedback to test how attractive we are or how successful it would be to propose to a loved one). Intuitive research strategies also feature prominently in counselling and psychotherapy sessions where practitioners collect 'evidence' and develop hypotheses to come to a better understanding of their clients and the presented problems. Moodley (2001, p.18) argues in this context 'that counsellors and psychotherapists are themselves engaging in research when they practise therapy since every counselling and psychotherapy session is basically a (re)search process'.

More specifically, most of us will have gathered some kind of experience as either researcher and/or research participant in a 'research project', for example by taking part in some survey research on the High Street or answering phone surveys, or by filling out personality and attitude questionnaires in magazines. The way we experience our research involvement – for example, as boring or interesting – will shape the personal meaning we attach to research (e.g. as a painstaking process or a fun thing to do).

PAUSE FOR REFLECTION

Have you ever participated in a research project, either as researcher or as participant? Think about what you liked/disliked about the experience.

Professional meanings

In the professional context of counselling and psychotherapy, research can have very different functions depending on the aims researchers want to accomplish with it. Among others, research can be used to:

- protect jobs and demonstrate that a service is effective;
- give voice to people who may be marginalised in society;
- provide an evidence base for new approaches for working with clients or for counselling and psychotherapy in new areas;
- prove that one approach is more effective than another one;
- protect clients from harmful ways of working or from unscrupulous practitioners;
- answer questions that are important for the personal and professional development of practitioners.

It seems obvious that the motivations behind research will influence how it will be perceived and what meaning it will have for research participants and recipients. For example, research conducted with the aim to empower clients will probably be seen in a favourable light, while strategic studies to prove the superiority of one therapeutic school over the others might receive a more ambivalent reception.

Professional meanings of research – e.g. as helpful or unhelpful for practice – are also affected by the experiences and reactions of research participants (clients, therapists) when asked to participate in research. How clients and therapists experience research as participants is still an under-researched area (Stone & Elliott, 2011; Tracey, McElearney, Adamson & Shevlin, 2009). The information box below summarises the design and evidence from three qualitative studies on this topic conducted in the last few years. In doing so it provides you with an example of how to summarise and critique research.

Information box 2.1   How do clients and therapists feel about participating in research projects?

Studies/Design

1. *The qualitative study of Unsworth, Cowie and Green (2012) investigated both therapists' (n=9) and their clients' (n=10) perceptions of the use of routine outcome measurement with computer software in the NHS context. Focus groups with therapists and individual interviews with clients were conducted and inductively analysed.*
2. *Stone and Elliott (2011) investigated clients' experience of research within a university-based research clinic (where clients participate in research in exchange for free treatment). In their small-scale qualitative study they analysed archive material of semi-structured interviews with 17 clients using grounded theory (see Chapter 12).*
3. *Tracey et al. (2009) conducted a qualitative study exploring 18 practitioners' views and experiences of the process of implementing an 'impact*

(Continued)

(Continued)

evaluation' for a school counselling service. A broad range of sources was used to gather data, including focus groups, recordings of meetings, documents, discussion boards and structured questionnaires. The collected material was analysed using thematic analysis (see Chapter 13).

Study findings

*The findings draw a mixed picture of **client** experiences of research as having both positive and negative aspects. Many clients seem to benefit in some way from the research (e.g. visual measures can help to reflect and track the process in therapy) and appear more at ease with routine outcome measurement than their therapists (Studies 1, 2). However, they also report difficult or hindering research effects, e.g. they feel inhibited by the recording of the session or have difficulties articulating their feelings or rating their feelings in terms of a number (Study 2). Especially in the research clinic setting, clients seem to feel a moral obligation to take part in the research and to evidence through their responses that the intervention has worked well for them (Study 2).*

*   ***Therapists'** experiences of participating in research seem to be equally ambivalent. They can feel anxious and resistant as they may fear their work is judged in the research process based on a set of scores (Study 1). They can also be concerned that the research demands will interfere with the therapeutic relationship and increase their workload (Study 3). However, through practice and over time, therapists seem to be able to see the potential benefits of the research for the recognition of their work and service, their practice development and professional identity (Studies 1, 3).*

Limitations

All three studies employed a qualitative research methodology with small samples that are not fully representative of the subject population, which limits the generalisability of the findings (the ability to apply the findings to a wider population from which the sample came). The studies were focused on the immediate effects of participating in research projects; it is therefore not clear how these experiences are represented in the long term. It can also not be ruled out that researchers' own opinions and desires (e.g. that research is experienced as beneficial) did not have an impact, perhaps unconsciously, on data analysis and interpretation (this effect is called researcher allegiance).

The research evidence presented above can inform you when planning your own study in an ethically sound way (you will learn more about research ethics in Chapter 8). It will help you to decide how to recruit and inform participants about your project and how to make sure that they benefit from participating in your research. Funding bodies for research in counselling and psychotherapy (e.g. National Institute for Health Research in the UK) typically require researchers to consult service users and take their views into consideration in planning and conducting research. The aim with this is to make sure that the research on a service has relevance to those who use the service – in other words, that it is experienced by them as valid and useful.

Social and cultural meanings

Social and cultural understandings and views of research have a subtle but crucial impact on the way people feel and think about research. In our modern societies, science is part of almost every aspect of our lives. This has not always been the case as the rise of modern science is closely linked to industrialisation, modernisation and technical and medical progress in the last century (McLeod, 2013). During this time science has advanced rapidly, and new discoveries and developments are now promoted globally by a huge knowledge industry encompassing universities, research institutes and mass media. Media and journalists are a significant source of information for the public on science and technology, and they present research in ways that influence the public view and understanding of research (see our example in Information Box 2.2).

Information box 2.2   'Infidelity can make relationships stronger!' – Media representation of research

When our research appeared under this headline in The Daily Telegraph *on 15 May 2010, friends and relatives swiftly phoned Andreas and Naomi to let us know that we were being quoted as saying that the solution to a rocky relationship was to have an affair.*

The story was picked up in various media outlets following a BACP press release about a presentation on infidelity which we did at the BACP research conference. The research findings we presented were based on an interview study with seven experienced Relate couple counsellors about their experience of working with infidelity. The conclusion of the study was that for (the minority of) couples who go to couple counselling following infidelity, **if** *they decided to work on staying together, and* **if** *they were prepared to look at how both parties might have contributed to a couple context in which the infidelity happened, then they might end up with a better understanding of each other and their relationship. Not exactly what the headline suggested.*

This incident exemplifies that it is hard to explain briefly the complex findings of most research in a way that does not caricature or misrepresent them. It also shows the media tendency to present research findings as 'truth' – after all, the finding here was based on the experience of a small group of albeit experienced couple counsellors.

In the public view, science is often equated with natural science, e.g. physics, chemistry and biology, drawing on images of researchers in lab coats and working away with test tubes in scientific laboratories. This mirrors the dominance of the 'positivist' approach to research (see Chapter 6) that assumes the existence of an objective reality, with the goal of research 'to act as a "mirror" to that reality in as objective and reliable a fashion as possible' (McLeod, 1999, p. 11). The mainstream, positivist approach to research, together with the quantitative methods as usually employed by positivist researchers (e.g. large samples and statistics), is generally seen as 'true' or 'hard' science compared to 'softer' qualitative approaches.

The rise and increasing influence of science in society has led to a strong emphasis on evidence and 'scientific proof' as important criteria in societal discourse and decision making (Cooper, 2011). Politicians and decision makers tend to favour positivist, quantitative research as this approach promises objective and reliable evidence for their decisions. Hence, in the discourse about science and evidence-based practice, other types of research and evidence are often neglected and devaluated. Together with the perception that research funding and research topics are in many cases determined by political and economic factors and pressures, this contributes to the perception that research and the interpretation of research findings are open to misuse to suit political ends. Examples of the influence politics and stakeholder interests can have on the funding and use of research are the practices in pharmaceutical research (Haley, 2012) and the Increased Access to Psychological Therapy (IAPT) programme in the UK (see discussion in Chapter 1).

Conclusion: De-mystifying research and integrating it with practice

PAUSE FOR REFLECTION

Think about how research needs to be conducted and presented to catch your attention and be of interest and relevance for you.

We have seen in the previous section that attitudes to and perceptions of research are influenced by the social, personal and professional meanings that are associated with research activities and outcomes. We have also heard that fears and concerns about research are often related to, or even caused by, a lack of confidence in one's own knowledge about and capacity to engage with research. It might therefore not come as a big surprise that trainees and students who enter counselling or psychotherapy training are often found to be ambivalent about both whether they are really interested in and whether they have the capacity to do research (Gelso, 2006). At the beginning of their training, most trainees have little to no knowledge of and experience with research, and typically their main motivation to do the training is to become a practitioner, not a researcher.

The good news is that there is consistent evidence that attitudes to research do modestly improve during training as students learn more about research and develop a research-related sense of efficacy (Perl & Kahn, 1983). However, for the initial ambivalence to be resolved, and for students to develop a research-related sense of efficacy, the quality and timing of the research training they receive needs to be right, as well as the extent to which their research experiences are integrated with other aspects of the counselling and psychotherapy training (e.g. clinical practice) (Gelso, 2006). Looking at the findings from Gelso (2006), Moran (2011) and Widdowson (2012a), we have identified and synthesised four factors or conditions that can play a key role in reducing anxieties and enhancing research attitudes and interest (see Table 2.1).

Table 2.1 *Factors enhancing research attitudes and interests*

Factor/condition	Recommendation for training providers	Recommendation for trainees
1. Early involvement	Experiential involvement of trainees in research components and activities as early as possible. Experience should be matched to trainees' skills level/minimal threatening involvement (e.g. facilitated by activities/reflective questions as used in this book).	*Don't worry too much and get your hands on research as soon as you can!*
2. De-mystifying 'perfect research'	Emphasis in research training that all research studies are limited and flawed in one way or another. However, while methodological issues are inevitable, research can still usefully add to an unfolding body of research.	*Your research doesn't need to be flawless; rather, try to balance possibilities and limitations!*
3. Learning and valuing different approaches to research	Taught plurality of research methodologies in training curriculum helps trainees to fit the method to the research question and their personality/personal preferences.	*Familiarising yourself with the range of methodologies helps you to choose the best approach for your research and you!*
4. Integrating research with practice	It is important in training to demonstrate links between research and practice. Practice can be a source of ideas for research (see the next chapter on choosing a research question). Similarities between research and practice and relevance of research for practice should be emphasised.	*Think about your personal and professional interests when planning and doing research!*

The recommendations derived from these four factors, not only for trainees but also for training providers, can help to de-mystify research and enhance attitudes to and perceptions of research. If you feel you need more ideas and examples of how research can be used to inform and enhance training/practice in counselling and psychotherapy, please try the Engagement in Research Self-Rating Scale (McLeod, 2012) presented in Activity 2.2 below.

Activity 2.2   The Engagement in Research Self-Rating Scale (ERS) (McLeod, 2012)

There are a number of ways in which research can be used to enhance counselling and psychotherapy practice. For each of the areas listed below, circle the response that accurately indicates your engagement in practice on the following scale:

1. *'I do not feel at all confident/competent in relation to using research knowledge and skills in this way'*
2. *'I feel slightly confident/competent...*
3. *'I feel moderately confident/competent...*
4. *'I feel considerably confident/competent...*
5. *'I feel highly confident/competent...*

1. *...Using research to inform my practice in relation to specific aspects of therapy (e.g. using homework activities with clients, building a collaborative relationship, etc.).'*
2. *...Using research to deepen my understanding of the issues and challenges experienced by specific clients and client groups (e.g. people who are depressed, clients from a different cultural background).'*
3. *...Being able to draw on research evidence to justify and argue for the effectiveness of my approach to therapy, when questioned by others (e.g. clients, colleagues, managers).'*
4. *...Evaluating the effectiveness of my practice, or the work of the agency/ organisation/placement where I am based.'*
5. *...Carrying out my own research to explore issues that interest me as a means of furthering my personal and professional development.'*
6. *...Using research instruments, such as questionnaires, to collect feedback from my own clients and/or track their progress in therapy.'*
7. *...Reading research papers to keep up to date with developments in the field.'*

Comment

The ERS is an example of a self-rating scale that can help to improve self-reflection and understanding of personal research attitudes and self-efficacy. It has been designed to collect information on the ways in which counsellors and psychotherapists make use of research skills and findings in their work. By adding the scores for each item you can calculate your overall score, which will be somewhere in the range between 7 (lowest possible score) and 35 (highest possible score). If your overall score is at the lower end, the ERS items provide you with some great ideas on how you might be able to make more use of research to inform and enhance your training and practice.

When you start to engage with research you will hopefully discover that there are more similarities between counselling practice and research than you might have expected. This is expressed in a trainee's quote from Moran (2011, p. 176):

> I think that is really exciting when I think of research in terms of – its about curiosity, it's about enquiry, it's about discovery, it's about examining, it's about process, that's what we do.

We hope this book will help you to discover how true these words are.

Suggestions for further reading

Barker, C., Pistrang, N. & Elliott, R. (2002). *Research Methods in Clinical Psychology: An introduction for students and practitioners* (2nd edition). Chichester: Wiley.
  This is an accessible introduction to doing, and thinking about, research – not only for clinical psychologists.

McLeod, J., Elliott, R. & Wheeler, S. (2010). *Developing and Enhancing Research Capacity in Counselling and Psychotherapy: A research training manual.* Leicester: British Association for Counselling and Psychotherapy.
  This manual contains a wide range of research training resources that can be used for teaching counsellors and psychotherapists, encouraging students to learn by doing rather than listening.

PART II
Beginning the research journey

THREE

Choosing a research question
Dr Elaine Kasket (Regent's University London)

Introduction: The start of your research journey

The word 'journey' suggests something different from the trips we take on any normal day, such as train rides through familiar countryside or the well-trodden route between home and work. 'Journey' suggests something out of the ordinary: a trip that may take a long time, that may feel arduous, and that may take us to little-known places. A journey of this kind begins with a curiosity, a wish to explore, and a desire or even a need to discover something new. We may view the prospect with apprehension as well as excitement, and at journey's end we may reflect on how meaningful it has been.

The fact that you are reading this book probably means that you are beginning or at least contemplating a research journey. Perhaps you have even been on the road for some time but have lost your way and need a fresh start. You may be driven by a desire to generate new knowledge that benefits both the practitioners and recipients of counselling and psychotherapy, to do research that matters in the way that was covered in Chapter 1. Your research may be in service of furthering your own educational or professional interests, or fulfilling others' requirements. Whatever your motivations, you may or may not have a clear map of the road ahead, and you should exercise care and attention at the start of your journey. Why?

In literal journey terms, you may have a notion to go to Borneo or Timbuktu, but you may not know much about these places, and if you rush off too impetuously, you may have a rocky road. If you want a better experience, you will need to ask more questions, gather more information, and plan carefully. The success or failure of a research journey also owes much to the original research question, and yet many novice researchers rush through this beginning phase.

The aim of this chapter is to guide you towards the best possible starting place: a good, solid research question. How do you know when you have arrived at one of these?

First, a good research question responds to a need by identifying something that we would benefit from knowing more about but which has not been sufficiently explored yet. It extends the boundaries of our knowledge rather than treading well-known territory. If something has already been looked at quite a bit, there is questionable usefulness in investigating it again.

Second, a good research question makes a difference. It asks the kind of question that, if you answer it, will meaningfully contribute to thought and/or practice in counselling and psychotherapy. If a question does not really matter to those who practise in the profession, if it will not ultimately trickle down to benefit the people we serve, it is probably not worth exploring.

Third, a good research question is viable. In other words, it is conceptualised and articulated in a way that is sufficiently focused, clear, and realistic. There are thousands of interesting questions to ask; some have never been answered because there is simply no way of practically and/or ethically investigating them, and some are not answerable within the context of the researcher's time-frame, resources, and/or access to participants.

This chapter contains exercises and examples to help you in forming a good question, including an account of the route that I followed to arrive at one of my own research questions. After you identify your starting point, the precise route you will follow, and your ultimate destination, will be intimately connected to your review of the existing literature, which is a focus of Chapters 4 and 5.

Finding your inspiration

Flipping through a stack of travel magazines, one is reminded what a big world it is, with so many wonderful, fascinating and diverse places to explore. Faced with such overwhelming choice, perhaps it is little wonder that people who are lost for holiday-destination inspiration may end up placing a finger on a spinning globe, seizing on a recommendation from a friend, or just reverting to the most popular, most familiar, or easiest destinations.

The breadth of human experience is even wider than the territories of the earth, and within that huge scope exist millions of questions. With all of the potential counselling-and-psychotherapy-related questions that there are in the world, which one will you ask? If you have no idea, you may be tempted to pursue the same strategies as the overwhelmed holiday-planner: pick something at random, get a steer from a supervisor, or do something easy. With focused work at the outset, however, you can end up with the preferable alternative: a question that is meaningful and useful for both you and others involved in the professions of counselling and psychotherapy. Information box 3.1 relates a personal example.

Information box 3.1   A research idea is born

In 2007 I joined the social networking site Facebook, which had only been open to the general public since September 2006. One day I took a break from the presentation that I was preparing for a death-and-dying conference and started looking for old friends who might be on Facebook. One of my name searches threw up an in-memory-of group for a teenaged girl.

> *Having never encountered this before, I found and explored the profile that the young woman had created in life. I noted many interesting things: people had continued posting comments and messages long after their friend had died, and much communication was directed towards the dead girl. I wondered how the continued existence of this teenager's social networking profile would affect the bereavement experience of those left behind, and what bereavement counsellors would make of this.*

Eureka! I had experienced that initial spark, the first inkling that there was a new journey that I might like to take. What can we notice about the experience described in information box 3.1 that might be salient for the research-question-finding process?

First, the inspiration did not take place in the contexts of working at my private practice, reading an academic journal, or talking with psychologist or counsellor colleagues; it did not happen in an active search for a question, but had occurred when I was in social rather than academic mode. By being 'tuned in' to the fact that everyday experiences can eventually translate into research, I was immediately able to frame my discovery as a potential topic.

Second, I was instinctively drawn to this as a fascinating topic to explore in research. Although sometimes deep personal interest can have a hindering or biasing effect on the process (which will be discussed in the 'Being reflexive' section below), it goes without saying that fascination drives research better than boredom.

Third, online social networking was then a relatively new phenomenon, open access to Facebook was new, and communication with dead friends via their in-life profiles was definitely an emergent phenomenon. All this newness made it highly unlikely to be a research area that had already been plumbed to its depths. I had a suspicion that I would find a gap in the existing literature, which encouraged me to investigate further.

Finally, the phenomenon struck me as an area that certainly might have important implications for both thinking and practice. I was not sure what these implications might be, what fields or disciplines might benefit from my carrying out research in the area, or what I should specifically focus on. In other words, more work was yet to be done: I had an inspiration, but not a research question.

I was lucky in stumbling upon a research territory that interested me greatly, that gave rise to researchable questions, and that proved to have significance for practitioners. If an idea has not hit you yet, there are many realms of your life – personal, interpersonal, professional, academic, societal – where inspiration may lie. To catch hold of that inspiration, it helps to keep your awareness sharp and engage in some focused thinking. Activity 3.1 is an exercise in noticing what emerges when you tune into five broad areas of experience. At this stage, try to suspend the actual search for a research topic and remain open, making notes as you go along and allowing yourself to free associate or brainstorm off of your observations.

Activity 3.1 Realms of inspiration

With focused attention to different realms of experience, numerous research inspirations may spring to mind. Consider the questions and ideas presented in Figure 3.1.

Study

Flip through the last few issues of academic and professional journals in the field. Look at conference proceedings. What is topical currently? Where is more research being called for? If you are on a course, look out in lectures and reading for areas of knowledge that are relatively unexplored or emergent (e.g. a newer therapy that does not have much evidence yet with particular problems or populations).

Work

If you are practising, which clients or issues do you most struggle with? Which are you most interested in/passionate/fascinated about working with? Why? Have you ever sought guidance or information on a clinical issue and struggled to find it? What are the big issues currently in the service or organisation where you work? What is happening in the profession?

You

What is most meaningful for you in life? What do you really value? What kinds of things make you upset, angry, or scared? What social, behavioural, psychological, or emotional phenomena do you wish you understood better? What topics of conversation really get you engaged? What is your favourite television or radio programme? What about that programme really draws you in? What events have most shaped you? Why are you a counsellor/ psychotherapist?

Wider society

What issues are topical on talk radio, in newspapers, on TV, in social media? What is 'trending'? What do you notice in other media, e.g. advertising? What stories are in the news that have caught *your* eye but do not seem to be getting much attention? What patterns or incidents have caught your notice 'out in the world': at your or partner's work, at university, at your kid's school, in government, at the shops, at the pub, in your social groups?

Other people

Talk to colleagues, supervisors, lecturers, and people you meet at conferences. Ask them to tell you the stories of how their own research interests and questions emerged. How do they see their own research as being applicable to practice, and beneficial for clients and society? Where do they feel more research is needed? If they had unlimited time, what would they research that they are not currently able to work on?

Figure 3.1

Once you have identified some areas of potential research, you may be tempted to forge ahead with your planning and to start looking at the literature. First, though, pause for thought. You may have many reasons – some within your awareness, some not – for feeling drawn to these topics. Your own beliefs, feelings and agendas have the potential to affect you, the research process, and the outcome. It is worth noting that this is true even for supposedly 'objective' research, as illustrated by studies that show that proponents of particular models of therapy have a tendency to design 'objective' and 'scientific' studies that somehow manage to find that their favoured form of therapy is the best. This is known as the 'allegiance effect' (Cooper, 2008; Munder, Gerger, Trelle & Barth, 2011).

Being reflexive

Chapter 2 covered your attitudes to research overall. Once you identify a potential research area, a whole new collection of attitudes will become relevant. An example of this would be going into the research process hoping to prove that women who experience domestic abuse both want and benefit from therapy. This may indeed be the case but it is important to design a study that has the potential to find otherwise. When a researcher realises that she carries baggage – feelings, hopes, assumptions, biases – with her at the beginning of her research journey, this is self-awareness. When that self-awareness is applied, through acknowledgement and management of the impact of the researcher on the research, this is reflexivity (see Chapter 12 also for discussions of these terms).

When we are reflexive, we realise the effect of our subjectivity on every phase of research, including project design, data collection, data analysis, and the presentation of findings (Finlay & Gough, 2003, p. 20). Let us focus on the 'project design' phase, which includes identifying your research question. Why is it so important to be reflexive at this stage? Information box 3.2 gives two illustrations.

Information box 3.2   Reflexivity and research questions

Javier:

Javier is pursuing a Masters in counselling and psychotherapy and was diagnosed with HIV midway through his course. It was a particular shock because Javier's boyfriend had concealed his positive status. For his Masters dissertation, Javier wants to look at disclosure of HIV-positive status between gay male partners. In discussing it with his research supervisor, Javier is suddenly beset with uncontrollable crying and feelings of intense rage. After much reflection, Javier and the supervisor collaboratively decide that he is 'too close' to the

(Continued)

(Continued)

research area. Javier ultimately chooses another topic that still has meaning for him but that does not have intense emotions associated with it. Had he carried on with the original topic, Javier might have become overwhelmed, gotten stuck, and/or infused the research with his own biases.

Zainab:

Zainab works as a couples counsellor at a Relate centre. Having noticed how few couples from her own British-Pakistani background present for counselling, she decides to investigate British-Pakistani males' attitudes towards couples therapy. A colleague queries why she is focusing specifically on men – is it because she has identified a gap in the literature? Zainab has not actually reviewed the literature yet; she had just decided that she was most interested in men's attitudes. It dawns on Zainab that she strongly believes that her own partner and her male relatives would never engage in couples therapy, and that she has assumed that refusal by the husband would be the main barrier to British-Pakistani couples seeking help for relationship difficulties. Zainab realises that she needs to bracket off her own expectations and go through a proper review of the literature to see what has already been done.

There are several different kinds of reflexivity (see Finlay & Gough, 2003; Willig, 2008), but the most important kind for this stage of your research is personal reflexivity. While the personal interests that have led you to a topic can make your research process more enjoyable and meaningful, they can also get in the way, as they did for Javier, or lead you to pick a topic without properly reviewing the existing literature and identifying a need, as Zainab did. Reflexive exercises can help you become more aware of your positioning relative to your potential research topics.

Activity 3.2   Reflexive exercises

Write 'The Story of Me and X': Write a narrative describing the history of your relationship with topic X, from the beginning – the time you were first aware of this area – to the end, where you decided you might research it. Richly describe what has happened with you and the topic, what emotions it provokes, and what you believe about it.

Write 'The Story of My Successful Research Project': Imagine that you are at the end of the research process, and suppose that it has gone just as you

---

would like. What would you hope to have discovered? How do you imagine dis-seminating the results, and what influence or contribution would you like your findings to have? (This exercise also helps uncover some of your investment in the research process itself. Sometimes doing research, or achieving a research degree, has significance (McLeod, 1999).)

Get feedback: Tell the people who know you best – your closest friend, your partner, your mum or dad, your therapist – that you are considering doing a piece of research on this topic. What are their reactions? What do they think about the topic, and the prospect of your immersing yourself in it? Create a journal about the conversations after they have taken place.

Do free writing: Put the general topic area at the top of the page, set yourself a period of time, and write whatever comes to mind.

Engage in a focused mindfulness exercise: Get into a comfortable posi-tion in a quiet place, bring the topic into mind, and simply notice whatever thoughts, feelings, or sensations come to you. Try to accept and welcome whatever emerges without judgement. After the exercise, write down what emerged.

The writing generated by the exercises in Activity 3.2 can form the beginning of a reflexive research journal that will be useful to you throughout your jour-ney. Read through the beginning of your new journal, think about Javier and Zainab, and consider what impact your positioning could have on a potential question. If you have reflected on multiple topics, by the end of the process you may have identified which one you would like to explore further. This means it is now time to chart a particular course through what may be a wide swathe of territory.

Refining your scope

Professor John McLeod speaks from a wealth of experience with novice researchers when he observes, 'Very often, people new to research generate questions that would happily supply a lifetime of endeavour for a lavishly funded research unit' (McLeod, 1999, p. 57). This section assumes that you are contemplating a piece of research on a slightly smaller scale! There are prag-matic and design aspects to viability that will be discussed in Chapter 7, but for now I will focus on one particular dimension of viability, which is a sufficiently specific research question.

Let us return to my own 'Eureka!' moment. Imagine that you are in the same situation, and that you begin a research project entitled 'death in the context of the internet'. *How will you know that your focus is too broad, too vague, and/or too ambitious?*

First, *you will feel overwhelmed by the literature.* You will be exploring literature on countless thanatological (death studies) topics, to include literature on models of bereavement, on spiritualistic beliefs and communication with the dead, and on mourning practices in different contexts. You will become exhausted by your review of all of the many ways death is dealt with on the internet, to include virtual cemeteries, online support groups, and all the different social networking sites. The task will feel impossibly huge.

Harry: 'What do you mean, we're lost?'

Second, *you will struggle to design and implement your research project.* Your lack of a clear, specific research question will translate into your being unable to ascertain the right methods of investigation, the right participants, and the right questions to ask them. If you try to think of a participant pool and data-gathering materials for your study, could you do it? You will come to realise that this could be a book (probably Sofka, Cupitt & Gilbert, 2012), but not a single research study.

Third, *you will be unable to succinctly and clearly describe your research.* You may be able to sketch out the parameters and give a superficial 'whistle-stop tour', but you will be unable to give a deep and meaningful sense of the research and to convey how the results will be of significance or benefit.

A number of techniques can be applied to a broad research area to whittle it down to a researchable question. Four of these 'lenses' and suggested activities to help you look through them are outlined in Table 3.1.

Using different lenses to examine your broad research ideas can help you find a researchable question.

Table 3.1 *Looking through lenses*

Time/place/person	Activity
McLeod (1999, p. 51) discusses this method and points out that 'the more specific the research is, the more likely that it will produce useful results'. 'How effective is Acceptance and Commitment Therapy?' is clearly too overwhelmingly broad and vague a question. 'How effective is a six-session package (*time*) of Acceptance and Commitment Therapy for couples with relational difficulties (*person*) seen in a private practice setting (*place*)?' is a massive improvement.	Examine your draft research question, breaking it down into its constituent components if that is helpful. Consider each dimension in turn and how your question might be usefully narrowed along that dimension.

Benefit & applications	Activity
One of the beneficiaries of your research will be you – you may gain experience, expertise in a particular area, presenting problem or population that may enhance your employability, a publication and/or conference presentation, an enhanced reputation, and perhaps a research degree. To be worth doing, however, your research will need to be meaningful and beneficial in spheres beyond the personal. How will it add to the *body of knowledge*? How will it help *practitioners* do better work? How might it help *services or organisations*? How will *clients* benefit from the increased knowledge and skills that your research brings to the field? How might *policy makers* be informed by more knowledge in this area? How could *wider society* benefit? Good research questions will have answers to all of these.	Make a table. In the first column, list the stakeholders and beneficiaries of your research: you, the body of knowledge, practitioners, services and organisations, policy makers, wider society. Describe the impact you imagine your research might have on each. If it is difficult to identify meaningful impact, refine or change your research trajectory further.

(Continued)

Table 3.1   *(Continued)*

Pragmatics & ethics	Activity
Your fantasy may involve large-scale/longitudinal research, but your reality includes constraints on your time, finances, materials, facilities, amount of assistance, and access to participants. Additionally, and crucially, most researchers of counselling and psychotherapy will be doing research that involves and affects practice, and this involves 'two strands of ethics, first, the ethics of scientific ... research and, second, the ethics of your professional helping practice' (Sanders & Wilkins, 2010, p. 253). You will need to identify a research question whose design bears formal ethical scrutiny, then put those ethics into action when you start your research.	Make a table. List the salient parameters: time, money, access, materials, facilities, ethics. In collaboration with a supervisor or colleague, and consulting the ethical guidelines of your profession, academic institution, and/or organisation, refine your proposal as necessary to produce a question that is ethically and pragmatically feasible.

Originality & contribution	Activity
It is difficult to justify undertaking a piece of research that merely rehashes work that has been done before. Ideally, your work will usefully extend the body of existing knowledge. If you are doing a Doctoral degree, this will be a requirement (Quality Assurance Agency, 2008). Sometimes novice researchers proceed with their project without being sufficiently aware of the literature to know whether their research breaks any new ground. An area of knowledge might be unfamiliar to you, but many may have travelled there before.	Before you go too far down any path, review the literature! Many a novice researcher has failed to identify a gap in the existing knowledge and has discovered that all their hard work is redundant.

Activity 3.3   Four lenses to achieving a researchable question

Complete the activities suggested in Table 3.1 to guide you in reaching a researchable question.

Applying different lenses to the 'death and the internet' interest area results in innumerable potential research questions. I ultimately narrowed my project by 'place' (Facebook only) and focused on particular people (recently bereaved young people who had lost friends via traumatic death) (Kasket, 2012). Hieftje (2012) also applied lenses involving place and person when she did her study on 'the role of social networking sites in the memorialization of [US] college students'. I will be applying a benefits and applications lens when I study bereavement professionals' conceptualisations of and attitudes towards mourners' ongoing online interaction with decedents' social networking profiles. Information box 3.3 includes some additional examples of well-defined research questions relevant to counselling and psychotherapy. You will note the time/ place/person specificity in evidence in each.

Information box 3.3   Specific and researchable questions

- *Does participation in research lead to changes in attitudes among clinicians? Report on a survey of those involved in a French practice research network (Thurin, Thurin & Midgley, 2012)*
- *A group-based treatment for clients with Obsessive-Compulsive Disorder (OCD) in a secondary care mental health setting: Integrating new developments within cognitive behavioural interventions – An exploratory study (Fairfax & Barfield, 2010)*
- *Therapeutic activities and psychological interventions by cognitive behavioural and psychodynamic therapists working with medically unexplained symptoms: A qualitative study (Luca, 2012)*

Preparing to launch

At some point you will have a question firmly in mind. Perhaps you are itching to get going – to apply for ethical clearance, to write an interview schedule, to start recruiting participants. First, though, pause again. Returning to our metaphor one last time, before you depart on a long trip you are likely to make some last checks: Is your plan solid? Have you overlooked anything? Have you anticipated problems and thought about how you will confront them? The same kinds of precautions will serve you well now.

In the 'Realms of inspiration' exercise (Activity 3.1), it was suggested that you talk to other people about their own research experiences. At this point, have further chats with individuals who are seasoned researchers, supervisors, and practitioners. Give them your draft research question, perhaps with a one- or two-minute précis. Invite constructive criticism around the characteristics of researchable questions outlined earlier:

- Do they feel that the research question *responds to a need* within psychotherapy and counselling? Have they experienced this as an area where more knowledge and guidance is needed?
- Does the question seem useful and beneficial? Do they feel that their own and others' knowledge and practice would be meaningfully enhanced if the question were answered? Do they feel individuals, organisations and society would benefit from this research?

- Finally, is the question clear and unambiguous? Do they hear any ethical alarm bells? Be transparent with them about your time and resources. Do they think that you will be able to manage this research?

If you 'road test' your question in this way before setting out, you will have a much smoother ride. Remember, however, to be open to hearing, considering, and possibly acting upon the constructive criticism that you have invited. If you find yourself arguing too vociferously in favour of proceeding, even in the face of others' doubts or concerns, go back to the reflexive exercises!

The course we have charted thus far is illustrated below. You began with a broad idea, a beginning sense of where you might like to go; you looked at your motivations for wanting to go there; and you moved into the process of refining your research question. You may have been guided in this by peering through the various lenses outlined earlier. To help ensure originality and contribution, you will likely already have consulted the literature.

The process of finding your research question is not strictly linear, as the loop-back from 'literature' to 'refining research area' shows (see Figure 3.2).
Although reading, understanding, and reviewing existing research is the focus of the next two chapters, it would have been impossible to discuss choosing a research question without reference to the literature. Research is

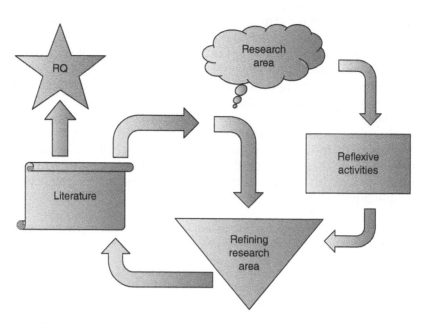

Figure 3.2   *The cycle of finding your research question*

not a straight road – it frequently involves doubling back and revisiting previous phases with fresh eyes and new information. You may move through many iterations of this particular cycle – possible question → literature exploration → possible question → literature exploration – before emerging triumphant with your ultimate question.

Conclusion

The research journey begins with the selection of an appropriate research question. A poor question will lead to you getting lost, or finding yourself in an alley with no way out. A good research question by contrast – one that is strong and enticing, one that speaks to a gap in the knowledge and has the potential to shape how practitioners work with clients – will motivate you to stay engaged with the research even through difficult times. Now that you are prepared with an interesting, meaningful, and viable focus of investigation, it is nearly time to take your next steps. First, though, one last check before you go.

Information box 3.4   Research question checklist

Have you...

- *...identified a question that is clear and specific?*
- *...identified a question whose answer will benefit someone?*
- *...established that there is a need for this knowledge?*
- *...identified a meaningful gap in the literature?*
- *...reflected on your relationship to the research question?*
- *...thought through how your investment in the research question could affect your research?*
- *...ensured you have the necessary resources to answer the question?*
- *...anticipated and addressed ethical concerns?*
- *...road tested your question with experienced supervisors, researchers, and clinicians, especially ones who are knowledgeable in your research area?*
- *...heard, considered, and possibly acted on constructive feedback received?*

Suggestions for further reading

Clough, P. & Nutbrown, C. (2012). *A Student's Guide to Methodology* (3rd edition). London: Sage.
   Chapter 1 covers the impact, purpose and change-making potential of research, and your reasons for doing your research study.

Finlay, L. & Gough, B. (2003). *Reflexivity: A practical guide for researchers in health and social sciences.* London: John Wiley & Sons.
  An excellent resource to help you be a reflexive researcher.

McLeod, J. (1999). *Practitioner Research in Counselling.* London: Sage.
  Chapter 3 provides exercises and guidance for finding your research question.

Punch, K.F. (2006). *Developing Effective Research Proposals* (2nd edition). London: Sage.
  Chapters 1–3 will help you brainstorm and clarify your ideas.

Sanders, P. & Wilkins, P. (2010). *First Steps in Practitioner Research: A guide to understanding and doing research in counselling and health and social care.* Ross-on-Wye: PCCS Books.
  Good overall text on situating your research within professional practice.

White, P. (2009). *Developing Research Questions: A guide for social scientists.* Basingstoke: Palgrave Macmillan.
  A resource completely dedicated to finding your research question.

FOUR

How to read and understand research
Dr Elena Gil-Rodriguez (Goldsmiths, University of London)

Introduction

How do you feel when you pick up a counselling and psychotherapy research article? Anxious? Reluctant? Bored? We saw in Chapter 2 that both trainees and practitioners are likely to feel ambivalent, or even negatively, towards the growing emphasis on research and research-related training requirements (as outlined in Chapter 1). No wonder that reading and understanding the research literature in counselling and psychotherapy can be a daunting prospect that we may wish to avoid! But an ability to read and evaluate the literature is a crucial skill, not only as an essential part of the journey that informs research for those conducting a research project or study, but also for practitioners if research findings are to be used to inform and improve counselling and psychotherapy practice.

In this chapter you will find guidance on how to read both quantitative and qualitative research critically, and to evaluate its usefulness and contribution to the field. This will be achieved through the provision of guidance on the differences in format between quantitative and qualitative research and a framework of evaluation for both paradigms that highlights how to evaluate the different sections of research articles. The chapter will also provide reading tips, along with suggestions for how essential information from a research paper may be summarised for further use so that reading that results from a search of the literature might be organised in a productive way. By the end of the chapter we hope that the prospect of reading research might make you feel a bit different – just like the reader of a counselling and psychotherapy research journal that counselling researcher Jane Speedy described watching on a train: 'Suddenly, just past Swindon, she started chuckling, then giggling and then finally burst out with great roars of belly-laughter' (Speedy, 2005, p. 65).

What do we mean by 'research article'?

This chapter will focus on empirical quantitative and qualitative research found in academic and professional journals. By this we mean research that involves the direct examination of the world through concrete experiences or observations and recording of data (Cooper, 2008; Locke, Silverman & Spirduso, 2010) as opposed to articles based on theory or opinion. In addition, the type of research article primarily featured in this chapter should have some element of peer review as a minimum requirement and should therefore be found in what are known as refereed publications (see Chapter 16; Sanders & Wilkins, 2010).

A research article can therefore be defined as a written document providing the history of a research study or journey from beginning to end. In brief, this should outline what was investigated, why this is worth researching, how the information was gathered and what the findings mean. The characteristics of the information provided will vary depending on the type of inquiry involved and the conventions of the discipline (Locke et al., 2010). In addition to write-ups of single studies, research studies which systematically combine and evaluate the results of multiple studies are very useful. This is because in the hierarchy of evidence, well-executed syntheses of research are more compelling than the best single study. This type of study includes systematic reviews, meta-analyses (a method of statistically comparing the results of multiple quantitative studies) and meta-syntheses (a method of drawing conclusions from multiple qualitative studies) (Walsh & Downe, 2005).

Distinct from single-study research and research syntheses, there is also a vast range of 'grey literature' available. Effectively, grey literature is information that is not published in peer-reviewed academic journals but may still be of use to researchers or practitioners. It includes documents such as unpublished dissertations, internal reports or manuals, and material from the web such as blogs and Wikipedia. Grey literature can be distinguished from the sort of research article that is the focus of this chapter in that there is a lack of scholarly or peer review for this type of information. Despite this lack of peer review, grey literature is still an important and valuable resource. For example, the Office for National Statistics (ONS) provides an authoritative source of information for a huge range of topics, including attitudes to mental health and rates of mental illness within populations (www.ons.gov.uk). What must be borne in mind, however, is that this type of information requires an even more careful evaluation of its quality and appropriateness because, unlike a peer-reviewed article in an academic journal, there is no preliminary evaluation of the quality of grey literature.

Activity 4.1   Reflecting on your beliefs, assumptions and perceptions

Spend ten minutes reflecting on what might hold you back from the task of reading and evaluating research. To aid your reflection, try to complete the following statement: 'Reading and evaluating research is…'. Using your own ideas and meanings, make a list of statements that reflect your beliefs, assumptions and perceptions.

Reading and evaluating research can be very daunting and even scary to the uninitiated. There are many reasons for this:

- The literature is vast, as any relatively simple keyword search via an electronic database will reveal (see Chapter 5). This is often experienced as the '*I am completely overwhelmed by the sheer vastness of it*' effect.
- Research papers tend to be written using a very specific format and language (or jargon) that can be almost as complex to negotiate as a foreign language. This is often understood as the '*it's all Greek to me*' effect. This can be highly off-putting to both students and practitioners and can even be experienced as profoundly deskilling and demoralising.
- It may be that individuals feel unable to critique published research due to their lack of expertise or understanding of both the topic area and how to go about evaluating the literature. This is often understood as the '*who am I to say, as what do I know about it?*' effect.

Understanding research can be challenging ...

The aim of this chapter is to help you to overcome these stumbling blocks by de-mystifying the process of reading and evaluating the research literature and providing you with a no-nonsense and succinct guide to reading and understanding research.

Tips for developing your critical reading abilities

There are ways to develop your critical abilities when evaluating published research in counselling and psychotherapy. The first step, as McLeod (2003, p. 17) states, is to read research reports with a 'questioning and somewhat sceptical frame of mind', i.e. being mindful of the limitations and uncertainties that may be present in the research, even when it is conducted in good faith and presented with integrity. The 'golden rule' here is: never accept anything you read uncritically. Just because something has been published, even in a quality peer-reviewed journal, it does not necessarily follow that it is 'true'. Evidence can often be interpreted in a variety of different ways. Other tips for becoming a smart reader include:

- Support your independent learning by starting with texts that present research reports with some analysis, such as those found in Gomm, Needham and Bullman (2000) or Girden and Kabacoff (2010).
- Buddy up with a fellow practitioner or researcher or form a study group and work on developing your critical evaluation skills in the group/pair setting. This strategy can greatly enhance your learning experience (two heads are better than one) as well as provide support and encouragement while you become more familiar with reading critically.
- Start 'reading smart' (Locke et al., 2010, p. 63) by annotating a hard-copy version of the text on your first reading. You can be as creative as you like with this process, using different colours to underline and highlight, writing notes in margins, drawing diagrams – whatever you find helps you start to assimilate the material that the authors are presenting.
- Once you have some clarity about the arguments being made, make a deliberate effort to apply a more critical eye. Ask yourself: Do I agree with this interpretation of this research/these findings? Can I think of another explanation? What have they ignored or not explained that is problematic?
- Use a record form such as that found in Table 4.2 below to structure your deeper and more critical reading of the article and record the outcome for future reference and easy recall.

Anatomy of a research article

The ability to read research confidently develops over time but one thing that will help you is developing a mental checklist of what types of information should be in the different sections of research articles. As discussed in Chapter 6, there are, broadly speaking, two types of research – quantitative and qualitative – and the ways in which they are written up differs. The format of quantitative research articles tends to follow a universally accepted way of presenting research findings, while qualitative research articles are more variable. And while some of the standards of quality by which research studies can be evaluated are similar across paradigms, there are also vigorously debated differences (see Elliott, Fischer & Rennie, 1999, 2000; Reicher, 2000). Learning what the two approaches share and how they differ is an essential part of understanding, and therefore being able to critically evaluate each. Despite these differences, a first evaluation of any research can usefully begin by assessing whether an article accomplishes some key things. Common features should include:

- a robust rationale for the study that is soundly situated in the topic area;
- appropriate research question(s)/hypotheses derived from a thorough review of the literature in the area;
- the matching of researching questions to the appropriate methodology;
- reliable data collection methods carried out with integrity to collect high-quality and valid data;
- carefully thought out and applied procedures;
- rigorous data analysis;
- thoughtful comment upon the limitations of the research and what the findings mean in the context of the topic area;
- a concise, transparent and rigorous write-up that clearly demonstrates these features.

With this overarching list of criteria in mind, we will now examine the different sections of the report in turn.

Abstract

The main function of the abstract is to expand on the title so that potential readers may evaluate whether it is worth continuing to read on. It should provide a mini outline of the study, including a rationale, key details about the methodology and the headline findings and conclusions. It should also not be misleading – e.g. overstate the results.

Introduction/literature review

In this section, the job of the critical reader is to evaluate if the purpose of the study is stated clearly and appropriately framed within the literature review.

1. A clear rationale/persuasive argument about the value of the study should be constructed and presented (often early on). It is not sufficient that no one has undertaken the research before – there should be an argument about why the study matters. This is often an argument about the social relevance/importance of the study.
2. The literature review should start broadly and become narrower so that there is more information about studies that are closer to the study being presented. Similarly, the arguments being made should move from the general (there is not much research on...) to the specific (the problem with the only current studies in this area are...). If done well, this 'funnel model' should lead, with compelling logic, to the decision to conduct the presented study.
3. The study topics/issues/variables (e.g. depression, masculinity and unemployment) should be convincingly defined early on and a rationale for the chosen definition should be provided. Ideally, alternative conceptualisations of these study foci should also be discussed.
4. The study topic should be introduced in terms of previous research and provide sufficient detail regarding what is known and what is not known so that the reader can understand how the study fits into current understandings in the area. In other words, the gap in the literature must be identified and the case for filling the gap should be explained.
5. The reader needs to consider whether the literature cited is broad enough or if anything is missing. For example, a study on depression in unemployed men should broadly (briefly) reference research on depression, unemployment and men, as well as all the intersections between these areas.
6. A methodological argument should be developed throughout the literature review so that decisions regarding research design and procedures are well justified, i.e. in terms of what has been found to be effective or ineffective in previous investigations.
7. Any conflicting findings noted in the relevant literature should be discussed and given due consideration.
8. The references cited should be comprehensive and should include both recent research and citations from seminal investigators in the field.
9. The literature review should end by clearly identifying the study research questions.

It is worth noting here that you may find some differences between the literature review in a quantitative study and that in a qualitative article. Matthews (2005) makes the point that, while reviewing the literature is a vital preliminary step for any research endeavour, the function of this process is likely to serve a slightly different purpose in the two paradigms. A key difference may be that in a qualitative paper the literature review may be brief and focused only on making a convincing argument for the study. There is often a correspondingly longer discussion section in such articles.

Method section

The differences between the method section in quantitative and qualitative papers are outlined in Table 4.1.

Results/analysis

Given the clear differences in the method section of qualitative and quantitative studies outlined above, you will no doubt be unsurprised to find that the results also tend to be written up differently. This section will therefore examine each paradigm in turn.

Quantitative research

Evaluating the results sections of quantitative studies is a common area of anxiety as it can feel very intimidating and off-putting. However, we would encourage you not to avoid or skip this part of a paper because you do not feel confident about your knowledge of statistics. You do not need to be a statistics whizz to have a go at evaluating some common concepts that you will find in this section of quantitative counselling and psychotherapy articles, and the information here is aimed at helping you make a start.

As before, there are some good general starter checks that you can speedily make to look for some basic indicators of quality and without needing to immediately focus on the details of the statistical analyses. For example, have a look at any graphs presented and check whether the scales for each axis are clearly identified. Does any diagrammatic or tabulated representation of the findings add up and make sense? Check whether the variables displayed in any table are clearly identified in the title and if statistically significant numbers are clearly marked. It is also worth looking at the basic data. For example, if a mean (average) for a questionnaire is reported, think about what that actually means. To exemplify, if the average client score on a 10-item depression scale with a 1–5 response scale is 20, that is a pretty low score. If this is the pre-therapy score, maybe it means the clients in the study were not really depressed.

A next step is to check your understanding of common statistical concepts in any paper that you read (see Chapter 10 for an explanation of some key terms as well as resources to extend your understanding). It is also useful to note whether the assumptions for the statistical tests conducted were checked and met, and whether there is any justification provided for why the particular statistical tests were chosen and/or the way the statistical analyses were conducted.

On a final note, try not to be discouraged by the complexities of statistical tests and how the results section in this type of paper is presented, and do bear in mind that your skill in evaluating quantitative research reporting will improve with time and practice.

Qualitative research

As mentioned earlier and discussed further in Chapter 12, there has been an extensive and lively debate over the past decade or so pertaining to issues of

Table 4.1 *Differences between the method section in a quantitative and qualitative article*

General principles and questions you might ask of the various components of the method section	What you would expect to see in a good quality...	
	Quantitative report	**Qualitative report**
Approach to the research: • Has this topic been adequately addressed?	Not typically discussed but a positivist (see Chapter 6) approach is assumed.	A brief outline of the philosophical assumptions/paradigms that underpin the research. These should be shown to be congruent with the research design.
Research design: • How clearly is the study design explained/described? • Is a rationale provided for the selection of the study design? • Was this information placed at an appropriate and helpful place in the report that improves the understanding of the remainder?	A named design with the primary variables and their relationships to each other described (see chapter 10 for more detail).	A named design with some indication of its intellectual heritage (e.g. anthropology, psychology, philosophy, etc.) (see Chapter 12 for more detail).
Sampling/participants: • How well are decisions regarding the nature, number and selection of participants conveyed and justified? • Have participants been treated ethically?	A clear rationale for the sample characteristics and selection with clearly specified inclusion/exclusion/ selection criteria. The sample should closely match the selection criteria. A thorough explanation of the selection/recruitment procedure and a discussion of any limitations of this process. A justification of the size of the sample, e.g. in terms of the statistics.	Participant demographics and any other relevant characteristics, depending on the findings. Rationale for participant selection. A clear outline of sampling and recruitment strategies with a clear discussion of any limitations of these processes. A coherent rationale for the sample size that is related to the design and purpose of the study and justified in terms of the methodology.
Instrumentation/measures: • How thoroughly are these aspects reported and justified?	All instruments/measures/ procedures clearly named and described. Where appropriate, validity and reliability of measures should be adequately demonstrated – remember that the results will only be useful in so far as the measuring tools are credible or reliable and this must be demonstrated through adequate reporting. A rationale for the selection of particular instruments or measures where there is more than one option.	Information about how any data collection stimuli (e.g. interview questions) were developed and the topic areas covered plus information about any piloting.

General principles and questions you might ask of the various components of the method section	What you would expect to see in a good quality...	
	Quantitative report	Qualitative report
Procedures: • How well has the data generation process been carried out? • How thoroughly are the procedures reported? • Is there sufficient detail described? • Do you know enough to repeat the study?	The protocol for the use for each instrument/measure/ procedure; the details regarding the recording of all data; the exact manner in which each intervention was applied to each participant. Adequate details regarding the statistical tests used and the processes involved in and justification for choices around analysis of the data. A clear statement with regard to how ethical issues were handled.	A detailed account of the data gathering process plus a justification of any data collection method. An account of any ethical procedures (e.g. obtaining fully informed consent/ debriefing, etc.) plus the length and number of interviews or focus groups, etc., and recording and transcription information. Full details of the analytic process/steps and an indication of how thoroughly this was carried out through comprehensive reporting and documentation of the procedure.
Quality: • Is there any consideration of how the quality of a qualitative analysis was addressed? • How well documented and reflexive is the research process? • How appropriate are the methods used? • How well have ethical issues been considered and addressed?	[Quality issues are not typically directly addressed in a section on quality criteria in quantitative papers as there is a clearer general consensus on what these are.]	A description of what the quality criteria for the study are, and how quality has been achieved and the forms of validation that have been attempted (e.g. member/peer validation, etc.).
Reflexivity: • Has this been addressed within the report?	[Not addressed in quantitative papers because quantitative studies assume an objective researcher stance.]	A rationale for adopting a reflexive approach. A positioning of the researcher in relation to the topic or population of interest (e.g. age, gender, first-hand experience of the topic area, etc.). An outline of any assumptions or biases that the researcher might bring to the investigation and how these have been managed throughout the research process, and in particular throughout the analytical process.

quality in qualitative research and how this might be assessed. In addition to this, the diversity of qualitative research means that the evaluation of reports in this paradigm is more complex. In response to these intricacies, various frameworks have been developed that outline the key principles for quality in qualitative research. The details of this debate and the ensuing frameworks are beyond the scope of this chapter. However, interested readers are signposted to Chapter 12 for a range of quality guidelines that are available for further reading and to facilitate the development of evaluative skills in this area.

Notwithstanding this abundance of frameworks and the ongoing debate, all of which can be somewhat overwhelming for the novice, there are a number of basic principles that can be applied when evaluating whether a qualitative results section is of good quality. At the most basic evaluative level, the reporting of the analysis should be clear and comprehensible – it should make sense to you, the reader, and should be coherent in terms of the rest of the report. The results (or analysis) should present an argument that is constructed from the analysis of the data, sometimes involving an interpretative account of the data, which should be convincingly evidenced with data extracts. The presentation of data extracts allows the reader to evaluate whether the researcher's interpretations are credible and grounded in the data; this might be a judgement about whether there are sufficient data extracts. Conversely, a sign of poor quality might be too many data extracts coupled with insufficient interpretation or analysis – the balance between the two components must be appropriate. A good quality results section will generally 'weave back and forth between assertions and evidence throughout the text' (Matthews, 2005, p. 805) representing 'a continual interplay of ... analysis and interpretation' (Morrow, 2005, p. 260). In addition, the evidence presented must support the interpretations. Clearly, it is problematic if the data presented does not seem to support the points that are being made. Another potential problem is when the research 'findings' mirror the questions that were asked of participants; if this is the case, what has been presented is not a proper qualitative analysis but a précis of what participants have been organised to say. Qualitative analysis is often more convincing if the results are unexpected to the researchers, and if there is clarity (e.g. from a description of the types of question asked in an interview) that participants were not led into certain sorts of responses.

One further point to make is that different qualitative methodologies have different conventions for the presentation of the analysis and a quick, basic quality check is whether this section is presented in a manner consistent with those conventions (e.g. see the section on write-up in Chapter 13 on thematic analysis). What you may also find is that occasionally the results and discussion section are merged together and the findings are discussed simultaneously with the relevant literature and discussion points rather than being presented alone. If this is not the case, then you should not expect to see any references to other research or theory in this section – this will be found in a separate discussion section where the findings of the current study will be discussed within the framework of the existing literature. A final comment regarding qualitative results sections is that they will, by their nature, tend to vary in presentation due to the vast array of different qualitative research methods that are available for use. The take-home message here is that your critical abilities in this paradigm will improve with time and practice, and the more you can read, the better.

Discussion/conclusion

A good quality discussion section in both paradigms should constitute a thoughtful discussion of the findings within the context and framework of the existing literature in the area. By this we mean that the ways in which the findings support, clarify and are consistent with, or contradict and challenge what has already been established and reported in previous research, should be explicitly discussed. To make a start in your evaluation, therefore, you might ask yourself to what degree the findings are adequately situated within the current existing knowledge and understandings that we have about the topic area and whether the knowledge base has been extended as a result of the study. Findings should be explicitly and clearly related back to the purpose of the study and the research hypotheses/question(s) and a good quality discussion section will outline and explain the basis upon which wider inferences have been drawn from the findings.

An essential component of any discussion section is a transparent and frank discussion of the limitations of the study. The purpose of this exercise is to acknowledge any biases or failings in the research and enable the reader to evaluate the impact of these upon the credibility and generalisability/transferability of the results. At this point the authors of a good quality article should make suggestions for further research that either address the limitations of the study and/or suggest the direction in which future research might go in order to build upon the findings.

Finally, counselling and psychotherapy research often has an emphasis on implications for practice, training and policy, so examining how well these have been described and outlined, as well as how robust and meaningful they are, is an essential component of the evaluative process. The question here is really 'so what?' – has the article adequately conveyed the study's impact and importance and what sort of contribution has it made to the field.

Activity 4.2   Reading critically

Find a relevant or interesting-looking article – quantitative or qualitative – and use this guide to critically read and make sense of the paper.

Organising your critical reading

The key to successful critical reading of the research literature, whether to inform practice or for a research study, is good organisation. Keep a record of your reading in order to avoid becoming overwhelmed by the detail found in research reports. A suggestion for a record form to aid this process is presented in Table 4.2. This can be customised to your requirements or you can develop your own depending on personal preference and the purpose of your reading (e.g. for planning your own research or to inform your practice).

Table 4.2 *An example record form*

Area	Idea of what you might include
Reference	Record the full reference/citation for the article
Literature review	• Indicate in broad terms the relevance or importance of the study. • Briefly describe how the study fits into what is already known in the existing literature, i.e. the gap in the literature. • Critical analysis – note any issues in the literature review (e.g. failure to include relevant literature).
Method	• Summarise the details pertaining to the sample, participants and how they were selected. • Describe/outline the context of the study, e.g. briefly outline where it was conducted. • Briefly outline the main procedural steps for the study. Use a diagram or a flow chart to describe the steps and any key relationships among them. • Outline the study data – how this was collected and the role of the researcher in the data collection process. • Describe the type of data analysis employed. • Critical analysis – note any issues identified in the method section.
Results	• Outline what the authors identify as the main findings from the analysis. • Identify what the significant findings are from your perspective and use your critical analysis lens to list any issues you have noted about the findings.
Discussion	• Describe what conclusions the authors have drawn from the findings (including implications for practice, training, policy). Identify whether the findings have addressed the purpose and rationale for the study. • Outline the limitations for the study as described by the authors and include any of your own that are related to areas such as methodology and quality. • Briefly outline the main points of the discussion and anything of value that you have learned from the article (positives and negatives). • Identify the core relevance of this study for your purpose (e.g. how it contributes to the argument you are making for this paper or your own research study).

Information box 4.1   Referencing management software

An alternative to the type of form shown in Table 4.2 is to use a referencing management software system, such as RefWorks (www.refworks.com), Endnote (www.myendnoteweb.com/) or CiteULike (www.citeulike.org/). Some of these systems are free (e.g. CiteULike) and some are not (e.g. RefWorks and Endnote), but many education institutions will be able to provide student access to this type of software. It is worth spending the time to learn how to use them as they can really help with organising and storing your investigations of the literature.

Whatever system you use, however, it is key to keep records and to make sure that when you are reading and logging your literature search that you are doing so as a critical reader. Simply saving abstracts or making a few desultory notes is not helpful when you are trying to remember why you thought that study was important. Taking a systematic approach will help you get into good habits as you develop your critical reading skills, and developing a disciplined approach to reading and understanding research will enhance your effectiveness, and confidence, in this task.

Conclusion

This chapter began with the aim of turning anxious or resistant research readers into enthusiastic and critical readers of research in counselling and psycho-therapy. Clearly, if readers find research articles uninteresting and difficult to read, part of the responsibility lies with the authors of research articles; the paper by Jane Speedy with the chuckling research reader that was quoted earlier is in part a critique of conventional research papers for being 'irrelevant, dry, academic and statistically inclined' (Speedy, 2005, p. 66). The argument of this chapter, however, is that readers of research also have a responsibility to work on their research literacy skills. Hopefully this chapter has helped you begin the journey towards research fluency; the list of further reading below will aid you to continue to develop the ability to read critically.

Suggestions for further reading

Aveyard, H. & Sharp, P. (2013). *A Beginner's Guide to Evidence-based Practice in Health and Social Care.* Maidenhead: Open University Press.

An easily accessible introduction to evidence-based practice (EBP) (see Chapter 1) that includes useful information about the types of research methods often used in counselling and psychotherapy research and hierarchies of evidence, along with a helpful chapter relating to the critical appraisal of research articles, all within the context of EBP.

Locke, L.F., Silverman, S.J. & Spirduso, W.W. (2010). *Reading and Understanding Research* (3rd edition). Thousand Oaks, CA: Sage.

A good place to start for developing skills in reading and understanding research as it provides detailed and practical advice without assuming any specific knowledge of research methods.

FIVE

Doing a literature review
Dr Meg Barker (Open University)

Introduction

The first stage of most research projects is to undertake a review of the literature to determine what research has already been conducted in the area. This helps the researcher to hone their own research questions and to determine how they plan to conduct their research. The purpose of the literature review section of the final report of the research project is to summarise this previous literature and to provide a clear rationale for the current research in the light of what has been done before. This section is often called the 'introduction' in a research paper as it introduces the reader to the area, funnelling down from the broad topic under consideration and why it is important, through a critical consideration of prior research which identifies any gaps in the literature, to the specific research questions or hypotheses of the current study.

This chapter covers both the process of searching for relevant literature and the process of writing the literature review. It should be read in conjunction with the previous two chapters because the process of literature review runs parallel with the choice of research question (Chapter 3), and obviously skills in reading and understanding research (Chapter 4) are necessary.

The purpose of the literature review is to:

- Outline the area you are researching.
- Explain why it matters (e.g. Does it have implications for policy or treatment? Is this a particularly under-researched group?).
- Summarise the research that has already been done in this area, particularly any key studies.
- Identify any gaps in this literature: to justify why your study is important and what it adds to the literature.
- Present your research questions (if qualitative research) or hypotheses (if quantitative research). These should be set out at the end of the literature review.

This list will be useful while you are writing the literature review, as well as afterwards, to ensure that it does all these things.

It is likely that you will write one version of the literature review prior to conducting your research, but return to it afterwards to redraft it in order to ensure that it does tell a clear argument leading up to your research (rather than simply summarising past research) and that it includes all of the key studies and theories. Note that the literature review for a research proposal does not need to be as extensive as that for a final research write-up (see Chapter 9).

As a general rule of thumb all of the research and theories mentioned in the rest of the paper should have been introduced in the literature review or introduction. However, it may be necessary to bring new material into the discussion and conclusions if the analysis suggests taking a different direction or engaging with a different area of research that you hadn't anticipated.

Conducting a literature search

Of course before you write your literature review you have to actually search through what has been done before. This stage is an integral part of the research process: it is through reviewing previous research that we can hone our own research questions (see Chapter 3), avoid unethical practices such as over-researching certain groups, and take account of what past researchers have learnt about the best ways of approaching the topic.

PAUSE FOR REFLECTION

Think about a topic you are interested in researching (perhaps one that you considered in previous chapters or are thinking about for a dissertation, thesis or paper). How would you currently imagine going about finding out what research has been conducted before on this topic?

As a very rough rule of thumb, to keep the process manageable, what you are looking for by the end of the literature search are around 5–15 key papers, chapters or books, which are the main ones you will base your literature review around, and around 20–40 additional materials (papers, books, reports, etc.), which you are likely to reference but are less central to your argument. These may be background reading or less specifically relevant papers which you will skim read and refer to rather than summarising in depth. Of course, such numbers depend somewhat on the level of study that you are at, and the length of the final report that you are working towards. You might need less for a brief research study on a foundation degree or diploma, and a good deal more (perhaps five times as much) for a full doctoral thesis of 80,000 words or so. However, the general process of searching for literature is similar whatever stage you are at.

This rule of thumb does not, of course, mean that you should conduct a literature search in a linear way, simply stopping once you have around 40 papers, books, reports and chapters. Rather, the literature search is a process of finding everything that you can of relevance and then whittling this down to the most essential work that you need to mention in your literature review. In fact, the hardest task in the process is often deciding what to leave out.

There is rather a dark art to the process of searching for literature, as you will find when you start to conduct literature searches yourself by typing words into search engines and databases. It isn't a simple matter that you type in the topics that you are interested in (e.g. 'bereavement and counselling' or 'eye movement desensitisation and reprocessing for victims of the London bombings'), and inevitably get back around 10 key papers or books, and an additional 30 or so quite relevant ones. Rather, you generally either get way too much (thousands and thousands of hits for your search terms) or way too little (one or two papers which might not be relevant at all to what you are doing). This is where breadth and focus come in (see also the section on 'Refining your scope' in Chapter 3). If you realise that there is already loads written on your topic, then you need to focus in ('bereavement of a child and person-centred therapy', for example). If there is hardly anything, you need to broaden out (to 'trauma counselling and therapy for victims of terrorist attacks', for example).

As you search you will want to see how many hits you get, in order to narrow or broaden your search terms. It is also vital, at this point, to make sure you include all of the materials that anybody else in the area (such as your markers, examiners or reviewers) would regard as crucial. For example, some topics are covered in more than one discipline so you may have to look beyond papers and books on counselling and therapy. For instance, bereavement is also addressed in health and social care, psychology and sociology. A useful suggestion that a piece of work is of central importance is when you spot it being referenced by several other writers in the area.

The literature review needs to cover each element of your research and any overlaps between them. For example, the Figure 5.1 illustrates the elements and their overlap for person-centred therapy with child bereavement. Your search would need to include bereavement, person-centred therapy, and children, as well as each of the overlaps (child bereavement, person-centred therapy and bereavement, etc.)

There are three main stages of literature searching:

First stage: Using search engines and other resources to accumulate a large collection of relevant materials.

Second stage: Reading through the abstracts, summaries, etc. that you have obtained and using these to find further materials.

Third stage: Considering all the material you have to determine which papers and chapters you need to read in depth, and where the gaps in the literature lie.

We will now go through each of these in a little more detail.

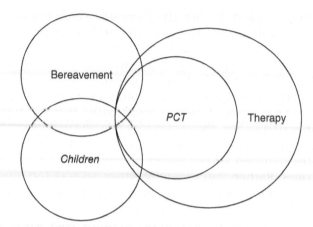

Figure 5.1 *Overlap between literature search areas*

First stage

There are various places to conduct your literature search, and it is usually worth using more than one of these as not every paper, book or article is listed in a single database, particularly if you need to search across more than one discipline.

Google Scholar is a great starting place which everybody can use regardless of which databases their college or university subscribes to. Type 'Google Scholar' into the Google search engine and then just use this in the same way as the regular Google. Google Scholar only links to academic papers, books and reports, avoiding the large amounts of non-academic materials you would get on the general search engine.

Increasingly, papers, and to a less extent chapters and books, are freely available online. However, quite often you will only be able to access an abstract or a few pages without payment. Used in conjunction with your university or college library, you should be able to access many of the full documents. Talk with your librarian about this.

The librarian can also point you towards databases that the university or college subscribes to, such as Psychinfo, Web of Science, or Medline.[1] It is worth being aware that there are spelling differences across countries. For example, it is 'counselling' in the UK, and 'counseling' in the USA, so use both spellings. Also, the terms by which researchers name things may vary by country, or may just not be familiar to you. For example, with 'bereavement' you would need to look up synonyms such as 'grief', 'mourning', 'loss', and 'death'.

---

[1]See this wikipedia page for frequently updated lists of academic databases and search engines: http://en.wikipedia.org/wiki/List_of_academic_databases_and_search_engines

Information box 5.1   Example of a literature search

Let's go through an example of the kind of search that you might do towards the beginning of a research project on mindfulness therapy. You can follow through this process on your own internet browser.[2]

- *I open up Google Scholar[3] and type in the word 'mindfulness'.*
- *This yields 70,700 results. I need to narrow down my search!*
- *Down the side of the screen I cannot check 'patents' and 'citations' (given these are unlikely to be central materials), and restrict my date to work within the last decade. That takes me down to 30,700 results. Sorting by relevance then enables me to see the most relevant materials on the first few pages.*
- *Scanning these I soon realise that mindfulness has been applied to many different problems. I can narrow down my search if I'm particularly interested in one of these: depression. Typing 'mindfulness and depression' gets down to 17,000 hits.*
- *I might further narrow down my search if I'm interested in a particular form of mindfulness, e.g. Mindfulness-Based Cognitive Therapy (MBCT). Searching for this gets me down to 8,040 hits.*
- *This might be a starting point for printing out and reading the first few pages worth of abstracts to get a feel for the field, and/or I might narrow it down still further. If you click the arrow box to the right of the search box you can fill in further search options. For example, if I'm not interested in depression related to pain and illness I could include those in the 'without' box.*

Sometimes there are particular journals which specifically publish papers in the area that you are interested in. In such cases it is useful to search their websites for anything of relevance. For example, if you are interested in relationship therapy for people in same-sex relationships, you may find specific relationship therapy journals (such as *Sex and Relationship Therapy*), and those on lesbian, gay and bisexual people (such as the *Journal of Homosexuality* and

---

[2]Actually, I now know rather more about this having recently written a book on the topic, for which I ended up conducting many such literature searches! If you are interested, the book is: Barker, M. (2013). *Mindful Counselling & Psychotherapy: Practising mindfully across approaches and issues*. London: Sage.

[3]There is a general guide to searching Google Scholar at: http://scholar.google.com/intl/en/scholar/help.html

Psychology & Sexuality) and search those. You'll get a feel for the key journals as you look through the search results.

Finally, it may be useful to visit a large library such as the British Library to search their documents, especially if there is a historical element to your research (for example, if you are studying the treatment of people with mental health problems over time and want to view old reports, books or policy documents). It is also useful to search online book stores because books don't always come up in journal searches.

Second stage

Once you have done your initial search you can obtain the full papers, books or reports for the most relevant looking materials by following the links or ordering them through your library. It is then worth looking through these to ensure that you have all the key references that other people are citing. I often come across a really important book or paper by looking at what is cited in other papers rather than through the search engine process.

At this point it may even be worth emailing key names in the field and ask them for any relevant papers or recommended reading. Many academics respond positively to a brief, interested email.

Ensure that you consider the quality of the materials that you have found at this point. Only clearly academic sources which have been properly peer-reviewed will count in your report so be very cautious of including general webpages, wikipedia pages, newspaper articles, blogs, and so on. The only real exceptions to this are when you are actually talking about the way that something is represented in the media or popular imagination, or when there is a 'grey literature' that you need to draw on (e.g. reports published by small charities or organisations on the experience of a specific group that has been under-researched; see also Chapter 4). In these cases, just ensure you are careful to flag up, in your writing, that you are aware that these are not academic sources and to make clear why you are using them.

TOP TIP

During the second stage of literature searching it is well worth making a reference list as you go along: either a word document with all of the references in (alphabetised and/or in topic sections) or using a programme which helps you to insert references into your writing (see Chapter 9 for information on how to reference). It can also be useful to make summaries as you go along (see Chapter 4).

Third stage

During the third stage of the literature search you will have determined which materials you want to read in detail and begin doing so. You will also now be getting a sense of the structure of the story you will tell in the literature review and where the areas are which have not yet been researched in depth.

You might well find it useful to cut up your abstracts and/or summaries of papers or chapters into separate pieces of paper, and then to sit on the floor and try to sort them into 'like' piles or related materials: this can give a good visual impression of the overall shape of the research in an area, and where there might be gaps for your own research. A similar thing can be done using computer files and folders if you work better that way.

'No I'm NOT waving!'

Activity 5.1   Conducting a literature search

Choose a counselling/psychotherapy-related topic of interest to you (perhaps one you are planning to go on and research). Conduct a literature search using the search possibilities which are readily available to you (e.g. Google Scholar, Amazon, your university or college's online library search, and any existing books or papers you have).

Identify the key materials that you would draw on, and what more general materials would be of help if you were going to write a literature review on this topic.

Comment

Keep hold of the list of materials that you develop for this activity as it will be useful as the basis of later activities where you'll have a go at structuring a literature review.

Conducting a literature search can feel overwhelming because there is often so much written on a topic. Also, each time you search you find new and potentially very useful material. At some point, of course, you just have to draw a line and determine to press ahead with what you have. This line will be an arbitrary one given that there is always more possible material, but it is important that you draw the line, rather than striving for completeness or perfection. Any marker, examiner or reviewer will be aware that nobody can read everything.

Writing up the literature review

Once you feel that you have sufficient materials and have become familiar with them, you are ready to embark on the process of writing. Often, however, it is not a matter of doing all your reading and then doing all your writing. Rather, you swing between the two, for example jotting down a structure for your literature review, then going back and re-reading the papers that are most relevant to the first section, then coming back to draft that section, checking back with your reading, and possibly even doing a further literature search, once you have a complete draft in case there is something you've missed, etc.

The literature review is likely to be pretty much the first thing that you write up of your research study. Therefore it is important to think a little about the writing process before you start. Embarking upon a major writing project is nerve-wracking for most people, even those of us who are very experienced writers. In addition to this, lots of people find writing the literature review harder than other parts of a report because it requires understanding and synthesising so much material while making a clear argument. You can help yourself a lot by planning *how* you are going to write before you begin.

PAUSE FOR REFLECTION

What are the main anxieties and blocks that you have about writing? What do you currently do to address these?

Writing can tap into areas of low confidence and self-esteem. Even the most experienced writer sometimes worries about being 'found out' as not knowing enough if they put their words on paper. There is a concern that what we write will be 'set in stone' for all time. Many people simply do not see themselves as a writer, perhaps because they were not the 'academic one' in the family, or their writing was criticised at school.

We can tackle such worries in many ways. First, it is useful to aspire to be a 'good enough' writer, rather than striving for perfection. You can't possibly please every potential reader of your work because different people like different things (in terms of tone, style and content) so define your audience and write for them (the most likely reader who is interested in the area and wants it clearly explained and to learn more). If you have time before you have to write a big project, you might find it useful to write smaller things (e.g. letters, blog posts, book reviews) to build up your confidence.

There are many things that you can do to make writing a long piece, like a literature review, a less daunting prospect. The worst thing to do is to stare at the blank screen trying to write the perfect first sentence. Instead, start with a mind-map, followed by a structure for your writing (see below). Building up like this breaks the task down into sections of a few hundred words at most. It is amazing how fast it can go when you break it into chunks.

Think about when and where you write best and create that environment. Many people find it useful to do writing for an hour per day, stopping after that if it is not flowing and going on to other, less daunting, tasks (like reading, structuring papers, dealing with data, conducting further literature searches, etc.). When you do sit down to write make sure that you do write for an hour. Don't worry about the quality or wording for the first draft. Just get down what you want to say in the way you would explain it to a friend. You can go through and polish the language later.

It often helps to start with a mind-map of the information that you obtained from the literature research to help you to see what there is to include, before going into actual writing. The information boxes below give you an example mind-map for my literature review on mindfulness therapies and depression, and invite you to create your own mind-map for the topic you explored in Activity 5.1.

Information box 5.2   Example of a mind-map

This is an example mind-map on mindfulness therapies and depression. It gives you an overview of the different areas of published research on this topic.

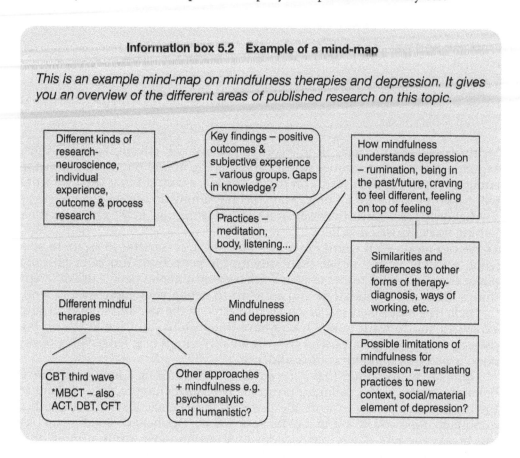

Once you have something like this you can go in and make a note of the specific references that you would want to include in each section (names and dates from your list). You could also use different coloured ink to highlight different types of paper (theory/research, quantitative/qualitative, CBT-based/other, etc.).

Activity 5.2   Creating a mind-map

Create your own mind-map for the topic you're interested in.

As mentioned, the first part of writing the literature review is to rough out a structure. Moving from the mind-map to the structure involves weaving the *content* that you want to draw on into a coherent *story*. Remember that the purpose of the literature review is to provide a rationale and justification for your research: why it is necessary and why it matters. You should be looking to convince your reader, not merely to describe what has been done before.

A good metaphor for the literature review is a funnel, starting with the broad topic and why it is of interest and then narrowing down gradually to focus on the specific area that your research is addressing. For example, here is an illustration of what the funnel might look like for my literature review on mindfulness and depression.

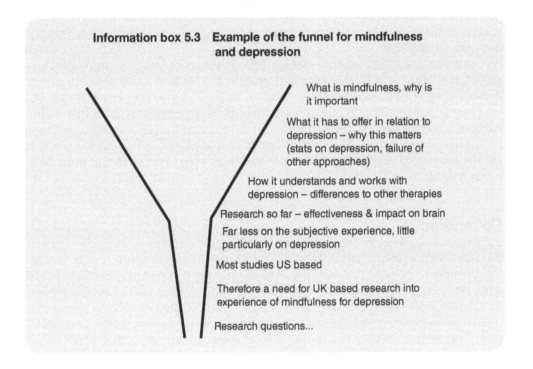

Information box 5.3 Example of the funnel for mindfulness and depression

What is mindfulness, why is it important

What it has to offer in relation to depression – why this matters (stats on depression, failure of other approaches)

How it understands and works with depression – differences to other therapies

Research so far – effectiveness & impact on brain

Far less on the subjective experience, little particularly on depression

Most studies US based

Therefore a need for UK based research into experience of mindfulness for depression

Research questions...

The idea is to draw the reader in and to infect them with some of the passion that you have about the area, as well as doing the practical task of summarising past research and justifying your own project.

Once you have a sense of the funnel it is a good idea to come up with the subheadings which will structure your literature review, breaking it down into sections of a few paragraphs each (e.g. each of the areas on the above funnel might be a subsection with a subheading). Once you have these written down you can start to consider what the paragraphs will be within each subsection, jotting down a few words for what you want to cover (with which references) in each paragraph. Remember that each paragraph should make one point and then expand on that, before flowing into the next paragraph. Soon you will have a side or two of paper with a complete structure for your literature review. Then it is just a matter of going through and turning each note into a full paragraph.

Your literature review should summarise past studies, but you need to ensure that you synthesise them together rather than simply providing a list of one study after the next. For example, you might want to cluster studies which use a similar methodology or have a similar focus into the same paragraph. Pull out any limitations of past research and gaps in the literature here (see Chapter 4 on reading and evaluating research) and keep returning to the matter of why this makes your own research worthwhile. Then summarise clearly how your research builds upon this past research, fills gaps, addresses methodological limitations, etc. End by clearly stating your specific research questions/hypotheses (see Chapter 3).

Once you are filling in your paragraphs, in terms of style, as previously suggested, it is often best to write the first draft in simple English, just as you would if explaining it to a friend, as this is often easier to write and ensures that you are clear and accessible. When you go through and polish this draft into a final version, you can work on getting the writing appropriately academic without losing this clarity (supervisors and more experienced academics can help you to get the tone right, and you can also use the papers that you've found most helpful as a model).

Conclusion

We have seen in this chapter that the function of the literature review is more than simply to present the past research on your topic: you also need it to justify your research and why it matters. Reading, summarising and evaluating previous research in your literature review will also help you to decide upon your own methodology (see Chapter 6) and to plan your research (see Chapters 7 and 9) as well as noting the major ethical issues in this area that you need to consider (see Chapter 8). The following checklist summarises some of the main 'dos and don'ts' when conducting a literature search and review.

Checklist of dos and don'ts

Do

- Search, read, search some more (repeat as necessary!)
- Remember to both broaden and narrow the focus of your literature search to get a reasonable number of materials

- Know when to stop searching (once you have identified what seems to be key)
- Collate a reference list as you go, rather than writing it at the end
- Work to organise and structure your literature search, for example by compiling research records (Chapter 4) or using a mind-map
- Think about the process of writing that works for you (and any blocks) before getting started on writing
- Foster a clear argument by building up your literature review from an initial skeleton structure
- Think about your intended reader: is your argument clear, accessible and engaging?
- Weave together past research rather than summarising one study after another
- Ensure that you justify your research and why it matters
- Make sure your literature review has the required funnel shape
- Ask others to read over your work to let you know what makes sense and what needs clarifying

Don't

- Feel like you have to find everything ever written on your topic
- Start writing your literature review from the first sentence without structuring it first
- Try to write when you're not in the right space for it (after the initial hour of writing)
- Attempt to write perfectly in the first draft (you can always go back and polish)
- Simply describe the literature – you need to craft an argument
- Worry if you have anxieties about writing – everybody does

Suggestions for further reading

The British Association for Counselling and Psychotherapy have produced an information sheet on conducting a literature review which is available through their website: www.bacp.co.uk/research/Information_Sheets/R1.php

There are a couple of specific books on how to conduct a literature review:

Hart, C. (2000). *Doing a Literature Review: Releasing the Social Science Research Imagination.* London: Sage.

Ridley, D. (2008). *The Literature Review: A Step-by-step Guide for Students.* London: Sage.

SIX

Introduction to research methodology

Dr Ladislav Timulak (Trinity College Dublin)

Introduction

Research is a systematic and rigorous quest for knowledge. It is embedded in a particular understanding and set of assumptions about the nature of carrying out research, a topic which is the subject of the philosophy of science (see Information box 6.1 for the definition of the philosophy of science). Different approaches to the understanding of reality (ontology) and ways of knowing (epistemology) developed into research paradigms (prevailing ways of thinking) and particular methodologies.

This chapter provides you with an overview of different research paradigms and how they are expressed in terms of current quantitative and qualitative research methodologies. It introduces you to the essential features of quantitative and qualitative methodologies (formulation of the research problem, research design, sampling, data collection and data analysis methods) as well as basic methodological aspects of research studies. The chapter will also present different research genres in the field, such as outcome research, process research, and other types of counselling and psychotherapy research.

Research paradigms

When thinking about a different understanding of reality and ways of knowing, you can imagine two arguing politicians who each present an opposite view on some issue (e.g. how to overcome an economic downturn). Each politician will portray their reality (macro-economic stability versus the well-being of simple people) and will use the evidence supporting it, while discounting the type of evidence presented by their opponent as erroneous. One position relies on hard statistical data that speaks about 'the reality', while the other one relies on first-hand accounts from people affected by the downturn, which represents 'their reality'. Each politician will represent a particular 'paradigm'.

Information box 6.1   Philosophy of science (based on Ponterotto, 2005)

Philosophy of science contains beliefs or assumptions regarding:

- *ontology (the nature of reality and being);*
- *epistemology (the study of knowledge, the acquisition of knowledge, and the relationship between the knower [research participant] and would-be knower [the researcher]);*
- *axiology (the role and place of values in the research process);*
- *rhetorical structure (the language and presentation of the research); and*
- *methodology (the process and procedures of research).*

PAUSE FOR REFLECTION

Try to reflect on your own assumptions regarding the nature of reality. For instance, if a client gives you their story of an argument with their partner, do you think the client's perspective is objectively true?

Ponterotto (2005), using the framework developed by Guba and Lincoln (1994), recognises four research paradigms (positivism, post-positivism, constructivism-interpretivism and critical theory) that shape the social sciences, including psychotherapy research. Ponterotto (2005) sees *positivism* as placing an emphasis on the assumption that there is one true reality, the assumption that the researcher and participant are independent and the assumption that there is no place for values in research (thus there is thorough control for biases). *Post-positivism* also places an emphasis on the assumption of one true reality but acknowledges that it can be known only imperfectly. It further recognises that the researcher may have some influence on the participant (phenomenon), but tries to limit that influence. It also sees no useful place for values in research. *Constructivism-interpretivism* sees reality as multiple constructed subjective realities influenced by the context and the interaction between the researcher and the participant, with the researcher acknowledging and attempting to bracket his/her own values and their influence on knowing. Finally, the *critical theory* paradigm views reality as multiple realities mediated by power relations and sees the interaction between the researcher and the researched as being values-mediated and hopefully aspiring to be transformational and empowering. Researchers in this paradigm hope that their values will influence the research and outcomes, and will lead to transformation and empowerment of the participants and the group they represent (for a comparison of the four paradigms, see also Table 6.1).

Table 6.1 *Comparison of four research paradigms (based on Ponterotto, 2005)*

Positivism	Post-positivism	Constructivism-interpretivism	Critical theory
One true reality	One true reality but can be known only imperfectly	Reality – multiple constructed subjective realities	Reality – multiple realities mediated by power relations
Researcher and participant are independent	Researcher may have some influence on participant	Interaction between the researcher and the participant	Interaction between researcher and researched being transformational and empowering
No place for values in research	No place for values in research	Researcher attempting to bracket his/her own values and their influence on knowing	Researchers hope that their values will lead to transformation and empowerment of participants
The rhetoric of presentation is objective	The rhetoric of presentation is objective	The rhetoric of presentation is subjective and cautions around subjectivity	The rhetoric of presentation is subjective and fully owns the subjectivity
Quantitative methods	Mainly quantitative methods	Mainly qualitative methods	Qualitative methods

Each of these paradigms is conducive to different types of rhetoric and methodology. Positivism and post-positivism use the language of precision and 'science', while constructivism-interpretivism and critical theory use a language that is personalised, embedded in personal perspective and in which the intellectual and emotional impact on the researcher is shared. Positivism and post-positivism most often find an expression in what is typically called quantitative research (see Chapter 10), i.e. research that involves control of variables and observation of effects or relationships that can be expressed in the numbers characteristic of the studied samples and generalised to the population that the research samples represent. For instance, if a therapy offered in the research study is effective for a particular type of client (e.g. clients with depression), then it is assumed that those effects will be observed with a certain probability should that therapy be delivered to clients with the same condition beyond the studied sample (i.e. it will work for other depressed clients).

Hope and Harry ponder research paradigms for their journey ...

Constructivism-interpretivism and critical theory paradigms are typically associated with qualitative research (see Chapter 12), research that often focuses on the description of complex phenomena as they occur under natural conditions, or participants' own experiences of various phenomena. These descriptions are then represented by the researcher in a condensed form but are still very close to the phenomena as observed or expressed/described by the participants. In some types of qualitative research the researcher may also be using his or her own interpretation of the phenomena, while he/she fully shares with the audience (readership of the research) the lenses through which the phenomena are observed. An example of qualitative research can be an interview-based exploration of why clients drop out from therapy. Although the researcher may just record the reasons stated by the clients at their face value, the researcher may also interpret them; for instance, the researcher may suggest a client was too polite to be truly honest with the researcher for fear of causing offence to the therapist.

Activity 6.1   Identifying research paradigms

Pick a study of interest to you. Read through its method section and try to identify which of the four paradigms described above influenced how that study was conducted.

Quantitative and qualitative research

Any research methodology, be it quantitative or qualitative, consists of a series of steps that lead to credible findings. These steps contain the formulation of the research problem (what we want to study, i.e. research question/s), research design (how we are going to go about it), sampling (who will be our participants/data source), data collection methods (how we are going to gather relevant information that will help us answer our research question/s) and data analysis (how we are going to analyse the gathered information and what we can infer from it).

Formulating the research problem

The formulation of a research problem in quantitative research is based on a thorough overview of existing research and conceptual thinking in a particular field. The researcher establishes what is known and what is missing and prepares a research design that would allow for arriving at the answer to the researcher's question(s). The research questions in quantitative research are often formulated in the form of hypotheses, in which the researcher conceptually defines the reality and tests whether his or her understanding of the reality fits or not. The research questions in quantitative research are typically (see Drew, 1980) either descriptive (e.g. what is the frequency of a certain behaviour in therapy), difference assessing (e.g. which therapy is better?) or relationship assessing (e.g. what is the relationship between the therapeutic relationship and the outcome of therapy?).

In qualitative research the research problem similarly often appears from a thorough immersion in the existing literature of the studied subject, but it may not necessarily be so, as often qualitative research is done in the areas where the research-based knowledge is missing. Indeed, Barker, Pistrang and Elliott (2002) observe that qualitative research typically poses exploratory questions, which are used when, (a) there is little known in a particular research area, (b) existing research is confusing, contradictory, or not moving forward or, (c) the topic is highly complex. Another feature of qualitative research is that the questions may evolve and change as the study proceeds, as the qualitative research strategy is characterised by flexible responding to new information as it is gathered. For examples of quantitative and qualitative research questions see Information box 6.2 (for more on the issue of how to come up with a research question see Chapter 3).

Information box 6.2   Examples of quantitative and qualitative research questions

Examples of quantitative research questions are:

- *Is CBT more effective than client-centred therapy in the treatment of depression?*
- *Is early therapeutic alliance a predictor of therapy outcome?*
- *Does the level of symptom reduction in clients in therapy depend on the length of therapy?*

Examples of qualitative research questions are:

- *How do clients in CBT for depression experience therapy and its outcomes?*
- *How do clients experience their relationship with the therapist?*
- *How do clients experience long-term therapy?*

Research design

The research question is addressed by a rigorous procedure that is referred to as research design (see Chapter 7 for more information). Quantitative research designs typically use an experimental manipulation in which the researcher manipulates what is referred to as the 'independent' variable (e.g. the provision or not of psychotherapy) and observes the impact of this manipulation on the 'dependent' variable (e.g. the client's well-being), while controlling for the influence of any 'interfering' variables. The main concern of any design is how it supports the validity of findings. Typically, we talk about construct validity (how well the research variables are delineated and how well they represent the hypothesised constructs), internal validity (how certain we can be in making causal claims), external validity (how well we can generalise from our sample) and statistical conclusion validity (how well we make conclusions on the basis of our calculations) (Cook & Campbell, 1979; Heppner, Wampold & Kivlighan, 2008; Kazdin, 2003; Shadish, Cook & Campbell, 2002).

Since the time of Cook and Campbell's (1979; Heppner et al., 2008; Kazdin, 2003; Shadish et al., 2002) seminal work, the experimental designs are typically classified as between-groups and within-subjects designs. In between-groups designs (such as RCTs, as introduced in Chapter 1), the experimental group (i.e. the one that undergoes the studied intervention – for instance, CBT) is compared to a control group, a group that matches the experimental group in all characteristics (e.g. gender, age, etc.) apart from the studied intervention (i.e. the participants do not undergo CBT). In within-subjects designs, the subjects (participants) are their own control. For instance, participants with social phobia could be observed over time in order to obtain their baseline characteristics. Following this, they could undergo exposure exercises targeting the phobia and they could then be measured again. Experimental designs optimally use a true randomisation, in which a particular research participant has an equal chance of being in the experimental group (e.g. in therapy) or in the control group (e.g. on the waiting list) or, in the case of within-subject designs, the independent variable (e.g. exposure exercise) occurs at random times throughout the duration of the experiment (therapy).

If it is not possible to organise a true randomisation, then we talk about quasi-experimental designs (Cook & Campbell, 1979; Heppner et al., 2008; Kazdin, 2003; Shadish et al., 2002). Quantitative research designs also include non-experimental designs and descriptive designs. The simplest example is that of correlational designs, in which we observe co-occurrence of certain variables (the relationship between them; e.g. what is the relationship between an early therapeutic alliance and therapy outcome?). More information on how to test and interpret a correlation between two variables can be found in Chapter 10. Quantitative research can be represented also by single-subject designs (involving only one participant). These single-subject designs can also be experimental (e.g. following the impact of randomly used exposure exercises in therapy for a specific phobia) or descriptive, where we observe a co-occurrence of examined variables that can be quantified (e.g. the level of insight following interpretation) (see also Chapters 14 and 15).

Design in qualitative research is best understood as a set of procedures that are flexibly used in order to acquire a rich picture of the phenomenon that is the subject of the research. In the case of qualitative research, we talk about the trustworthiness of the research study design or the credibility of the study, rather than validity (Elliott, Fischer & Rennie, 1999; Morrow, 2005). Credibility of a qualitative study is established by several procedures, such as triangulation of data collection or data analysis methods, auditing of the research analysis, validation of the conceptualisation of findings by research participants, etc. (see also Chapter 12).

McLeod (2011) sees several traditions influencing qualitative research: hermeneutics (with its focus on the interpretation of texts), phenomenology (with its emphasis on the description of the essence of the experience), ethnography (with its focus on the participants' observations), rhetoric (with the focus on making a convincing argument) and social justice commitment (with its acknowledgment of the values-based stance of the researcher). The actual qualitative designs (Creswell, 2012; McLeod, 2011) include phenomenological research, ethnography, grounded theory, narrative research, thematic analysis, discourse and conversation analysis, case study research, heuristic research and action research (see also Table 7.2 in Chapter 7).

One can also find studies that combine both quantitative and qualitative research strategies. Such designs are referred to as 'mixed methods' designs and represent a pragmatic approach to research (cf. Creswell, 2003).

Sampling

Once we are clear about the procedure, i.e. how we are going to answer our research questions, we have to locate participants who will undergo our research procedure. Quantitative methodology is primarily concerned with the *representativeness* of the sample and the subsequent generalisability of the results from the research sample to the population that the research sample represents. Apart from the representativeness of the sample, the major issue is the *sample size*, as the bigger the sample size the more precise is the estimate of the actual score in the population. The sample size is also decisive if we want to observe differences among compared groups, or if we are testing the strength of the relationship among the variables, because with the increase in the sample we increase the likelihood of reliably detecting even small effects/relationships.

Sampling in qualitative research is not necessarily led by representativeness and generalisability, although in some qualitative studies those concepts may be relevant for the sampling strategy. Qualitative research is rather characterised by purpose (Creswell, 2012), which in some cases may mean a relevant case, a theory-based case, a critical case, or a politically important case being studied. The size of the sample again depends on the purpose of the study. Sometimes it may be one case (a critical case), other times the sampling is open until saturation appears (i.e. new cases do not bring new findings). More information on sampling can be found in Chapter 7.

Data collection

Data collection methods in quantitative research include self-report measures (questionnaires), observer-based measures, projective measures (in which the participant is asked to respond to unstructured material in an open-ended matter), physiological measures (e.g. blood pressure), artefacts (products of human activity such as guidelines, rules, written books, etc.), and so on. The common thread of the use of measures in quantitative research is that the measures yield responses in a quantifiable manner (e.g. a self-report measure asks how often you had suicidal thoughts in the last week). Another feature of data collection methods in quantitative research is that in order to increase the reliability of the 'measurement', the measures are constructed in a way that several items (questions) feed into the same factor/domain (e.g. they ask about depression in several ways). Validity of such quantitative measures is also established on the basis of their correlations with similar measures (convergent validity), or the lack of correlation between dissimilar measures (discriminant validity) (Heppner et al., 2008; Kazdin, 2003; Shadish et al., 2002). Other forms of validity may also be assessed, such as whether the measures results correspond to a relevant criterion, e.g. a measure of depression corresponds to a diagnosis assigned by an expert (criterion validity), or whether the content of the measure covers all aspects of the construct (content validity).

Qualitative data collection methods often rely on unstructured or semi-structured interviews, but also include qualitative surveys, unstructured or semi-structured observations, the gathering of artefacts, recollections or think-aloud protocols (in which the participants report on their own actions as they are happening), or projective techniques (using ambiguous stimuli and associations to explore participants' thoughts and feelings, e.g. Rorschach Inkblot Test). In qualitative research, data are collected in a non-numerical way and the raw data often consist of words (rather than numbers). Another feature typical for the qualitative methods of data collection is flexibility. As the data are obtained, they may inform and influence further data collection strategies.

Many methods, e.g. projective methods or the examination of products of human activity (artefacts), can be used to collect quantitative as well as qualitative data. For instance, if we count how many people who are given a picture and are asked to come up with a story about it, mention particular aspects of the story, we gather quantitative data; however, if we focus only on the described meanings of the stories, we are looking at the qualitative aspects of the story. Tables 7.1 and 7.2 in Chapter 7 outline a selection of common quantitative and qualitative data collection methods.

Data analysis

Quantitative data analysis can be either descriptive or inferential. Descriptive statistics are used to summarise results of the data in the study, while inferential statistics give us an estimate of the real values of the measured variables in the population from which we took our sample (more information on both descriptive and inferential statistics can be found in Chapter 10). Qualitative data analyses tend to be either more descriptive or interpretative in nature (Elliott & Timulak, 2005). Kvale (1996, 2008) classifies qualitative approaches to data analysis as: (1) meaning condensing methods (that are trying to abbreviate the data), (2) data categorising methods (that are clustering the data according to similarities), (3) narrative methods (that are putting the data into stories),

(4) meaning interpreting methods (that are trying to interpret the data), (5) ad hoc meaning generating methods (that are less systematic and the researcher registers interesting information contained in the data in an ad hoc manner). Various qualitative designs have their own approaches to data analysis and they typically represent a combination of the methods presented by Kvale (for more see also Chapters 12 and 13).

Activity 6.2   Comparing quantitative and qualitative research papers

Select one quantitative paper and one qualitative paper on a topic of interest to you. Now compare:

1. *What kinds of research questions are asked in the respective studies?*
2. *What design is used in the respective studies?*
3. *What data collection strategy is used in the respective studies?*
4. *What data analysis strategy is used in the respective studies?*

Genres of psychotherapy research

Counselling and psychotherapy research is typically organised around the 'genres' that cut across qualitative and quantitative methodologies, and these genres are typically determined by the research focus. Psychotherapy research genres are similar to movie genres. Genres develop alongside the emergence of pivotal directors who change the field and create something that, viewed with hindsight, becomes a specific genre. Some genres thus become recognisable. Some become more popular and some less so. Some expand and some die out. Some may have subgenres, some combine other genres. In current psychotherapy research, we primarily recognise outcome research (which focuses on answering the question whether psychotherapy works) and process research (which focuses on answering the question how psychotherapy works). We can also find studies on other relevant aspects of psychotherapy (such as clients' or therapists' characteristics, supervision, training in psychotherapy, the setting where psychotherapy is practised, etc.; for more see Timulak, 2008b).

Outcome research

Counselling and psychotherapy outcome research utilises many data collection measures. These are instruments or methods that were specifically developed for psychotherapy research or are particularly suitable for it. Thus we have various self-report measures (e.g. Clinical Outcome in Routine Evaluation – Outcome

Measure, CORE-OM; see Chapter 10), observer-based measures (Hamilton Rating Scale of Depression – HRSD), physiological measures (e.g. urine in the case of addiction outcome research), qualitative in-depth interviews, etc. In quantitative research, many of these measures can be used in a way that allows us to determine whether the client's pre-post change was reliable (i.e. it was bigger than could be found by chance) and clinically significant (i.e. its volume brought the client to a state similar to the one typical for normative, non-clinical, healthy people) (cf. Jacobson & Truax, 1991). The magnitude of change achieved in a particular study is often also expressed per average client (per mean) in the form of effect sizes (Cohen, 1988). This allows for comparison of studies. Chapter 10 provides more information on outcome research and common statistical terms and procedures.

PAUSE FOR REFLECTION

Think about whether change is best measured at the end of therapy or six months later. What counts as therapy 'working' and who is best qualified to make this judgement?

The current 'gold standard' of outcome research is the randomised controlled trial (RCT). As outlined in Chapter 1, an RCT represents a form of experimental design with a random assignment of clients among the studied conditions (e.g. therapy versus no therapy or one type of therapy versus another type of therapy) and tight experimental control (everything is similar in the conditions bar the active treatment). The experimental control is expressed in the use of treatment manuals (which instruct the therapist how to behave in the session) and quality and adherence checks of the delivered treatment (a measure of whether or not therapists follow the manual). The issues of an appropriate control group (e.g. is the waiting group without any intervention an appropriate control or should the clients be receiving some form of treatment so that the pure placebo effect of the studied treatment can be controlled for), the follow-up (examining whether the changes due to therapy last), the outcome measurement (what is the best way of measuring therapeutic change?), the sample size (what is the necessary sample size so we can detect the changes between the compared groups?), etc. are considered in this type of research. A discussion of the pros and cons of RCTs can be found in Chapter 1.

Alternatives to RCTs include experimental and descriptive case studies (i.e. the studies that examine only one case or a few cases). Usually case studies are used when the effectiveness of a particular type of therapy for a certain problem is not yet known and/or a therapy has to be developed. Other alternatives are trials based on clients' preferences (in which the clients are given a description of several types of therapy and are invited to choose the one that they feel is right for them – the effectiveness is then examined taking the preference into

account); naturalistic studies (examining outcomes of therapy in routine practice, usually on very big samples – some of those studies are sometimes referred
to as practice-based evidence, see Chapter 1 and Barkham, Hardy & Mellor-
Clark, 2010); surveys mapping consumers' satisfaction (studies that look at satisfaction with therapy and not necessarily only whether it was effective); and
qualitative outcome studies (which invite clients to share in their own words
what impact therapy has had on their life) (for more details on outcome
research, see Chapter 10; Barkham & Barker, 2010; Timulak, 2008b).

A special branch of outcome research is dose-effect research, which studies
how many sessions are needed for improvement or full recovery of clients in
therapy. Finally, another genre of outcome research comprises research examining what outcomes are achieved by particular client groups (e.g. older clients,
female clients versus male clients, etc.) or particular therapists (again, for
instance, depending on the therapist's gender). As outlined in Chapter 4, the
results of individual outcome studies are often accumulated through quantitative meta-analyses and systematic reviews that allow for the acquisition of an
overall picture of the field of study (e.g. an average outcome of therapies for
depression).

Process research

Counselling and psychotherapy process research often uses methods of gathering data that were developed specifically for studying psychotherapy processes,
i.e. what happens in the course of therapy. Self-report questionnaires, like the
Working Alliance Inventory, are an example. The methods used are either par-
ticipative (the client and the therapist provide data) or non-participative (they
are observer based). As to the genres of process research, we can find process–
outcome research that looks at the relationship between process variables (e.g.
the therapeutic alliance) and therapy outcome. We can also find descriptive
process studies that investigate different aspects of the therapy process, e.g. the
impact of interventions (such as interpretation), significant moments (e.g. the
client identified helpful and unhelpful events in the course of therapy), retro-
spective reconstruction of relevant aspects of therapeutic process (e.g. the client's view of any conflicts in the therapeutic relationship), etc. Finally, one can
find theory-building studies that investigate the plausibility of change models
in therapy (e.g. how painful emotions such as shame, fear and loneliness are
transformed in therapy). For more details on process research, see McLeod
(2010a) and Timulak (2008b).

Other types of therapy studies

Psychotherapy research also includes studies looking at aspects other than process and outcome, which cover a range of issues directly or indirectly relevant for

counselling and psychotherapy. Research genres beyond process and outcome research include:

- Research focused on clients and factors in the client's life ('extratherapeutic' factors; Lambert, 1992): Studies investigating, for example, the prevalence of specific psychological disorders in the population, the ways in which clients seek help, or reasons why potential clients never seek counselling or psychotherapy, and clients' preferences for therapy approaches and therapists.
- Research focused on therapists: Studies exploring, for example, therapists' personal attitudes and worldviews, interpersonal skills and how therapists develop in the course of their career. Stimulated by the differences in therapist outcome in routine outcome measurements, therapist factors and characteristics are now also more considered in process and outcome research (e.g. research on practitioners with exceptionally and consistently good results; McLeod, 2013).
- Research on psychotherapy training and supervision: Studies exploring, for example, the benefit/disadvantage of having mandatory personal therapy as a part of therapist training or the learning-conducive qualities in a supervisor. Hill and Knox (2013) provide a review of the research on the effectiveness of clinical training, including training for trainees and practising professionals as well as individual supervision.

Activity 6.3   Recognising the genres of psychotherapy research

Take a look at the most recent issue of the journals Psychotherapy Research *and* Counselling and Psychotherapy Research. *Look at the abstracts of the papers and try to identify what 'genre' or genres (as studies may cut through more than one genre) are represented in each of the published papers.*

Conclusion

As I said at the beginning of this chapter, research is a systematic and rigorous quest for knowledge. It is influenced by the researcher's view of reality and acceptable ways of knowing. These underlying assumptions led to the development of methodological traditions such as quantitative and qualitative research. Each of these traditions asks particular research questions and addresses them with a particular strategy that has become recognised by their community of scientists as rigorous and persuasive, which means that the findings obtained through them are seen as valid or trustworthy. Each of these traditions has its particular strengths, but also specific limitations. For instance, quantitative research can tell us a lot about the generalisability of certain findings (e.g. how many people improve on a specific measure of distress at the end of therapy), but cannot tell us much about the nuances of their improvement as perceived by clients themselves. On the other hand, qualitative research may provide an in-depth analysis of the nuances of a change in the experienced distress, but cannot tell us that much about their generalisability to a wider population.

The interaction of social science research strategies (quantitative versus qualitative) with the types of question that have been asked by psychotherapy researchers (such as whether therapy works (outcome) or how it works (process)) has led to the development of particular genres of psychotherapy research (e.g. case studies, RCTs, process–outcome studies, dose–effect studies) that have both established and developing 'rules' about how they are best conducted. These rules are recognised by the community of researchers. Being knowledgeable about both the genres and the rules allows the researcher (and new researchers, like potential readers of this chapter, in particular!) to place their research questions (and potential strategies to answer them) in the context of the psycho-therapy research landscape.

Suggestions for further reading

Heppner, P.P., Wampold, B.E. & Kivlighan, D.M., Jr (2008). *Research Design in Counseling* (3rd edition). Belmont, CA: Thomson Brooks/Cole.
This book provides an in-depth presentation of primarily quantitative research in counselling and psychotherapy.

McLeod, J. (2011). *Qualitative Research in Counselling and Psychotherapy* (2nd edition). London: Sage.
This book provides an in-depth presentation of qualitative research in counselling and psychotherapy.

Timulak, L. (2008b). *Research in Psychotherapy and Counselling.* London: Sage.
This book provides a presentation of counselling and psychotherapy research genres.

SEVEN

Planning your research: Design, method and sample

*Dr Terry Hanley (University of Manchester),
Clodagh Jordan (Trinity College Dublin) &
Kasia Wilk (University of Manchester)*

Introduction

As is evident throughout this book, none of the chapters stand alone. This chapter is no exception. In particular, we would like to highlight that this chapter develops upon the guidance on choosing a research question in Chapter 3 and outlines how the initial research question needs to be refined and focused to plan a research project. Furthermore, it shows how knowledge about methodologies and methods, as introduced in the previous chapter and further elaborated in Part III of this book, helps to guide the decisions about appropriate design, method and sampling for a research project. The purpose here is therefore to sew plenty of seeds which can be nurtured with the support of other chapters. More specifically, this chapter will encourage you to think about the choices that individuals make when designing research projects and hopefully drum home the message that forward planning is essential for a successful research project (and that many difficulties and failings in research can be overcome with a little more effort at the outset of the project).

Choosing a research design

Let's start with a relatively broad research question, 'Does humanistic counselling work with clients with mild to moderate depression?' Such a question is not uncommon within the world of counselling and psychotherapy and the answer can have significant consequences for how money is distributed to service providers. Unfortunately, the answer is not as straightforward as it may seem. It would be nice to come up with a definitive 'yes' or 'no' answer, but there are numerous complexities inherent in the question. For instance, 'What does "work" mean?', 'What is humanistic counselling?' and 'What is mild to moderate depression?' Each of these concepts is incredibly complex and the answers are often embedded

Planning is very important for a successful research journey …

within our perception of how the world is constructed (see Chapter 6 for a consideration of how our view of the world will impact upon the research we undertake). Such a perspective leads some to conclude that we should view counselling and psychotherapy research through a 'human science' lens, rather than the 'natural science' one so often adopted within medical model settings (e.g. Rennie, 1994). These epistemological debates rage on within the world of counselling and psychotherapy and can greatly influence the research designs that we adopt in research.

Information box 7.1   A story of a research project – finding a research design

Jane worked in an online counselling service for young people and decided that she wanted to hear from the young people with whom she worked. Specifically, Jane wanted to systematically find out what they thought about the service they were accessing. In coming to this research area, Jane was mindful that she did so with many preconceptions. For instance, although she had initially been sceptical about online counselling, her work had changed this perception to a much more positive one.

PAUSE FOR REFLECTION

Think about how your attitude to and beliefs about counselling and psychotherapy might influence the research *design* that you may choose.

With the above in mind, it is clear that those researching therapy need to be clear about their motivations for asking particular questions and their rationale for the research designs that are adopted. A common pitfall for those undertaking research for the first time is the mismatch between the research question and the research design. For instance, a researcher may solely want to know if a particular approach 'works' (i.e. demonstrates a reduction in distress during a particular intervention period), but then may adopt a design which is more discursive in nature and which utilises qualitative data (see Chapter 12). Unfortunately, the more discursive data that are collected may be interesting, but are unlikely to answer the research question. In contrast, such an approach would potentially prove more fruitful if the research question focuses upon how the particular approach might be perceived as being helpful to the participant in question. Ultimately, the creation of a successful research design is likely to be greatly influenced by the congruent link between it and the research question posed.

Activity 7.1   Potential research designs

Spend 10 minutes brainstorming and making notes about some potential research designs that could be used for this research question: 'What do young service users think about online counselling?'

So, given the above, what types of question might help to guide your choices in research design? There are a multitude of possible questions, but here we present some key ones:

- Do you see your question as being exploratory in nature (e.g. to gain insight into a particular phenomenon), descriptive (e.g. aiming to capture the essence of a known phenomenon at a point of time), or causal (e.g. to investigate a relationship between phenomena)?
- Are you more interested in experimental/controlled conditions in which to study your research question? Or are you more interested in natural/life-like conditions in which to study your research question?

As should be evident, the answers to questions such as these will greatly shape the research that you conduct and the utility of the findings you obtain (see also Chapters 10 and 12). For instance, controlled causal research is often prized in psychology but challenged for its ecological validity (i.e. can something that is controlled reflect the complex real world; see the discussion on RCTs in Chapter 1), while, in contrast, naturalistic causal research might capture a more accurate sense of the real world but it comes at a price of being messy and hard to contain (which means that making generalisable claims may not be possible). In addition to questions about the type of study you want to conduct, practical considerations also play a major part. For instance:

- How long do you want to/can you spend studying this phenomenon?
- How might the research project fit into your existing life commitments?

Such considerations are essential when conducting any research project. Ultimately, conducting research therefore needs commitment and a successful research design that will reflect both your area of interest and your life situation.

Keeping the above considerations in mind, let's have a look now at different types of research design. Information box 7.2 lists some of the general types of research design that are often encountered in counselling and psychotherapy research.

Information box 7.2   Examples of general types of research design in counselling and psychotherapy*

Fixed versus flexible research design

Some research designs lend themselves to a very rigid structure while others have the potential to shift as they are conducted:

- *Example of a fixed design: Does humanistic counselling reduce symptoms of depression in older adults? Utilising the Beck Depression Inventory pre- and post-treatment.*
- *Example of a flexible design: An evolving longitudinal exploration based on a series of interviews of how humanistic counselling is perceived by older adults with a diagnosis of depression.*

Descriptive versus experimental research design

Some designs aim to describe a particular phenomenon in detail while others aim to test a particular set of conditions using an experiment:

- *Example of a descriptive design: A qualitative case series describing clients' experiences of humanistic counselling following a major accident.*

(Continued)

- *Example of an experimental design: Randomised controlled trial (RCT) comparing the efficacy of humanistic and CBT-oriented counselling in reducing depressive symptoms, with control-group design and random allocation of clients to groups (see Chapter 1 for more information on RCTs).*

ᵃ *Please note that these design types are not mutually exclusive. See Chapter 6 for further classification of research designs.*

Moving from methodology to method

At this juncture we start moving away from considering the issues around choosing a suitable research design, to considering what you need to do to make your research design work. In particular, in this section we hope to provide a brief introduction to the difference between the 'methodology' adopted and the 'method' utilised. We also provide a brief introduction to the different types of quantitative and qualitative research design and the data collection methods that you might use in your work.

So, let's begin with what is the difference between the 'methodology' adopted and the 'method' utilised? This is a question that we commonly encounter with beginner researchers and it can cause a lot of confusion. If we start with the concept of the 'method', a helpful way to conceptualise this is that it is the research tool used to collect and analyse data. This can include, for example, an interview (one way of collecting data) and a thematic analysis (one way of analysing the data, see Chapter 13). In contrast, the concept of 'methodology' is much broader and reflects your motivations for adopting the design that you have chosen: 'A "good methodology" is more a *critical design attitude* to be found always at work throughout a study, rather than confined to a brief chapter called "Methodology"' (Clough & Nutbrown, 2012, p. 39). In short, it is why you did the research in the way that you did and it is pervasive within your written work.

Different types of research design (exploratory, descriptive or causal) are commonly broken down into two broad categories: quantitative and qualitative (see Chapter 6 for more information about these approaches). Furthermore, each of these categories has widely used data collection and analysis methods associated with them. In Tables 7.1 and 7.2 we outline a selection of common quantitative and qualitative design types and the associated data collection methods (due to space restrictions, we do not present data analysis procedures here or describe the data collection methods in detail).

Let's also not forget that the project is not going anywhere without careful consideration of ethics (see Chapter 8, for a fuller discussion). Any design needs to consider the full impact that the study will have upon those involved.

Table 7.1 *Common quantitative research designs and data collection methods*

	Quantitative research
Design types	*Longitudinal research (reflecting upon a phenomenon/variable over a sustained period of time)*
	E.g. Is humanistic counselling effective in reducing symptoms of moderate depression 10 years after treatment? A longitudinal study following adolescents into adulthood post-treatment.
	Pre-Post test (reflecting upon change of a variable at the onset and end of an intervention – e.g. therapy)
	E.g. How effective is humanistic counselling in reducing depression over 20 therapy sessions? Using self-report outcome measure.
	Cohort studies (utilising specific groups of people over a period of time)
	E.g. Post-natal depression and humanistic counselling: measuring the effectiveness of short-term treatment with first-time mothers.
	Comparison studies (comparing one phenomenon/variable with another)
	E.g. Depression and therapeutic outcomes: comparing person-centred therapy with cognitive behavioural therapy in reducing depressive symptoms.
Data collection methods	*Questionnaire or survey* – e.g. Beck Depression Inventory
	Structured interview – e.g. Structured clinical interview for DSM-IV, section related to assessing if a patient meets diagnostic criteria for depression.
	Observation – e.g. Parent observation of child for low mood or irritability, symptoms of depression
	Measurement – e.g. Measurement of weight gain or loss (as this one diagnostic symptom of depression)

Table 7.2 *Common qualitative research designs and data collection methods*

	Qualitative research
Design types	*Ethnography (an approach that involves generating a deep understanding of a grouping of people by sharing a lot of time with them)*
	E.g. Can humanistic counselling work with asylum seekers? Applications and observations from the field.
	Case study (reflecting upon a single case in detail – a case may be a person, service, community etc. – in order to provide insight into a particular issue)
	E.g. Working humanistically with depression in children: the case of Laura.
	Phenomenology (research which focuses on a particular aspect of people's experience of a chosen phenomenon)
	E.g. Exploring the lived experience of depression in second-generation South Asian women.
	Grounded theory (adopting a very bottom-up attitude to making sense of the information collected in order to generate a theory about an underlying common process)

(Continued)

Table 7.2 *(Continued)*

	Qualitative research
	E.g. What theory best explains the therapeutic effects of humanistic counselling with moderately depressed clients?
	Participatory action research (involving the community to address a particular issue needing change)
	E.g. How do community health centres utilise humanistic counselling with depressed clients?
	Narrative research (Involves gathering detailed stories to help understand a topic or issue)
	E.g. What stories do depressed clients tell us about receiving humanistic counselling?
Data collection methods	*One-to-one interviews* (unstructured or semi-structured)
	Focus groups (led by a facilitator and involving a group of participants discussing a particular topic)
	Observation (unstructured or semi-structured)
	Document analysis (e.g. thematic content analysis of autobiographical material about personal experience of depression)
	Qualitative survey (focused on meaning and words rather than numbers and categories)

Information box 7.3   A story of a research project – choosing a research design

When considering what research design and methods to use, Jane was clear that she wanted to gain a deep understanding of the online relationship from the user perspective. After attending research seminars on her counselling course, and with some guidance from her research supervisor, Jane decided that she wanted to conduct a qualitative research project. In particular, due to nuances in the environment, and because Jane wanted to get a rich picture of the clients' experiences, she decided that it would be most appropriate to conduct individual face-to face interviews with those involved.

Ethical issues posed by the planned research needed to be considered in the design of her project. It involved making sure that participants were well informed of the research procedures and would be making an informed choice to participate. Jane therefore had to provide information sheets and consent forms which outlined the participants' rights to withdraw participation. She had to explain how confidentiality would be ensured by protecting collected data through encryption and by using anonymous quotes in her report, and she had to describe how the findings would be disseminated. Jane ensured that her participants were able to ask questions before agreeing to take part. She also made sure the interviews took place in a safe and secure location that would not put her participants or herself at risk.

Sample

Once you have refined your research question the next step is to decide who, and how many people, you are going to work with. Below we discuss these issues in relation to quantitative and qualitative research designs.

In quantitative research, sampling is the process of choosing who you will work with in your research project. Usually, these people will represent a particular 'population'; this is a term which refers to the entire group of people that you wish to draw conclusions about. From this, your 'sample' then becomes the members of the population that you have chosen to include in your research. In quantitative research designs it is important that your sample is as representative of your population as possible (see Chapter 6). Information box 7.4 outlines the sampling techniques that are mostly used in quantitative research.

Information box 7.4   Sampling techniques

Sample of convenience/opportunity sampling: *This method simply means choosing participants for inclusion in the study who are the easiest to access. Although this sampling procedure does not ensure representation of the population, it is easy, cheap and time-effective. Convenience sampling is also used in qualitative research.*

Simple random sample: *This ensures that each member of the population has the same chance of being selected for the sample. It could involve picking a name from a hat.*

Systematic random sample: *Like it sounds, this is a more formal way of random sampling. For example, you choose a number 'x', obtain a list of people or observe a flow of people, and select every xth person.*

Stratified random sample: *This is implemented when you need to eliminate the effects of a co-founding variable, such as age or ethnicity. The method involves separating your group into 'strata' (e.g. by age or ethnicity) and then carrying out a simple random sample or a systematic random sample for each strata or group.*

Quota sample: *Here, you ascertain what your population looks like in relation to specific characteristics (e.g. percentage of people in the group who live in urban versus rural areas), develop quotas established by these characteristics, and then select people for each quota.*

Purposeful sampling is often utilised in qualitative research. This means that the researcher deliberately chooses participants who have experienced the key concept or issue that is being explored. There are a number of purposeful sampling procedures that you can use to select your sample and each has a different purpose. For instance, some adopt a maximal variation sampling approach where participants who have different perspectives on the key concept or issue are chosen (this is a heterogeneous sample), while others look to recruit individuals who are similar in key ways (this is a homogeneous sample), for example as in the qualitative method IPA (see Chapter 12).

Once you have decided upon your sampling technique, it's important to consider how many people are to be involved. Remember also that your task will be to justify the sample size in terms of the research question, the methodology utilised, the data collection method and the chosen analysis method.

Within quantitative research, the confidence that you can place in your results is affected by the size of your sample, and as you have already read in Chapter 6, the larger the sample size, the more likely you are to approximate the population from which you wish to draw conclusions. Essentially, when considering quantitative sampling, it is important to ensure that your sample is large enough for statistical procedures to be applied so that you can draw assumptions that reflect the chosen population with confidence. It is very important to reduce sampling error where possible. Where the population's statistical characteristics are approximated from a subset of the population, rather than the entire population, it is important to calculate results that reflect the 'true' population score and not just your sample estimate (see Chapter 10 for more information). To decide on an adequate sample size for quantitative research there are sample size formulas that you can use (for more on this, see Field, 2009). If your research design is an experiment, it is possible to turn to power analysis formulas which are used to work out the minimum sample size that you need so that it is reasonably possible to reveal an effect of a certain size. If your study is a survey, you can implement sampling error formulas to identify the appropriate sample size (for further reading on sampling error formulas, see Field, 2009).

Qualitative research is a completely different ball game when it comes to judging when enough is enough. One concept that is often discussed is that of 'data saturation', although it is worth noting that not all qualitative approaches subscribe to this approach. Saturation is the cyclical process of data collection and analysis which is repeated until no new conceptual information emerges. When this occurs it is time to stop collecting data. According to Glaser and Strauss (1967), if a researcher stays loyal to the values of qualitative research, the sample size should follow the theory of saturation, where the gathering of new information will not lend any new understanding to the research question. Therefore, saturation is generally used as a guiding point for qualitative research sample size (Mason, 2010). However, other factors dictate how quickly saturation is achieved. Charmaz (2006, p. 114) proposes that the research question is the ultimate driver of the design and sample size, and that a small study with 'modest claims' may reach saturation faster than a larger study. Ultimately, the sample size of qualitative research varies widely; it is the methodology that is adopted and access to participants that often guide the decisions.

Information box 7.5   A story of a research project – sampling and recruiting

Within Jane's qualitative study of online therapy with young people an opportunity sample was adopted. Participants were recruited through advertisements on the website that she worked on. Jane recruited six ex-clients of the online counselling service (not her own ex-clients) who were willing to be interviewed about their work with counsellors. Although she hoped for more participants, she ultimately stopped recruiting when (a) new themes no longer emerged in her data analysis and, more practically, (b) time limits on the project meant that the study had to come to an end.

The sampling method chosen was straightforward but in her write-up Jane acknowledged that it was possible that the young people who volunteered to participate did so because they had had particularly positive experiences of online counselling; she recognised that this sampling method might not 'catch' participants who were less satisfied with their counselling experience. Also, the method of data collection – face-to-face interviews – might have prevented some young people who had problems with transportation from choosing to participate.

The practical side of research

One factor to consider is the place that the research is going to have in your life. Research takes a lot of hard work and effort. Hanley, Lennie and West (2013) outline how it is important to consider the support that you have in place for completing such study. For some, this might be a supportive family, for others it might be having a quiet space away from other students in which to work. It is worth reflecting upon what you will need to complete the project in the long run at the outset of the project – after all, research can be a very costly business. For more advice on this important element of research, see the 'Student top tips' in Chapter 17.

In addition to having space in your life, most researchers find it helpful to pilot or trial a specific method before engaging fully in the research project. This is particularly helpful if you are not familiar with your chosen method and want to 'test' it out first to see how it can work with your research question. For example, doing one interview or collecting a few sample questionnaires to see if the interview schedule or questions provide appropriate data can clarify your approach and save you a lot of time later on. Through this process you may find that data analysis will involve much more work than you initially thought, or that your method may not be the best fit for obtaining your data. By testing out the design with a small sample, you may save yourself the unpleasant surprise down the road of not being prepared for the potential constraints and challenges that can accompany particular methods.

Pilot testing is also useful for understanding how easy (or not) it will be to recruit participants, a key practical issue for the success of any research project. Information box 7.6 provides you with a number of methods people often use to recruit research participants.

Information box 7.6   Methods for participant recruitment

Colleagues/students/clients: *Recruiting participants from people that you are already in contact with is an easy way to gather participants. Note that while there are advantages that come from recruiting from a group that you belong to (being an 'insider' researcher), there are also ethical issues about recruiting people you know (such as friends and colleagues). The ethical issues around recruiting clients are particularly complex, but there can be advantages in involving clients in research (Etherington, 2001).*

Formal service agencies and support groups: *Contacting relevant service agencies and support groups whose service users are eligible for your study may be another good starting point when recruiting. Note that many organisations may require you to apply for organisational ethical approval from them, which can mean that you have to undertake two ethics processes.*

Advertising: *Recruiting participants through the use of emails, flyers or newspaper, television and radio advertisements is another popular method of generating participants.*

Snowballing: *Snowballing is a recruitment strategy where current participants are asked to recommend or recruit eligible future participants from among their friends or acquaintances.*

Social networking sites and web forums: *Social networking sites and web forums are another option for participant recruitment. Note that permission typically needs to be sought from the web forum coordinators and that some websites have policies about posting invitations to participate in research on their forums. In addition, professional bodies may have specific ethical guidance for conducting research online (e.g. British Psychological Society, 2007).*

Information box 7.7   A story of a research project – practical issues

Within Jane's studies, finding space to study became a major issue. In addition to juggling her studies with a full-time job, she also had a close bereavement during this period. This meant that finding time to prioritise her research became difficult. She worked with her research supervisor to develop a strategy that fitted with her life commitments. This involved breaking down the research into doable chunks and reconsidering the initial design of the study. Importantly, Jane piloted her design and realised that her interviews would take a considerable amount of time to analyse. This led to the decision to recruit fewer individuals to the study than originally planned. Ultimately, although it was difficult to find time to complete the work, the support of the supervisor and the revised design meant that the project remained manageable and was completed in time.

Conclusion

Activity 7.2   Does size matter in research?

Spend 10 minutes contemplating the following arguments with a view to considering your own attitude to the importance of size in research.

Quantitative methods fail to capture the richness of human experience. There may be 1000 people involved in the study but it is impossible to claim that it is the therapy they have received (or at least the therapy that is claimed they have received) that has been beneficial.

Qualitative research is just storytelling in the guise of research. I wouldn't want to refer my family members for medical treatment based upon the views of a few people, so why would I do so with their psychological health.

Comment

Reflect upon whether your responses contradict the choices that you would make in research design. For instance, do you gravitate towards qualitative research but find yourself questioning its usefulness?

Within this chapter we have provided a whistle-stop overview of issues related to research design. As indicated at the outset of the chapter, many of these issues are developed in other chapters and you may find the recommended reading useful in extending this even further. Good research design is essential to the completion of successful projects so here is a final list of recommendations:

Do

- Make your decision making transparent and clear (e.g. in your research report).
- Choose a research design (qualitative or quantitative) that is suitable for your research question (which can often be informed by your personal motivations and preferences).
- Make sure your choice of data generation method(s) corresponds with the design that is adopted, which in turn is underpinned by the research question posed.

Don't

- Choose a method without first developing a sound rational that fits with your methodology of choice. There is a multitude of methods that can be employed in a research design, and every method will have its own body of associated literature.
- Select participants for your research study without forethought. Make sure you carefully consider *how* these participants will be selected and the number of people involved and why these are the best participants to answer your research question.
- Plan a project that is too big to be feasible in the time allowed. Make sure you create a design that is 'doable'. Researchers should be practical and work to create a research design that will succeed in the time available for the project. This will involve doing plenty of preparation, considering the fit with the researcher's life situation and piloting your design for unforeseen flaws.

PAUSE FOR REFLECTION

After reading through the sections above, what types of design do you gravitate towards (in terms of doing and using)? Now revisit the first reflective question we posed at the beginning of this chapter, but this time reframe the question to consider how your attitude to research design might influence the therapeutic approach that you may choose/ offer to others?

Suggestions for further reading

Creswell, J. (2003). *Research Design: Qualitative, quantitative and mixed methods approaches* (2nd edition). London: Sage.
   This is an excellent textbook that continues discussions about research designs.

Hanley, T., Lennie, C. & West, W. (2013). *Introducing Counselling and Psychotherapy Research*. London: Sage
   This introductory text reflects in more depth on the personal journey of engaging with counselling and psychotherapy research.

EIGHT

Ethical considerations
Prof. Tim Bond

Introduction

Research ethics have become increasingly important over the last fifty years, especially for research that involves people. For forty of those years the main focus was medical research and psychological experiments, designed to study people in the clinic or laboratory. In the last ten years, the range of research has widened to include any type of research involving people, including the observation of people behaving naturally, a collection of life histories and any research based on interviews or questionnaires. This means that almost all of the research undertaken by counsellors and psychotherapists is now informed by research ethics. This will usually include meeting some compulsory requirements, particularly submitting to ethical review prior to starting the research, which may be imposed by professional bodies, universities or other organisations.

PAUSE FOR REFLECTION

What do you expect from reading about ethics? How do you approach ethics in your practice as a counsellor or psychotherapist? How will this inform your approach to research ethics?

Ethics are about the careful consideration of what is right or wrong. They provide ways of distinguishing what is good or harmful in conducting research and promoting the good. I have deliberately put the emphasis on ethics supporting the search for what is good. I have done this because, in my experience, most researchers want to do good. I expect that you share this desire. By undertaking research, you are probably not only hoping to improve your own practice, but also want to achieve something that will benefit clients or assist other practitioners to work more safely or effectively with their clients.

As someone who researches and writes about ethics, I know how quickly the positive message of ethics can be overwhelmed by a focus on what ethics prohibit and the fear of being disciplined by the 'authorities'. Whenever someone says to me, 'Tell me what I am allowed to do', I listen carefully to whether someone has a healthy balance between doing what is required of them and taking personal responsibility for their ethical judgement and actions. Excessive compliance turns ethics into no better than following orders and suppresses active attention to the experience and well-being of others. On the other hand, excessive reliance on personal judgement fails to stand on the shoulders of others who have responded to ethical challenges, sometimes involving serious abuses, and runs the risk of naively repeating avoidable mistakes. It's a balance. Research ethics require the application of existing rules and processes but never without watchfulness for the rights of others and the impact on the people affected. Ethics energise and inform ethical actions. These different elements of ethics combine to support ethical mindfulness (Bond, 2010, p. 242), which is essential for any professional practice, including research.

In the next section, I will consider the ethics that we can hold out as 'good' in research.

The ethically good researcher

Let us imagine a counselling trainee named Mary who needs to undertake research as part of her training. She has been working with clients with eating disorders and wants to research how the experience of having an eating disorder influences the ways that mothers approach feeding their children. She is interested in the messages mothers would like to give their children about food and how easy or difficult this is to achieve. She intends that this study will inform her future practice and that she might learn something of use to other counsellors.

Activity 8.1   Thinking ethically

Spend 10 minutes imagining that you are undertaking this research. Brainstorm and make a list of all the groups of people directly affected by or likely to be affected by this research. Use your ethical imagination, informed by empathy, to consider the proposed research from the different perspectives of participants, their children and as the researcher. What would be most ethically desirable and undesirable from each of these perspectives?

I have spent a lot of time over the last year reading and analysing different approaches to research ethics issued by government departments, professional bodies and charities that fund research or are dedicated to promoting the quality of research. Like many others, I have found identifying shared principles quite tricky, there being considerable variations in the detail of what falls within a particular principle. However, when I step back from the detail, I can see a framework of five positive ethical positions that would be equally applicable across the range of biomedical and social sciences. I will set out what these ethical positions appear to be and how they could provide points of guidance for any researcher. They provide the ethical principles that are relevant throughout the research journey, from beginning to end. These principles are:

- Integrity
- Rigour
- Respect
- Being trustworthy
- Responsibility

They inform our use of the ethical toolbox (see later) and our actions throughout the research journey.

How do the five ethical principles apply to researching counselling and psychotherapy?

Integrity

To have integrity as a researcher means undertaking the research in a genuine spirit of inquiry by being open to finding the unexpected and the puzzling, alongside maintaining high standards of honesty and transparency throughout the research process. For Mary, in our example, this means starting her research with questions that she wants to know the answers to. She expects, indeed hopes, to find surprises and contradictions to her own expectations. She follows her selected methodology scrupulously and reports her findings honestly and is transparent about how she reached her findings. In most research, it is impossible to report every twist and turn of the research process in detail. The final report is a carefully considered selection of the main points that answer the research question. However, Mary discusses all her doubts and major decisions with her supervisor and answers all questions as honestly as she is able. She is determined not to conceal awkward contradictions and tensions between findings in case they will be helpful in uncovering new findings or better interpretations of her findings. Mary is determined to be ethical throughout the whole of the research process from beginning to end and sets a very high standard of integrity for herself of honesty and transparency to others, especially to people with relevant insight, such as her research supervisor.

The opposite of integrity is dishonesty, misrepresentation and concealment of what the research suggests might be true (see, for example, the recent scandals in social psychology where researchers in the Netherlands were found fabricating and manipulating data for their publications).

Rigour

How can we know that the knowledge produced from the research meets quality requirements for research-based knowledge? To say that 'Research found that ...' is to make a quality claim for a superior type of knowledge based on the systematic and carefully considered application of research processes. At its most basic level, rigour requires that the research is undertaken at an adequate level of academic standards and competence. Academic standards require that the design, the methods and manner of implementation are consistent with the research question being investigated. Rigour is not about one approach to research being superior to all others. Rigour is about ensuring a good match between the issues being researched, the research design and the methods being used, with the researcher actively managing the strengths and limitations of both (see also Chapter 7).

For example, it is impossible to measure accurately the effectiveness of a therapeutic intervention without some systematic comparison with a similar group of people with the same condition or difficulty who form a control group (see discussion of RCT, as introduced in Chapter 1). The control group might receive no treatment, perhaps by being kept on a waiting list as a point of comparison with those receiving treatment, in order to make an accurate measure of the impact of receiving the intervention. This meets the ethical requirements of being academically rigorous but, given that the waitlist condition entails waiting to access treatment, raises new ethical issues about what to do if the treatment proves to be particularly effective. Should the people in the control group be taken off the waitlist and offered the new treatment? This is an ethical question, which requires consideration against other ethical principles, particularly what would be respectful or trustworthy?

What if it is not possible or considered desirable to have a control group? Would the principle of rigour forbid any investigations into the effect of a particular intervention? The answer is 'no', so long as the research is not claiming to be providing evidence about effectiveness; in this case, the research could be about clients' or therapists' reflections on the use of an intervention. Rigour, therefore, is basically about the compatibility between the method and the knowledge being sought or claimed. Following the guidance on research methods elsewhere in this book will enhance rigour.

Mary's research interest in mothers with their own personal experience of eating disorders and the messages they would like to give their children about food is fundamentally a qualitative inquiry that requires appropriate methods (see Chapter 12). Mary will need to consider whether it is more rigorous to research a larger number of mothers' experiences more superficially or to research fewer mothers in greater depth. Mary and her supervisor will have to weigh up which will provide the more rigorous and informative findings.

The opposite of rigour is academic muddle and carelessness, leading to putative 'findings' that are not adequately based on an appropriate research design and methods.

Respect

Showing respect for the rights and dignity of research participants is at the core of what it means to undertake research ethically. There has been a long history of researchers being so committed to investigating a particular topic, as rigorously as possible, and with a strong belief that they will benefit society, that they have lost sight of the consequences for their research participants – even to the point of exposing them to physical or emotional harm (see Tuskegee example below).

Ethics require that the researcher:

- assesses the likelihood of any harm to the research participants from taking part in the research;
- seeks to minimise any potential harm *and* ensures any unavoidable risk of harm is justified by the potential benefits of the research;
- ensures that all participation in the research is truly voluntary and offered on the basis of freely given and informed consent; and
- informs participants that they are allowed to withdraw from the research at any point.

These safeguards are underpinned by independent ethical review which is required for all research involving human participants in health and social care settings as well as for research undertaken in universities. The exact procedures and formal requirements vary between organisations but typically will require a risk assessment, an information sheet for participants and the use of a consent form or method of ensuring that clients have given a properly informed consent. These requirements for demonstrating respect for the rights and dignity of research participants are considered in greater detail in the next section.

Many of the ethical requirements around respect for research participants' rights and dignity are now also legal requirements, particularly under data protection legislation. Processing personally sensitive information, which would include most counselling research, requires the 'explicit consent' of the person involved (Data Protection Act 1998, Schedule 1, para 1(b)).

The opposite of being respectful is being prejudiced and manipulative, as in the Tuskegee Syphilis Study (Jones, 1993). This is an infamous example of pretending to offer free medical treatment to already syphilis-infected African-American men when the researchers were really only collecting tissue samples to record the long-term progression of the disease. The researchers not only prevented the men from being treated, but also allowed spouses and children to become infected. The project was only made possible by racist prejudices against the participants and it eventually led to an American President publicly apologising to survivors and their relatives for being the victims of racist research (CDC, 1997).

The Tuskegee case is extreme but much less extreme examples of ignoring the rights and dignity of participants can have serious consequences for the participants and cause significant damage to the future willingness of people to participate in research.

Being trustworthy

Not all research requires a strong relationship based on mutual trust. The completion of questionnaires, psychometric testing and factual data gathering can be relatively impersonal and may be considered rigorous because of its objectivity. However, Mary is proposing to gather peoples' experiences and the meaning they give to those experiences. Moreover, the topic concerns the relationship between mothers and their children, a deeply personal and personally important topic for participants. In this case, being respectful is necessary but not sufficient. This type of qualitative research requires considerable attention to the relationship, rather like when you provide therapy. It requires the researcher to be attentive to being trustworthy in order to enable the participant to talk freely and frankly. In the BACP *Ethical Guidelines for Researching Counselling and Psychotherapy*, trust is defined as 'a quality of relationship ... that is to withstand any challenges arising from inequality, difference, uncertainty and risk in their work together' (Bond, 2004, p. 4).

Activity 8.2   How to be trustworthy

Being trustworthy requires you, as the researcher, to build 'a quality of relationship [1]... that is sufficient to withstand any challenges arising from inequality [2], difference [3], uncertainty [4] and risk [5]...' with your participants.

Take 15 minutes to imagine yourself as a participant in your proposed research (or in Mary's research project) and consider how each of the five elements associated with being trustworthy might arise and what the researcher can do to build trust.

I created this definition of trust for BACP in order to stimulate the researchers' ethical attention to the participants' needs and experiences from their viewpoint. When we design research it is easy to become so focused on the challenges of conducting the research that we lose sight of what matters to participants and the significance of the relationship in gaining or losing their goodwill and willingness to participate fully. In therapy, the relationship has been empirically calculated to make a significant contribution to the outcome (Norcross, 2002). Its contribution to qualitative research is unknown but widely accepted as significant. Activity 8.2 is designed to encourage you to think about the types of issues that might impact on your participants' willingness to engage in your research.

One of the reasons why I recommend that you give careful thought to what it means to be trustworthy in your research is that it helps you to appreciate the participant's point of view more fully and to think through their expectations of you as the researcher (see also Chapter 2 for participants' experiences with research). Being trustworthy is central to the values of counselling and psychotherapy. Research adds to the challenges of being trustworthy because it carries with it a potential conflict of interest for the researcher between the best interests of the research participant and obtaining the best research findings.

The opposite of being trustworthy is to use deception to encourage participation. See again the Tuskegee Syphilis Experiment (1932–1972) described above for a widely condemned example of deception by pretending to offer treatment when really collecting medical samples and studying the natural development of the disease. The combination of deliberate deception and suspected racism against under-educated poor black rural workers in this study produced much outrage and was one of many scandals that triggered legally enforced research ethics in the USA (Israel & Hay, 2006, p. 33), largely based on a principle of respect. Another famous and controversial example of deception in research is Rosenhan's (1973) study on 'being sane in insane places' where fake patients were used to test the validity of psychiatric diagnosis. Nowadays, there are such high levels of ethical concern about the use of deception in research that its use is restricted and only considered justified if there is no other way of undertaking the inquiry, the deception is kept to a minimum, and participants are properly debriefed afterwards.

Responsibility

A researcher's responsibility is primarily directed towards the consumers of their research and the wider community. It involves giving careful consideration to how the research findings are communicated and their contribution to the well-being of society. As Mary is researching a topic of considerable sensitivity to her participants and a topic around which some members of the public may hold ill-informed or prejudiced views, ethical responsibility will require considerable care in how Mary communicates the outcome of the research in order to ensure the outcomes are as beneficial as possible to the people studied and for people in similar situations. The families may live with the consequences long after the research is completed. However, if Mary finds cause for concern about the mothering of children in her study, it would be responsible to report these findings accurately, without exaggeration, in order to prompt positive action or learning for future services.

'Sorry Toto, but we have an ethical duty to protect our research participants.'

The basic ethical toolkit for research

The way research ethics have developed over the last ten years is to emphasise three basic 'tools' as essential to any review process prior to starting the research and, more widely, as essential safeguards for participants. The detailed requirements for ethical reviews vary between organisations and between universities but will typically include three components: a risk assessment, an information sheet and a consent form.

Risk assessment

The risks in counselling and psychotherapy research are usually psychological and social rather than the physical risks to health involved in biomedical research. For example, someone may become upset or distressed by the subject of the research. Counselling and psychotherapy research is frequently intrusive, in the sense of investigating personally sensitive information, and is made acceptable by promises about safeguards around privacy and confidentiality. Breaches of confidentiality or anonymity can have serious consequences for the participant as they may result in harm to the person's reputation or loss of privacy. Where participants are vulnerable adults or children, they require additional care over their protection from harm and ensuring the quality of their consent (see the useful resources and guidance section below). Risk must also be considered in terms of whether the research might negatively impact the mental health treatment of a participant.

Research ethics traditionally view each research participant as an individual and calculate risks and safeguards on this basis. However, this is often over-simplistic. It is not unusual for qualitative research to have potential impact on people beyond the immediate participants. For example, Mary's research is focused on mothers and their experience but inevitably the mothers will be talking about their children and possibly other family members who are not formally part of the research process. What are the ethical rights of people implicated in the research but not directly involved? At the very least, their identity ought to be protected. This can only be achieved if you also anonymise the identity of your participants in order to prevent friends and family members guessing the identity of people mentioned in interviews. Legally they are entitled to having their reputation protected from being 'brought into disrepute' under the law concerning defamation. If significant information is being collected or reported about these 'surrogate' participants, then it is ethically desirable and, in the view of many, necessary to obtain their consent for this.

Information sheet

This acts as the basis for the informed consent of the participants. It should provide all the basic information that your participants may need in order to give their informed consent prior to participating in the research. The exact content of the sheet will vary between projects. Information box 8.1 provides a useful checklist.

Information box 8.1   Information sheet contents

- *Title of research.*
- *Brief invitation to take part.*
- *Either the reason why this person has been approached or the criteria for being included in the research.*
- *Purpose of the project.*
- *What will be involved in taking part? This should be written from the participants' point of view. What activities will they be expected to undertake? How much time is this likely to take and when will these activities occur?*
- *Clear statement that participation in the research is voluntary and that participants are free to withdraw at any point without there being any impact on the services being offered to them.*
- *What protection is being offered to information concerning participants? The norm is to offer confidentiality and anonymity with secure data storage. Sometimes it is more appropriate to offer the opportunity to have a contribution acknowledged – where participants would wish this to demonstrate their commitment to a cause or promote public awareness. Will participants have the opportunity to comment on transcripts of interviews or a draft of how you are reporting the research?*
- *Are there any limitations to confidentiality or anonymity? For example, in order to protect children or vulnerable adults from abuse or neglect.*
- *Any expenses or payments for taking part?*
- *What will happen to the results and how will they be reported?*
- *Will participants receive a summary of project findings as a way of acknowledging their contribution?*
- *Who should be contacted to ask further questions or volunteer to take part? Provide contact details.*
- *Remember that you will need to honour whatever you offer in the information sheet so be realistic.*

Consent form

In the USA, there is a strong legal requirement to use a properly written consent form that is signed and dated by the research participant, and this is reflected in much of their literature. You will find that it is also a normal requirement in the UK but variations are more likely to be approved where there are good reasons for doing so, for example because participants struggle with literacy, or signing a form raises significant cultural obstacles. As the consent form is one of the main strategies for respecting the participant's rights and dignity, it is important to find an appropriate way of discussing their consent and ensuring that the consent is recorded either on paper or by some other form of audio or video recording. Some participants with learning difficulties may benefit from the use of pictures to help them express their wishes. Specific issues around giving consent need also to be considered in doing research with minors, prisoners and people with a psychiatric diagnosis (see useful resources and guidance section). Regardless of how the consent is obtained, there are a number of points that would ordinarily be covered in order to ensure that someone is adequately placed to give their consent voluntarily and that this consent is based on adequate information. See Information box 8.2.

Information box 8.2   Consent forms

There are many different examples of consent forms on the internet. The consent form can be very simple for straightforward projects or quite complex for some projects. Here are some suggestions for research involving the collection of data by interview or questionnaires.

Title of project

I confirm that I

- *have read and understood the information sheet*
- *had the opportunity to consider the information provided and ask questions which have been answered*
- *am participating voluntarily and am free to withdraw at any time*
- *understand that whether I participate or not will not have any effect on the services I receive from ... [to be included if participants are current or potential users of services linked to the research]*
- *require information about me will be kept securely and its confidentiality will be protected*
- *agree to my data being seen by [insert name(s)] [include – on an anonymous basis – if appropriate]*
- *understand that information about me will be destroyed if I withdraw [or – the analysis of information will cease from the point that I withdraw]*
- *will be offered the opportunity to comment on information about me/on transcripts of my interviews/on a draft of the research report [to be included as appropriate]*
- *agree that information given by me may be communicated on a confidential basis to the appropriate agencies in order to prevent harm or neglect of children or vulnerable adults [to be included as appropriate]*

I agree to take part in this study

Name: Signature: Date:

Researcher name and contact details

The participant and researcher should each have a copy of the completed consent form.

Good practice in writing consent forms and information sheets for participants

Good practice is to:

- use the simplest language possible;
- avoid technical terms and jargon whenever possible;
- keep sentences short;
- test drafts on people with similar backgrounds to the intended participants whenever possible to check that obvious points or concerns have not been missed.

As part of preparing to write consent and information sheets it is helpful to imagine yourself into the position of your participants. Empathy for the people affected by your actions is an essential first step to being ethical. Testing drafts on potential participants, or on people who can speak from that position, helps to check the quality of your ability to imagine the issues that might concern participants. Learning from this process may also help you to revise your design or help you to be more sensitive to your participants' perspectives in how you run the research.

Conclusion

In this chapter, I have introduced you to the major ethical principles relevant to researching counselling and psychotherapy and some of the ethical toolkit used by researchers. Familiarity with the ethics of being a counsellor or psychotherapist is a good starting point but the change in focus from offering help to inviting someone to participate in research changes the ethical context and some of the challenges.

PAUSE FOR REFLECTION

What do you consider to be the major ethical difference in how you will conduct your research (or Mary's research) in comparison to providing counselling or psychotherapy? How will you respond to these differences?

This chapter can only be a relatively brief introduction. Research ethics are a mixture of principles and practical actions. Often, it is the personal moral qualities or virtues of the researcher that underpin the ethical integrity of the research (McFarlane, 2009). In the useful resources list below, I have suggested sources that I know students and practitioners have found helpful in meeting the ethical challenges of their research.

Information box 8.3   Ethical checklist

This checklist has been adapted by the author for small-scale projects by students and counselling services from 'The Recommended Checklist for Researchers', prepared by UK Research Integrity Office and available from www.ukrio.org

Before conducting your research

1. *Have you checked for any legal and ethical requirements concerning your proposed project?*
2. *Does your research ask questions that will provide knowledge that is sufficiently new and/or useful to justify the voluntary contribution of your participants?*
3. *Is your proposed research design and methodology appropriate to the questions being asked?*
4. *Do you have the necessary skills to undertake the research, if necessary supported by knowledgeable supervision?*
5. *Have you considered the research from the perspective of participants to identify any risks from their point of view and take appropriate measures to counter or minimise those risks?*
6. *Have you ensured that participants have freely consented to take part in the research on the basis of adequate information and know about their right to withdraw at any time?*
7. *Has your research been approved by any required ethical review?*
8. *Have you considered how you will acknowledge the contribution of others, including practitioners, researchers and writers, whose work has contributed to your project?*
9. *Have you communicated how participants or other contributors can raise questions, concerns or make complaints?*

When conducting your research

1. *Are you following your research plans systematically in ways that match your ethical approval or any other promises made to participants, for example in information sheets and consent forms?*
2. *Are you following best practice concerning the collection, storage and management of data and information concerning your research subjects?*
3. *Are you discussing the progress of your research honestly and transparently with a research supervisor in order to check out ethical and academic challenges as they arise?*

(Continued)

(Continued)

When finishing your research

1. *Will you report your research findings accurately, honestly and within a reasonable time frame?*
2. *Have you honoured any promises to participants and significant others about how their contributions will be used and reported?*
3. *Have you acknowledged the contributions of others and avoided plagiarism?*
4. *Have you ensured the security and, at the appropriate time, the secure disposal of personally identifiable data?*
5. *Has your research met all the ethical, legal and contractual obligations identified at the beginning of the research and during the research process?*

Useful sources of guidance and information on research ethics

Codes and guidelines

Bond, T. (2004). *Ethical Guidelines for Researching Counselling and Psychotherapy.* Rugby: British Association for Counselling and Psychotherapy. www.bacp.co.uk/research/ethical_guidelines.php (accessed on 16/6/13).

British Psychological Society (2010). *Code of Human Research Ethics.* Leicester: British Psychological Society. www.bps.org.uk/sites/default/files/documents/code_of_human_research_ethics.pdf (accessed on 16/3/13).

Medical Research Council (2012). *Good Research Practice: Principles and Guidelines.* Swindon: Medical Research Council. www.mrc.ac.uk/Ourresearch/Ethicsresearchguidance/Researchpractice/index.htm (accessed on 16/6/13).

UKRIO (2009). *Code of Practice for Research.* Falmer: UK Research Integrity Office. www.ukrio.org/what-we-do/code-of-practice-for-research (accessed on 16/6/13).

Practical research ethics considered in useful depth

Farrimond, H. (2012). *Doing Ethical Research.* Basingstoke: Palgrave Macmillan.

Iphofen, R. (2009). *Ethical Decision-making in Social Research.* Basingstoke: Palgrave Macmillan.

Oliver, P. (2010). *The Student's Guide to Research Ethics* (2nd edition). Maidenhead: Open University Press.

Researching children and young people

Alderson, P. & Morrow, V. (2011). *Research with Children and Young People*. London: Sage.

BERA (2011). *Ethical Guidelines for Educational Research*. London: British Educational Research Association. www.bera.ac.uk/system/files/3/BERA-Ethical-Guidelines-2011.pdf (accessed on 16/3/13).

Researching online

British Psychological Society (2007). *Conducting Research on the Internet: Guidelines for ethical practice in psychological research online*. Leicester: British Psychological Society. www.bps.org.uk/sites/default/files/documents/conducting_research_on_the_internet-guidelines_for_ethical_practice_in_psychological_research_online.pdf (accessed on 16/6/13).

Acknowledgement

I am grateful to colleagues in the Department of Counselling at the University of Malta and the editors of this book who commented on my ideas as they developed and earlier drafts of this chapter. Final responsibility rests with me as author.

NINE

Writing a research proposal

Dr Mark Donati (London Metropolitan University)

Introduction

This is the last chapter of Part II, which has aimed to help you begin your research journey. This reflects the fact that 'writing a research proposal' is very much the culmination of the various steps represented by the preceding chapters: understanding the importance of conducting research in counselling and psychotherapy, identifying a relevant topic, carrying out a literature review, clarifying a research question and identifying an appropriate way to investigate it. These are steps that provide the necessary foundations to actually start doing a piece of research, which is the focus for the subsequent chapters of this book. However, before you can begin your research, you and others involved in supporting it need to be sure that there is a sound rationale and plan to underpin it. This is where the 'research proposal' comes in. The aim of this chapter is to help you understand the purpose of a research proposal, what one looks like and how you can go about writing one for your project.

What is a research proposal and why write one?

A research proposal is a concise summary document that seeks to describe *what* your research is about. It needs to make a convincing argument for *why* the research should be done, and to explain *how* it will be done. From a practical point of view, it needs to demonstrate that the intended project is feasible within the constraints of time and resources available to you, and that you have the ability to successfully complete the research.

A bit like starting up a new business, undertaking research involves a lot of planning and then gaining the support of others who are investing in the project. A research proposal is therefore similar to a 'business plan', which will demonstrate to others that you have a good idea and know what you are doing, so you can secure the backing you need to make it happen. Just as a good business plan will demonstrate that there is a genuine gap in the market and the proposed venture that can address it, a good research proposal will identify a gap in knowledge and the study that will address it. So a research proposal can be understood as a way of gaining a warrant to support a project and a test of whether your research idea is sound and 'ready to go'.

Two areas in which you are likely to come across a requirement to write a research proposal are as a student on a certificate, diploma, undergraduate, Masters or Doctoral programme that involves undertaking a research project; or if you are a researcher applying for a grant or authorisation from an organisation, such as a research council, charity or the NHS, to undertake a piece of research. Consequently, the people who will be reading and evaluating your proposal may include dissertation supervisors or members of review panels who have responsibility for approving or granting funding for research projects. It is important to know who your audience is when you are writing a proposal, so you can tailor it to them.

'I'm sorry Sir. You can't get through without a research proposal.'

It is not uncommon for people undertaking research to feel anxious about the prospect of writing a research proposal, so much so that they may even prolong the amount of time they spend reading and reviewing literature and put off sitting down to write a proposal until they feel they have been utterly comprehensive in their preparatory work. While such anxieties are common and understandable, it is really important not to put off the task of beginning to write your proposal, or to see it as something you can only start doing once 'everything is clear' in your head. This is because the process of writing a proposal is a very effective way of identifying which parts of your project you are relatively clear and confident about, and which parts may require further thinking. Chapter 5 includes advice on how these kinds of issues and worries can be tackled in the literature review process.

PAUSE FOR REFLECTION

How do you feel about writing a research proposal? What kinds of thoughts does it bring up for you? Do you think you are 'ready' to write one? Which bit of your proposal (see below) do you feel it would be easiest to start with?

The key sections of a research proposal

Research proposals are structured documents that provide headings and sections that the researcher is asked to complete. These sections ensure that researchers provide the information that those reviewing will need to evaluate it. It is therefore important to ensure that your proposal provides the necessary information, otherwise you may not receive approval, or you may be asked to re-submit which will delay you getting started with your research. The exact content structure and length of a research proposal is likely to vary depending on the purpose for which it is being written (e.g. for a PhD or research council funding), the professional context (e.g. counselling or medicine), and the type of investigation being proposed (e.g. qualitative or quantitative research). However, most research proposals incorporate the following areas:

- Title
- Abstract
- Research question and rationale
- Background literature and theoretical framework
- Methodology and sampling
- Ethical considerations
- Resources and costs
- Timetable
- Dissemination plans

> **Activity 9.1   Thinking about proposal writing**
>
> *Find out whether there is a particular format, headings or guidelines you will need to follow in writing your proposal. Is there a set word length for the proposal or various sections of it? And is there a submission deadline you need to be working to?*
>
> *Consider who the 'audience' for your proposal is and what in particular they might be looking for? How familiar will they be with the study area? How much knowledge can you assume they know when you write the proposal?*

Title

You will also be asked to provide a working title for your research study. A good title should be simple and informative, and convey clearly the topic and nature of the research, for example: 'Personal development in counselling psychology training: a qualitative study of the views and experiences of trainers and trainees'. Sometimes researchers find it difficult or feel reluctant to give a title to their research before they have undertaken it, but the requirement to articulate what your research is about in a succinct way is a good test of how clear and focused your thinking is at this stage. You can almost always modify your title later if the project shifts a bit.

Abstract

An abstract is a short summary located at the beginning of the proposal, which 'abstracts' key information for the reader about your project. It is normally between 150 and 250 words in length and provides a brief description of the research context, question and rationale; the research participants; the methods used to gather and analyse the data; and the intended contribution of the research to the current body of knowledge.

Research question and rationale

In this key section you will be asked to state the specific research question that your proposed study is seeking to address. As discussed in Chapter 3, your research question lets the reader know the precise objectives and focus of your study and, like your title, is another good indicator of how clear your thinking is. If you are undertaking quantitative research, you will also need to state any hypotheses you will test in order to answer your research question.

Having stated your research question, you will then need to explain the rationale or justification for it. This involves presenting a set of reasoned arguments and evidence which lead to the following conclusions:

- there is a demonstrable gap or deficit in the current state of knowledge in the topic area;
- this gap has significant implications for professional practice in the topic area;
- the piece of research you are proposing will help to address this gap;
- the findings from your study will make a specific and valuable contribution to professional practice theory and research in the field.

Although you may have carried out a lengthy literature review to develop your research idea, at the end of this process you should be able to sum up the rationale for your proposed study in just a few sentences, which illustrate the key steps in your argument and evidence. Information box 9.1 provides an example and Activity 9.2 suggests an exercise that will help you to articulate clearly the rationale for your study.

Information box 9.1   Articulating your rationale

Here is an illustration of the steps one might take to build an argument which provides a rationale for a study on anorexia nervosa:

- *Anorexia nervosa is a very serious condition*

  - *Evidence – thousands impacted annually; severe impact on families; cost of treatment; mortality rates high*

- *Treatment for anorexia nervosa is often unsuccessful*

  - *Evidence – quantitative outcome studies; high drop-out and relapse rates; lack of evidence for treatment protocols; proliferation of treatments*

- *It is not clear why treatment is often unsuccessful*

  - *Evidence – quotes from major authorities; conflicting accounts and suggestions in the literature*

- *There is a lack of research that asks people with anorexia nervosa for their perspectives*

  - *Evidence – references to current research literature*

- *A better understanding of anorexia nervosa service-user perspectives might inform and improve treatment for this group*
- *Proposed study: recruit participants who have dropped out of treatment to develop an understanding of why they did so and how their treatment might have been improved.*

Activity 9.2   Now you try

Sit down with a colleague, friend or supervisor and try to explain your study's rationale to them succinctly, to test its clarity and coherence. Sometimes, naïve colleagues can be very incisive in asking questions about the point and value of your proposed research! Then try to capture the rationale for your study in writing, using the approach outlined in Information box 9.1. You can then use this like an essay plan to help you write the rationale for your study on your proposal form.

Background literature and theoretical framework

As well as explaining the research question and rationale for your study, your proposal will need to describe the literature that already exists in your topic area. This helps to summarise current knowledge and practice in your area, and illustrates the gaps referred to in your rationale, which have led to your research question.

Progress in the fields of counselling and psychotherapy is supported by a continual dialogue between practice, theory and research (see Figure 9.1). So when summarising your literature, you will need to explain the key theoretical ideas that underpin professional practice in your area and provide the key reference points for your research. These ideas constitute a 'theoretical framework' that informs your research question, and how you will interpret your findings later on. The background/literature review section of a proposal is often the longest and the one which people find hardest to write. A well-constructed literature review, with clear sections and arguments that follow logically from each other and which gradually develop a focus that leads to your research question, will provide the foundation for a clear concise summary of these components in your proposal. Detailed guidance on how to plan, complete and write up a literature review is provided in Chapter 5.

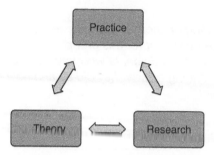

Figure 9.1 *The relationship between practice, theory and research in counselling and psychotherapy*

Referencing

Details of all the literature referred to in your proposal will need to be included in your proposal. This involves providing brief citations within the text itself and a full 'reference list' summary at the end of your proposal that contains all of the sources cited. Accurate and complete information about the literature that underpins your proposal is essential to enable others to understand the foundations of your work and to allow them to locate it for themselves, if they wish – e.g. if they are also researchers. Referencing is also important as it provides the reader with information about the type and extent of evidence underpinning your research. For example, if a statement you make is underpinned by a consistent body of empirical evidence, which you clearly reference, as opposed to a theoretical idea that has yet to be tested, knowing this can help the reader evaluate the statement.

A number of different referencing systems exist which provide researchers with clear conventions to follow when writing references. For example, there are different requirements for how to write a reference for a chapter in a book you have read as opposed to a paper in a published journal or an electronic source. The referencing system most commonly used in Psychology and Psychotherapy writing is the 'APA style' of the American Psychological Association (APA). APA produce a 'Publication Manual' and a website (see 'Further information and resources' below for details) that provide comprehensive, user-friendly information and tutorials on how to write references, as well as advice in other areas of academic writing, such as how to structure and format research papers, use language effectively, and present tables and graphs.

Methodology and sampling

I have suggested that a proposal seeks to explain *what* your research is about, *why* it should be done and *how* it will be done. The 'what' should be clearly addressed by your title, research question and literature review, and the 'why' should be covered in your rationale. The remainder of your proposal will therefore focus on explaining the 'how'. Central to this will be a description of your proposed methodology and sample.

As explained in Chapter 6 and illustrated in Chapters 10–15, a variety of methods are available to carry out research within the fields of counselling and psychotherapy. Moreover, different types of research are suited to asking different kinds of questions and gathering different kinds of data. In your proposal, then, you will need to state the type of research and data you will be using to answer your research question. You should also attach samples of the interview questions or questionnaires you will be using to your proposal as appendices. In addition, you will need to state the specific method you will employ to analyse your data. Remember that there may be a variety of possible research questions and studies that come out of your literature review, so when developing your proposal it is helpful to ask yourself what kind of methodology you will feel most comfortable and competent using (see also Chapter 7).

As well as describing your methodology, your proposal should also make it clear why you think the approach you are adopting is the best one for answering your question. For example, the kinds of limitations identified in your topic area may point to the need to conduct further research of a particular kind in order to develop the field. For instance, the example in Information box 9.1 suggested a need for more qualitative client-centred data to build a better picture than is currently available from the existing quantitative outcomes data on anorexia nervosa.

Once you have explained your methodology, you will need to show that you have thought about where you will get your data from. In other words, who will your participants be? If you have already made contact with an organisation that has agreed to provide you with access to participants, it is worth saying this in your proposal. Some proposals will require you to provide evidence of agreement (e.g. a letter from the organisation manager). You will also need to explain how you will select people to participate in your study. This may include explaining any particular characteristics participants need to have or not have in order to be eligible. This is sometimes referred to as 'inclusion' and 'exclusion' criteria. For example, will participants in your sample need to:

- Be of a particular age, ethnic or professional group?
- Include both male and female participants?
- Have experience of a particular form of therapy, either as a client or a practitioner?
- Have a particular kind of psychological problem or set of symptoms?
- Not be too distressed or too vulnerable to participate in your study?

These kinds of practical questions may also have important implications for the 'viability' of your study, as explained in Information box 9.2.

Information box 9.2   Is your research 'viable'?

A central consideration in developing and evaluating a research proposal is 'viability'. In other words, is the proposed research doable? For instance, there is little point in spending time developing a proposal that requires gathering data from a sample of participants whom you will struggle to find, or find in sufficient numbers, within the timescale and resources you have available. You should also consider whether the kind of study you are planning will require access to an NHS sample of service users or employees. If so, it is likely you will have to undergo a lengthy application and review process to gain authorisation and ethical clearance before you can go ahead (see 'Further information and resources' below). This is likely to extend the overall time it will take to complete your research, which could make an NHS-based project unfeasible if you need to complete your project or course within a set time period. Note, too, that some counselling and psychotherapy organisations will also have their own processes, forms and rules for approving research to take place in their organisation. It is important to find this out early on in your research planning process.

If you foresee viability difficulties with a project you were hoping to undertake, consider whether it is possible to adapt your research so that you can still carry out a meaningful study in the same topic area. For example, is there a way to recruit participants using a non-NHS sample, such as a private or voluntary sector organisation where clearance procedures may be more straightforward? Is it possible to shift your study's focus to clinicians rather than clients, or to a non-clinical sample, which will still produce useful data? If you think you are unlikely to find enough participants to do a quantitative study, might it be possible to recruit sufficient numbers for a qualitative study? If such adaptations are not possible to preserve the viability of your original area of interest, it may be necessary to identify a different, more viable topic area, in discussion with your supervisor/course tutor.

Ethical considerations

Your proposal will need to show that you are aware of the ethical dimensions of your research project and how these will be addressed. As discussed in Chapter 8, the well-being and informed consent of participants is a central consideration. Your proposal will need to explain how you will provide potential participants with information about:

- The title, nature and aims of your study, who is carrying out the research, what it involves and how they may be affected (e.g. emotionally or physically);
- How their decision to participate or not in your study will not affect any services they receive;

- Their right to withdraw from the study at any point;
- The kind of data they will be asked to provide, and how this will be recorded, stored, used and reported in your research;
- How the findings of the research might be published or shared with others, and whether they can have access to a summary of the findings;
- How the confidentiality and anonymity of the data they provide will be protected;
- How they can go about making a complaint if they are unhappy about how they have been treated in the research;
- Further sources of support or information they can access.

It is a good idea to create a 'participant information sheet' to provide such information to potential participants in a clear and accessible way. The information sheet should also include your contact details should they wish to participate or find out more (see Information box 8.1 in Chapter 8 on information sheet contents). You should also ask participants to sign a consent form confirming that they have been provided with this information before they agree to participate (see Information box 8.2). If you are undertaking research at a university, it is likely to have its own ethics review form and process, so you should check what these are (as already stated, you should also make sure you understand the ethics requirements and processes at any organisation where you may be recruiting participants or carrying out your research). When considering the ethical dimensions and processes that your project may involve, it is advisable to consult with your supervisor as well as any research ethics guidelines provided by your professional organisation (see 'Further information and resources' below).

PAUSE FOR REFLECTION

Could participating in my research affect, upset or compromise participants in any way? If so, how will this be minimised and managed by my research design?

- How should I explain the aims of my study – in my participant information sheet – in a way that is interesting and accessible to a lay audience?
- Could the findings from my study offend or upset other people or organisations? If so, do I need to rethink any aspect of the proposed project?

Resources and costs

In your proposal you will need to itemise the resources needed to complete your project, as well as any financial costs and how these will be met. If you are submitting a grant application, this section will be particularly important as it will set out the budget for your research project and show how the money invested will be spent. You should give a detailed breakdown of things like: computer software, library access, books, papers, stationery, postage, equipment (e.g. recording devices), facilities (e.g. rooms for completing interviews or questionnaires), travel costs, supervision, conference attendance, printing and binding costs, etc. Where there is a cost implication, you should give a realistic estimate of what this is and explain who will be paying for this.

Timetable

As well as the physical and financial resources required, your proposal will need to include an estimate of how long the research is going to take to complete. This should be based on a breakdown of the subsequent stages of the research, which might include:

- Research proposal review and ethical clearance
  - This may be broken down into smaller stages if part of an NHS process, including dates when research review panels are likely to meet and provide feedback on your proposal
- Participant recruitment and data gathering
- Data analysis
- Writing up
- Submission
- Examination (if your research is being completed for a degree award)
- Dissemination

Against each stage you should indicate (in months or weeks) when that part of the project will be happening. Try to be realistic in your estimates of how long the different stages will take and discuss this with your supervisor, particularly if your previous experience of research is limited. For example, depending on the size and context of your study, it could take anywhere from one to six months to complete data collection, possibly more if you are planning a longitudinal study or if you run into unexpected difficulties recruiting participants. Similarly, data analysis may take several months, particularly if you are conducting qualitative analysis and transcribing interview data. Depending on how much writing you have been doing as you go along, and the size/academic level of the project you are carrying out (e.g. diploma versus Doctorate), writing up your project is also likely to take several months to complete, including getting feedback from your supervisor on a draft of your work before you produce a final version for submission. An additional factor that will influence how long it takes you to complete you research is how much time and space you have in your life, alongside other personal and professional commitments, to dedicate to your research, so be realistic with yourself and others about what is likely to be involved. Remember that in any large project, breaking the task down into smaller chunks, with interim deadlines and milestones, is a helpful way to manage the overall process, sustain momentum and motivation, and have a way of monitoring progress.

Dissemination

Having argued for the necessity and value of your proposed study, it follows that your research will only make a contribution in your field if others get to hear about it! Dissemination is the all-important stage of communicating the findings of your research to the communities where you think they should have an impact. This may include other practitioners, researchers, actual and potential service users, service managers, government departments and policy makers. Having a plan for dissemination will be especially important if you are looking to secure funding from a funding body or if you are carrying out research at the Doctoral level. Chapter 16 provides a comprehensive discussion on the dissemination of research.

Conclusion

Writing a research proposal marks an important step and achievement in your research journey, and delineates your transition from the initial planning phase to the active stage of carrying out your research. While the prospect of writing a proposal may initially feel daunting, once you get started you will find that it is an invaluable way to help you develop the conceptual and practical clarity of your project, which you will need to make it a success. The more thorough your thinking and planning at this stage the more likely you will be to enjoy the process of carrying out your research. Moreover, having your proposal reviewed and approved by others will give you confidence in the value of your research idea and give you the green light to get started!

Further information and resources

Information on APA style and referencing can be found at:

- APA (2012). *APA Style*. Available at www.apastyle.org/ (accessed on 21/12/12)
- APA (2006). *The Publication Manual of the American Psychological Association* (6th edition). Washington, DC: APA Publications.

The following organisation websites are helpful if you want to find out more about potential sources of research funding in counselling and psychotherapy:

- BACP (2012). Finding research funding. Available at www.bacp.co.uk/research/Finding_Research_Funding/ (accessed on 21/12/12)
- UKCP (2012). Research funding. Available at www.psychotherapy.org.uk/funding_opportunities.html (accessed on 21/12/12)

- BPS (2012). Busaries and research support for postgraduates. Available at www.bps.org.uk/careers-education-training/undergraduate-and-postgraduate-psychology/bursaries-research-support-post (accessed on 21/12/12)
- DH (2012). Funded research. Available at http://prp.dh.gov.uk/category/funded-research/ (accessed on 21/12/12)

Further information can also be found by entering 'counselling or psychotherapy research funding' into your internet search engine. It is also worthwhile exploring the websites of individual universities, which may provide funding for postgraduate student research through their own bursary or studentship schemes.

If you are considering carrying research within the NHS, further information about clearance procedures can be found at the following websites:

- NHSdirect (2012). Information for researchers. Available at www.nhsdirect.nhs.uk/Commissioners/WhatWeOffer/ResearchServiceEvaluationClinicalAudit/Research/InformationForResearchers (accessed on 21/12/1)
- IRAS (2012). Integrated research application system. Available at www.myresearch-project.org.uk/ (accessed on 21/12/12)

Further sources of online guidance on writing research proposals can be found by typing 'writing a research proposal' into your internet search engine.

Suggestions for further reading

Perren, S. (2010). *How to Write a Research Proposal*. BACP Information Sheet R9. Lutterworth: British Association for Counselling and Psychotherapy.
This is a short but informative information leaflet that provides a helpful overview of the process of writing a research proposal.

Punch, K. (2006). *Developing Effective Research Proposals* (2nd edition). London: Sage.
This book provides a more comprehensive account of the process of developing and writing up a research proposal, and includes discussion of different approaches, conceptual frameworks and practical exercises.

PART III
Methodologies and methods for doing research

PART III

TEN

Quantitative methods
Elspeth Twigg (Independent Research Consultant and Data Analyst)

Introduction

In today's straitened and competitive times, having reliable evidence that the service you provide to clients yields substantive benefits can make the difference between renewed funding and the closure of a much-needed service. As discussed in Chapter 1, just *knowing* that you are making dramatic improvements in people's lives is not enough: there are political and economic pressures which mean you need to be able to quantify those improvements. This context means that it is increasingly required that counsellors and psychotherapists should be not just practitioners but 'scientist-practitioners', able to use scientific methods, procedures and research in their day-to-day practice. The level to which this is required varies but the increasing focus on outcomes monitoring means that some understanding of quantitative methods can be a huge benefit to practitioners.

This chapter provides an introduction to quantitative research methods, which are frequently used to answer a wide variety of questions in the field of counselling and psychotherapy.

Information box 10.1 Examples of quantitative research in counselling and psychotherapy

- *Numbers of panic attacks experienced per week by clients attending with acute anxiety (i.e. symptom severity at start of treatment)*
- *Pre-post therapy change in frequency of self-reported anxiety symptoms in clients presenting to the clinic*
- *Relationship between change in therapy (frequency of symptoms) and client factors (e.g. client's level of social support)*

(Continued)

(Continued)

- *Relationship between change in therapy (frequency of symptoms) and therapist factors (e.g. therapist level of experience with working with panic attacks)*
- *Relationship between change in therapy (frequency of symptoms) and organisational factors (e.g. average waiting times in the clinic)*
- *Number of significant therapist disclosure events in different therapeutic approaches (comparison)*

Although the uses of quantitative research are many, one key area in which they are particularly used is the field of outcomes research: looking at 'what works' and why. For this reason, the focus of this chapter is on the use of quantitative methods to assess outcomes in counselling and psychotherapy. At this point it is important to acknowledge that while statistics and quantitative methods are undoubtedly useful, it is unrealistic to believe that their appeal is universal. You may at the moment find yourself among the up to 80% of graduate students in social and behavioural sciences reported by Onwuegbuzie and Wilson (2003) as experiencing 'statistics anxiety'.

PAUSE FOR REFLECTION

How many of these common thoughts and worries about using quantitative methods in practice would you agree with?

- I don't understand statistics
- My clients won't want to waste time form-filling
- The questionnaires will take ages – and they're a waste of time anyway
- Nobody looks at the results
- Statistics can be twisted to tell whatever story 'they' want
- I don't believe a few questions can honestly show anything about how my clients are doing
- Filling in forms takes time away from the important task: the counselling
- I don't want to risk interfering with the therapeutic relationship by making clients fill out the forms
- I know how my clients are doing, I don't need bits of paper to show me
- 'Big-brother' can use the questionnaire results against me

Can you think of any others which aren't listed here? Try to keep these worries in mind as you read this chapter. Hopefully, by the time you've finished you will be reassured – and maybe even enthused.

Chapter 2 discussed trainee fears and assumptions about research but it's important to acknowledge these issues again here and encourage you to think about your own fears and assumptions as you read this chapter.

Chapter aim

It is not our intention to bring you to an understanding of complex statistics by the end of this chapter, but rather to provide you with an introduction to quantitative methods, using examples relating, in particular, to outcomes-focused research. We aim to furnish you with an understanding of the key statistical concepts you are likely to come across in routine practice and to help you collect and use data optimally, as well as understand statistical reports and findings.

We set out to challenge misconceptions that may be held by practitioners, to draw together contemporary clinical experience and research literature, and to demonstrate that the new requirement of therapeutic use of quantitative measurement has the potential to be of significant benefit to practitioners, clients and services. Throughout this chapter we will use three outcome measures which are commonly used in UK settings (CORE-OM, PHQ9 and GAD7) as resource examples and will take readers through a series of straightforward procedural steps which can help them benefit from the use of any one of the common outcome measurement tools currently in UK use.

Outcome measures

Counselling and psychotherapy services are increasingly required to routinely measure client outcomes using questionnaires. The majority of services in both the private and public sector must produce, at the very least, an annual report on service performance. Indeed, Improving Access to Psychological Therapies (IAPT) (DH, 2007; see also Chapter 1) services are currently required to submit data monthly for reporting and counsellors working in these services are obliged to have their clients complete measures (questionnaires) at each session. But how best to measure 'outcome'? There are ever-increasing numbers of outcome measures available to clinicians but for research to be valuable it needs to be easily replicated and compared with other studies. Consequently, it is advisable, where possible, to use a commonly-used and previously-validated outcome measure. A *validated measure* will have satisfactory test-retest stability (scores for clients who are not undergoing treatment will not change substantially week by week due to the way the measure is constructed) and high internal consistency (usually measured by Cronbach's alpha – Cronbach, 1951). In other words, the measure will be reliable over time within its target population.

**Information box 10.2   Outcome measures commonly used in
UK psychotherapeutic settings**

**Clinical Outcomes in Routine Evaluation – Outcome Measure (CORE-OM)
(Evans et al., 2000; Mellor-Clark, Connell, Barkham & Cummins, 2001)**

*A 34-item, global self-report (i.e. client completed rather than assessed by
the practitioner) measure recommended for use with over-16s. Shortened
versions (e.g. CORE-10, CORE-A, CORE-B) are available, as are practitioner-
completed assessment and end of therapy forms. Benchmarks are available
for Primary Care (2006, 2011), Higher Education Counselling and Workplace
Counselling.*

Generalised Anxiety Disorder Assessment (GAD-7) (Spitzer et al., 2006)

*GAD-7 is a 7-item, self-report questionnaire designed to screen and meas-
ure the severity of seven common Generalised Anxiety Disorder symptoms in
patients. It has also been shown to be useful in screening for posttraumatic
stress disorder (PTSD), panic and social anxiety.*

Patient Health Questionnaire (PHQ-9) (Kroenke, Spitzer & Williams, 2001)

*The PHQ-9 is a 9-item, self-report measure assessing each of the nine DSM-IV
criteria for a major depressive episode. Translations are available, as are ultra-
brief, 2-item versions. GAD-7 and PHQ-9 are both part of the IAPT suite of
recommended measures and are available at no cost.*

There has been some debate over the years (e.g. McLeod, 2001) as to the value
of using self-report measures and there are undeniably drawbacks (e.g. if a client
is having a good day then, even if they are asked to report their experiences over
the past one or two weeks, it may be that their current mood affects their
responses). However, there are also benefits, particularly in terms of cost and
ease of administration. Furthermore, research shows that clients can reveal
something in their self-report measure responses which they are not comfortable raising with the therapist (Lambert, 2010), which can then be discussed in
the session.

   This kind of outcome measurement is all part of the 'practice-based evidence'
(PBE) movement (Barkham, Hardy & Mellor-Clark, 2010) in the UK, as introduced and discussed in Chapter 1. The focus of this chapter will be on PBE collected from real-life settings, because this is what trainees and practitioners will
encounter most frequently in their practice (since this is the easiest type of
quantitative data for most people to collect).

Other data sources

In the field of quantitative analysis, much of the data, such as client-completed outcome measures for clients attending a clinic, will be self-report data. But data can come also from other sources: therapist/teacher/parent-report; physiological measurements such as blood pressure and heart rate; counts of the numbers of people making specific choices, are just some examples.

Activity 10.1   Data collection

Spend five minutes making a list of all the people in a client's life who might have a view on whether therapy 'worked'. Then make a list of all the types of data that could be used to provide evidence that therapy 'worked'.

Comment

In both cases, the list might be pretty long. You might include not only the client themselves, but also their partner, children, relatives, friends and work colleagues. In terms of evidence, in addition to self-reported depression (PHQ-9), anxiety (GAD-7) and general psychological functioning (CORE-OM), you might have mentioned self/other questionnaire-rated improvements in a host of domains, such as self-esteem, perceived effectiveness at work, or as a parent. In addition to questionnaire data, you could consider physiological and behavioural indices such as increased hours of sleep, lower alcohol intake, reduced cortisol (stress hormone) levels, etc.

Activity 10.1 demonstrates that quantitative research is not only about data analysis, but also about data collection. Further, without rigour in data collection there is limited value to the results of any quantitative analysis. Chapter 7 has provided guidelines on best practice in conducting research but the key aspects (the 'quality criteria') in terms of quantitative outcome research are detailed below.

'Doing' quantitative research for outcome measurement

There are several key stages in undertaking successful quantitative research for outcome measurement:

1. *Define your 'research question(s)':* This first step is critical, since a poorly-defined research question can make the entire study meaningless. See Chapter 3 for more on this.

2. *Identify the optimal way of measuring relevant data*: If using measures, wherever possible use an existing measure which is already validated and allows comparison with other similar studies.

3. *Decide on who you are going to ask (your sample) and how you will identify your sample*: Sometimes it is not possible to ask everyone for whom the research question is applicable, in which case you need to determine a suitable way of identifying a subgroup which is still representative of the group as a whole. You need to ensure your sample is sufficiently large for your results to be statistically sound (there are sample size formulas for the adequate sample size for quantitative research, see for example, Field, 2009).

4. *Focus on data quality*: The quality of the data gathered in the first instance is key and data should be collected for every eligible client at agreed, appropriate time points. If you only collect data from the clients who engage and do not drop out, your therapy may look more successful than perhaps it actually is.

5. *Clean your data*: No matter how carefully data has been collected, there is always the possibility that errors may have crept in. This is particularly the case if large amounts of data have been batch-entered. Check dates carefully if you are going to be looking at waiting times or durations of treatment. Only correct a value if you can be 100% certain that you know what the actual value should be, otherwise exclude that particular value from any relevant analysis.

6. *Analyse your data*: Decide on the best way to analyse your data to answer the original research question, or questions. Ideally, a researcher should have no bias, although this may be difficult to achieve. Using statistics can help mitigate any potential bias as numbers cannot lie!

7. *Present your results*: Provide sufficient detail on the sample, methods and results to support your conclusions.

PAUSE FOR REFLECTION

Think about what you've read about outcome measures so far and how they can be used.

- Can you think of how you might use them therapeutically?
- Do you recognise how important it is that everyone follows the same procedure? What can you do to make sure this happens?

An example of good practice in the use of outcome measurement in a single counselling service (in this instance, the CORE-OM) is detailed in Twigg (2012).

The value of an outcome measure, such as the CORE-OM, varies depending on how it is used. You can simply give it to your client at the start and end of therapy and pass it to someone else to deal with so you never even see the client's score. Or you can look at the completed measure at the start of the therapy session and discuss significant responses with the client. If you do this at each session the measure can be a valuable tool in helping you and the client track progress.

Although 'practice-based evidence' is not as prescriptive as 'evidence-based practice' (see Chapter 1), it is still important that procedures are standardised to some degree so that results are comparable. If one therapist gives the client their outcome measure to complete at the start of the session and the other at the end, the latter is likely to be biased by the work in the session. It is a good idea to at least agree within the practice on standard procedures and to try to follow guidelines as closely as possible.

Quantitative methods and outcome measures don't only allow services to look at client outcomes and service performance; pooled data (from several sources) can be used in generating benchmarks (see Information box 10.3).

Information box 10.3   What is benchmarking?

Benchmarking is a process whereby services or individuals can compare their performance on particular indicators against other, similar services. To facilitate this, data from many, similar services are pooled and summary data (e.g. means) provided. For example, the CORE System Group (2010) have gathered data for over 64,000 clients seen by 1,038 practitioners in 35 primary care service settings on waiting times, clinical outcomes, assessment outcomes (i.e. proportion of clients assessed who are accepted for therapy) and types of therapy endings, and these data were used to establish the published benchmarks (see www.coreims.co.uk/Support_User_Benchmarking. html). These benchmarks are freely available and a useful resource for practitioners and services. Benchmarks for Higher Education counselling services and Employee Assistance Programmes are also available. Similar large-scale datasets are available for GAD-7 and PHQ-9.

As an example of the usefulness of benchmarks, a service might choose to look at the proportion of their clients with premature/unplanned endings to therapy and compare this with national benchmarks for similar services. If their rates were unusually high, then the service managers and clinicians could work together with service user groups to look at possible reasons for and solutions to the problem.

The advent of the internet and increases in computing power mean that ever more information has become available. It is now possible to collect data, with relative ease, on a scale which was previously unimaginable. Statistical methods can help to make sense of that data and make data more manageable. Statistics are thus a powerful tool for counsellors and psychotherapists.

Statistics

Sadly, the word *statistics* strikes fear into the heart of many, but it needn't be so. Sure, there are complex statistical analyses – multilevel modelling, time series analysis and the like – but there are also relatively simple statistical processes. Understanding even a few of these more straightforward statistical terms and methods can prove very useful.

On a research journey, statistics can help you to explore strange new worlds and to boldly go where no researcher has gone before ...

Descriptive statistics

Descriptive statistics are used to summarise a sample. Commonly encountered descriptive statistics are listed and explained in Information box 10.4.

Information box 10.4   Common statistical terms defined

Sample size – *the number of individual cases (e.g. people) in the sample.*

Frequency – *the number of times a particular value occurs in the sample.*

Frequency distribution – *a summary of the number of times each possible value occurs in the sample.*

Mean (the average score) – *Calculated by dividing the sum of all valid scores by the total number of valid cases.*

Mode – *the value which occurs most frequently in your data. It is possible for a sample to have multiple modes.*

Standard deviation – *the average amount of variability in a set of scores. If standard deviation is large, then that means the average distance from each data point from the mean is large (so there is a lot of variability in the data). Although it is possible to calculate standard deviation yourself, it is much easier to ask Excel or other, similar software to do so for you.*

Variance – *is a value which shows the variability of scores in a sample. Calculated by finding the difference between each data value and the mean for the sample, squaring those differences and adding all the results together.*

Median – *the middle value, if all values are arranged in ascending order.*

Sometimes it can be hard to see how you would go about getting from numbers on a piece of paper or screen to the summary statistic you want. Below is a worked example to guide you through the process.

Worked example:

A counsellor obtains CORE-OM data for 10 clients (i.e. sample size = 10) at intake and wants to look in more detail at their scores. Clients' scores are shown below (no clients missed items on the measure).

Andy	Jools	Eric	Jane	Sid	Hafsah	Lucy	Rafiq	John	Bert
17	12	9	25	18	11	18	13	12	9

Mean score   = sum of all scores/number of cases
               = (17 + 12 + 9 + 25 + 18 + 11 + 18 + 13 + 12 + 9) / 10
               = 144 / 10
               = 14.4

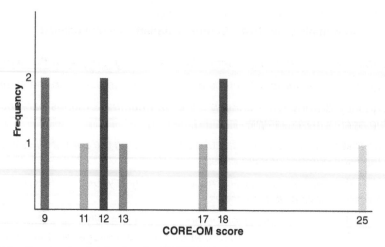

Figure 10.1 *Frequency distribution for CORE-OM data*

Ranked scores (arranged from lowest to highest)

9	9	11	12	12	13	17	18	18	25

Median score = mid-value of ranked scores = midpoint of 12 and 13 = 12.5
Modes are 9, 12 and 18.
Range = distance between lowest and highest scores = 25 – 9 = 16
Standard deviation (calculated using Microsoft Excel) = 5.0

Commonly encountered statistical terms (and what they really mean)

Research is often interested in *score change* – the difference between a client's score at the start of treatment and at the end – and in quantifying the magnitude of this change.

Reliable change (Jacobson & Truax, 1991) or *statistically significant improvement* is a change in score between two time points which is large enough not just to be a result of any possible measurement error introduced as a consequence of using a particular measure. The reliable change index is calculated using the standard deviation and reliability (Cronbach's alpha) of the measure in question.

Clinical change (Evans, Margison & Barkham, 1998) may also be called *clinically significant change or recovery*. Clinical change is the clinical outcome of interest in IAPT and, simply put, means a move from above to below an established clinical cut-off. This change does not need to be statistically significant (reliable).

An *effect size* allows the 'size' of the difference between the means of two samples (e.g. a treatment and control group) to be quantified in a single value; it is basically an index of how significant the difference is.

$$Effect\ size = \frac{Experimental\ group\ mean - Control\ group\ mean}{Standard\ deviation}$$

It is usual to use the pooled standard deviation (i.e. the standard deviations of each group, added together), but in some instances the standard deviation of the control group is used. Effect sizes are often used when looking at pre- and post-therapy scores and when comparing different interventions.

For example, a service has the following pre- and post-counselling CORE-OM data for 30 clients: Pre-therapy mean = 17 (SD = 6); post-therapy mean = 8 (SD = 7).

$$Effect\ size = \frac{17-8}{6+7} = \frac{9}{13} = 0.7$$

Cohen (1992) suggested that 0.2 can be considered a small effect size, 0.5 a medium effect size and 0.8 a large effect size. However, the context also affects what effect size we might expect. If we are comparing two active treatments, rather than a treatment and control group, then we would expect both treatments to have an impact on client outcomes and thus the effect size is likely to be smaller.

Confidence intervals are calculated from a sample of data and provide us with an estimate of how reliable a figure is. They are a function of the standard deviation of the sample. Sample size also has a large impact on confidence intervals, with larger samples generally yielding narrower confidence intervals and thus enabling us to place more credence in the result.

But what exactly is a confidence interval? It is unlikely that values obtained from a sample are exactly the same as those which would be obtained if we looked at the population as a whole (which is often unfeasible). Confidence intervals give us a range of values within which we can say, to a specified degree of certainty, the actual population value lies. A 95% confidence interval will contain the actual value 95% of the time. It is most common to use 95% or 99% confidence levels.

*95% confidence interval = sample mean ±1.96 * sample standard deviation*

It is also useful to note that, if you are looking at changes in score between two time points (difference scores), a confidence interval which does not include 0 implies that there are significant differences between the two samples. Similarly, if you have confidence intervals for the mean of two samples and those two confidence intervals do not overlap, then you can say, with the appropriate level of certainty, that the populations from which those two samples were drawn differ.

Worked example (continued):

The 95% confidence interval for the mean pre-therapy score of our counsellor's 10 clients would be 14.4 ± 1.96 * 5.0 = (4.6 to 24.2) – we can be 95% confident that the *actual* population mean lies somewhere in that range. As we can see, the small sample size means that the range of values within which we could expect the population mean to lie is 19.6 points! Using confidence intervals adds valuable information and lets us see how accurate our estimate is likely to be.

Six months after she started seeing her clients, our hypothetical counsellor wants to look at their outcomes. None of the original 10 clients are still in therapy: three clients (30%) had unplanned endings to therapy and post-therapy CORE-OM data were available for only five of the seven clients who completed therapy. So, outcome data are only available for 50% of the clients seen by the counsellor. Although it can be difficult to collect end-of-therapy data for clients who have unplanned endings to therapy, it should not be overly onerous to collect data for all clients who complete therapy and we would have hoped-for outcomes for at least seven clients. Note, however, that this type of issue with incomplete data is not untypical – research with the CORE-OM showed that while the average percentage of clients completing the questionnaire at the start of therapy was 83%, at the end it was only 39% (Bewick et al., 2006). Clearly, it is harder to be sure that counselling in a service 'works' if the stats are based on a minority of clients. Anyway, pre-post scores were:

Table 10.1

CORE-OM score	Andy	Jane	Lucy	Rafiq	Bert
Pre-score	17	25	18	13	9
Post-score	6	13	7	3	7
Pre-post change	*9*	*12*	*9*	*10*	*2*

A *reliable change* in CORE-OM score is five or more points, so four clients (80% of those with post-therapy data) showed a reliable improvement. For this change to be *clinically significant* the client's score must also have moved from above a defined cut-off (in the case of the CORE-OM this threshold is 10) to below. So, three of the four clients whose scores reliably improved also demonstrated a clinically significant improvement. Although Jane's score improved markedly, it remained above cut-off at the end of therapy and hence her improvement was reliable but not clinically significant. Since Bert started off relatively less distressed (<10) he also does not show clinically significant change: his score could not move from above to below cut-off as it started below cut-off.

Bear in mind that although 80% of our hypothetical counsellor's clients with pre-post data showed a reliable improvement, this also means that only 40% of the original sample showed a reliable improvement. This highlights again how important it is to collect data on as many clients as possible in order for the data to accurately reflect the true outcomes for clients. Of course, it is quite possible, and indeed rather likely, that clients who drop out of therapy will not show the same improvement as clients who complete therapy, so moving to collecting data at every session may make for improved accuracy but may also make *reported* recovery and improvement rates drop.

Statistical analyses

The types of statistical test that can be applied to your data depend on whether data are *normally-distributed*, what *type(s)* of data you have collected, whether the data are *independent*, and whether the *variances are equal*. These concepts are explained in the Information boxes 10.5 and 10.6.

Information box 10.5   Normal distribution

For certain parametric statistical tests to be appropriate (such as t-tests, see Chapter 11), data should be approximately normally distributed (see Figure 10.2). Data which follows a 'normal' distribution is symmetrically distributed with a single mode in or very close to the middle of the distribution. The frequency of individual values decreases as you move further away from the mode, producing a bell-shaped curve. This distribution is called 'normal' both because it is symmetric and because it occurs frequently in nature.

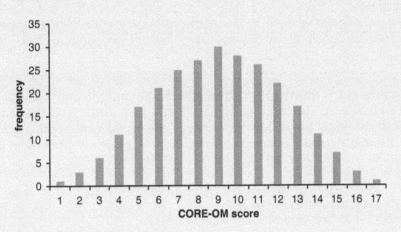

Figure 10.2   *Normally distributed data*

Central Limit Theorems state that for large samples (larger than 30 is a generally held rule of thumb but there is no sound, statistical, basis for this figure) distributions tend towards normality and can be assumed to be normal for the purposes of analysis.

Information box 10.6 Types of data and statistical concepts to help you know which statistical family to use

Types of data

Nominal *(categorical) data fall into discrete groups, such as males and females or academic year group.*

Ordinal *data, such as position in a race or responses on a 1–5 rating scale, are data which can be logically ordered. Intervals between each value are not necessarily the same.*

Interval *data, such as temperature, can also be logically ordered, but there is the same gap between each value. It lacks a 0 value, however.*

Ratio *data, such as distance, are similar to interval data but there is a clearly-defined 0 and hence ratios can be calculated: 50 metres is twice as far as 25 metres.*

It can be hard to determine if data is truly independent, *i.e. that a score on measure A is not somehow dependent on or related to a score on measure B. A rule of thumb is that data on the same individual (such as measures taken at different time points) or on matched pairs of individuals are not independent.*

The requirement for equal variances *means that if you are comparing groups, their variance should be roughly equivalent (see Information box 10.4).*

Statistical tests fall into two broad categories: parametric and non-parametric tests. *Parametric tests* include t-tests (see Chapter 11) and the ANOVA family of statistical analyses. In parametric testing, the usual central measure is the mean. Parametric tests are more 'powerful' and generally preferable to their non-parametric counterparts. In order to use parametric tests:

- your data needs to be normally distributed (or consist of more than 30 cases);
- data needs to be at least interval;
- samples must have approximately equal variances.

Non-parametric tests (or distribution-free tests) include the Kruskal-Wallis test and the Mann-Whitney U-test. The usual central measure is the median. Non-parametric testing is particularly useful with small samples and should be used if you do not think your data meet the requirements for parametric testing – it is never wrong to use a non-parametric test, it may just be less appropriate and it has less power (or ability to detect a statistical difference). Data can be ordinal (set in particular order by its position on a scale, such as race position) or nominal (grouped according to a certain characteristic).

Information box 10.7   Statistical significance

Once you have performed your statistical test, you need to know if the results confirm your expectations (your hypothesis). To do this, you look at the test statistic, which gives the probability that the difference or relationship observed happened by chance. It is common practice in psychology to accept levels of probability less than 0.05 as being statistically significant (i.e. we can be sufficiently sure that the result is not due to chance). This means that there is only a 1 in 20 chance that the statistically significant result is actually an error. The closer the test statistic is to zero, the more credence we can place on the observed difference/ relationship. However, large samples will often yield statistically significant results which are not meaningful. This is a difficult concept to grasp but Chapter 11 explains statistical significance in more detail.

Correlation

A correlation coefficient is a single value which summarises the relationship between two variables. Correlation coefficients can lie between -1 and 1, with coefficients close to 0 meaning that there is little or no relationship between the two variables of interest and coefficients close to ± 1 implying a strong relationship. There are several correlation coefficients available and the appropriate coefficient to use depends on the data that are being analysed. The coefficients which you are most likely to encounter are the Pearson (product moment) correlation coefficient (r) and Spearman's (rank) correlation coefficient (ρ (rho)). Pearson's coefficient is used to measure linear relationships, assuming the data meet the assumptions previously outlined for applicability of parametric testing. Spearman's ρ is used if one or both sets of data consist of ranks, or if the data do not meet the requirements for parametric testing which were set out earlier. Spearman's ρ looks at the strength of the relationship between two variables, regardless of whether this relationship is linear.

When looking at the results of correlation testing, it is important to bear in mind that 'correlation does not imply causation': just because two variables are correlated does not mean that one is necessarily influencing the other. There may be other factors at play, or the result may be chance. For example, there is a correlation between going to bed fully clothed and waking with a headache. You might conclude that not getting ready for bed properly causes headaches, or you might think that the amount you had to drink the night before was a factor! However, a strong correlation does mean that the statistical question you have posed merits further, more detailed, investigation.

Student's t-test, more commonly known as the t-test, is a parametric test which compares the mean of two samples. T-tests can be independent or matched pairs (they are also applicable when measures on the same individual at more than one time point (repeated measures) have been taken). Further detail on the t-test is given in Chapter 11.

Analysis of variance (ANOVA), or the F-test, is used when more than two groups are being tested, rather than using multiple t-tests. If it is used on only two groups, then it produces the same results as the t-test. As with the t-test, there is an underlying assumption that variables are normally distributed. Furthermore, although equal sample sizes are not required, large disparities in sample sizes may mean that variances in the two samples differ and thus affect results.

ANOVA looks at the amount of variance in a *dependent variable* (DV) explained by other, *independent (causal) variables*. For example, we might be interested in how much the changes in CORE-OM scores were explained by clients' marital status, gender and employment. The dependent variable in this instance is the difference between pre- and post-treatment CORE-OM score and the independent variables are marital status, gender and employment. If there are several independent variables measured in a study, then a particularly useful feature of ANOVA is that it can also be used to distinguish the main effect (variance in a dependent variable which can be attributed to one, particular, independent variable) and interaction effects (variance in a dependent variable which can be attributed to two or more independent variables working together). In other words, gender may heavily impact therapy outcome (main effect) for clients, or it could be that being a single woman is associated with large reductions in CORE-OM score, whereas being a single man is not (interaction effect with gender and marital status).

If the results of an ANOVA test are statistically significant (i.e. $p < 0.05$ for 95% significance level), this implies that the independent variables are having an effect on the dependent variable.

Information box 10.8   More complex forms of statistical testing

ANCOVA – *a blend of regression and ANOVA which allows you to add covariates (continuous variables, such as age, which are not part of the model itself but which may impact on your DV) to your model. This removes the effect of that variable on the statistical analysis. So, when looking at CORE-OM outcomes, we might think that age has an impact on score change and want to remove the effect of age from the analysis.*

MANOVA *(multivariate ANOVA) – used when there are two or more dependent variables (e.g. CORE and a client satisfaction rating).*

Regression analysis – *often used in making predictions and is a family of techniques which looks at the relationship between a dependent variable and one or more independent variables.*

Factor analysis – *used when there is an observed correlation between variables, this method attempts to describe variance in terms of a potentially*

---

lower number of unobserved variables, or factors. Factor analysis is useful when trying to understand patterns in data.

Structural equation modelling – is a method that statistically tests causal models between variables. It is useful for developing and testing theoretical assumptions.

Multi-level modelling – allows non-independent data to be analysed. For example, it allows the outcomes of individual clients to be grouped by the counsellor they worked with so that the outcomes of different counsellors can be compared.

However, such tests are beyond the scope of this text. If you are interested in learning more, then we recommend you consult one or more of the excellent books recommended in the further reading section at the end of this chapter.

Statistical software

It is possible for a service or individual to collect and analyse data using generic software (such as Excel, SPSS, R) or using software specifically designed for outcome measurement in psychological therapy and counselling services (such as CORE Net, PCMIS). Detailed in Information box 10.8 are some of the more commonly used software packages and systems available.

Information box 10.8   Statistical software

Generic analytic software packages

Microsoft Excel is a widely-used spreadsheet application. Data is arranged in rows and columns. It can easily be asked to perform simple statistical operations and is very useful for graphical illustrations of data and data editing. However, accessing more complex statistical operations requires an understanding of programming.

IBM SPSS can be menu-driven or use 'syntax' (simple code). Using syntax allows analysis to be quickly replicated. Rows typically represent cases (e.g. individuals, specific groups) and columns represent measurements (e.g. age, score, gender). Graphical output is somewhat limited compared to Excel but data analysis such as t-tests and other more complex tests can be more straightforward.

(Continued)

(Continued)

Other packages include:

SAS; R (free to download from www.r-project.org/); AMOS; HLM; LISREL

Analytic software specifically for use in counselling/psychotherapy settings

CORE Net *(www.coreims.co.uk/Buy_Net_Software.html) is a customer-configurable, web-based data entry system originally designed for entry of CORE-OM, Therapy Assessment and End of Therapy data. Over 30 outcome measures, including GAD-7 and PHQ-9, can optionally be added to the system and the system can be tailored to meet IAPT needs. The system facilitates regular collection and tracking of client outcome data and has various graphing and reporting capabilities. Client data can be batch-entered, entered by the client on-screen, or emailed to the client for completion.*

PC-MIS *(www.pc-mis.co.uk/) is a web-based, customer-configurable data entry system designed by the University of York's Mental Health Research Group and is the Patient Case Management Information System for the IAPT programme 'Designed by Clinicians for Clinicians'. The system helps services to collect data effectively and manage clinical caseloads, and to automatically generate reports from that data.*

IAPTUS *(www.iaptus.co.uk/) is the most frequently-used system for IAPT patient case management and reporting. The system provides a user-friendly mechanism for analysing patient data.*

Conclusion

We appreciate that there may be many challenges involved in undertaking quantitative research, but we hope that this chapter has given you some insight into the benefits of understanding and using such research. Some of the potential challenges are outlined below, along with potential benefits. You may be able to think of others.

Benefits

- Gives an understanding of what is happening (effects of medication/treatment, changes in symptoms)
- Easy to compare data collected for different clients/groups

- Can be used for large samples and offers the possibility to generalise findings with greater confidence
- Easy to aggregate data and test theories
- Can be replicated to confirm results
- Enables researchers to investigate causal relationships
- Findings from quantitative research are often more convincing for mainstream science, funding bodies and governments

Challenges

- Relies on the assumptions from positivism (see Chapter 6): there is a fixed, observable world which we all experience in the same way
- Often doesn't allow room for exploration of diverse individual meanings or deeper understanding of complex and ambiguous issues
- Constrains participants to report on their experiences in terms of categories and fixed-response questionnaire formats designed by researchers
- Making sure the right data is collected in the first place
- Data quality: ensuring that data is 'clean'
- Knowing which statistical tests are appropriate and understanding the results
- The focus on measurement may affect the therapy process

At present the NHS is moving towards a 'payment by results' system and the use of outcomes data is likely to become increasingly commonplace. However, practitioners may naturally feel wary of this and concerned that outcomes data for their clients could be used unfairly to judge their performance. While this is a reasonable fear, there are significant benefits to engaging in the use of outcomes data in terms of refining and improving your own practice. For example, there is increasing evidence from researchers such as Michael Lambert (2010) that using outcome monitoring and feedback can improve performance. Chapter 1 provides you with evidence illustrating how difficult it can be to be objective in your own assessment (e.g. self-assessment bias, as reported by Walfish, McAlister, O'Donnell and Lambert (2012)). The use of quantitative methods, and particularly routine outcome measurement, enables practitioners not only to evaluate their own performance properly, but also to use the data to ensure that patients are progressing satisfactorily and to improve their practice.

While data collection is seen as purely an administrative/managerial task, with no clinical yield, it will always be difficult to secure good quality data. By engaging clinicians in using the data which they collect and showing them what that potential yield can be, we can enthuse them about the use of quantitative data in improving client and service outcomes and at the same time improve data quality. It is our hope that this chapter will have helped you to see the value of this type of data collection and analysis for improving counselling and psychotherapy from the service level to the level of individual clients.

Suggestions for further reading

Barkham, M., Hardy, G.E. & Mellor-Clark, J. (Eds) (2010). *Developing and Delivering Practice-based Evidence: A guide for psychological therapies*. Chichester: Wiley-Blackwell.

A comprehensive account, written by US and UK experts in the field, on how to conduct practice-based research. The content is appropriate for practitioners working alone or in groups and for psychological therapy services.

Field, A. (2013). *Discovering Statistics using IBM SPSS Statistics* (4th edition). London: Sage.

Latest edition of this very popular text, guiding and entertaining readers simultaneously. Although the mood is light-hearted, the book covers a huge range of topics, from the very basics through to complex statistical tests such as logistic regression and multilevel linear models. It provides step-by-step instructions along with guidance on interpretation of results.

Field, A. (2013). http://statisticshell.com/html/apf.html

Lecture materials and other useful stuff produced by Andy Field to help you understand statistics.

ELEVEN

How to use t-tests to explore pre-post change

Elspeth Twigg (Independent Research Consultant and Data Analyst) & Dr Paul Redford (UWE Bristol)

Introduction

Having taken a broad look at quantitative methods in Chapter 10, we now move on to look in more detail at one of the most frequently encountered statistical tests when comparing two samples: the t-test. You may already be using outcomes measures with clients and, if not, then you may perhaps do so in the future. Outcome measures can be very useful in looking at individual client change but this utility can be extended to investigate whether scores for groups of clients differ in terms of specific criteria, as discussed in Chapter 10. We shall look in more detail below at the different ways you can use a t-test in your practice, but of course the t-test (of which there are a number of variations) is only one of a number of statistical techniques that are often used in counselling research. One of the reasons for its popularity is that it is a fairly robust procedure as well as one that can be conducted relatively easily using available software (such as MS Excel or other spreadsheets). In essence, the t-test is one way in which we can quantify and examine differences between group means, provided we are only looking at two groups.

When we collect data from two groups it is likely that both individuals' scores within the groups and the average scores of the two groups will vary. In fact, it would be unusual if the scores were exactly the same. However, the question arises as to what degree of difference there needs to be for us to conclude that this difference is 'statistically significant'? This is how a t-test can help. A t-test examines the difference between two mean scores (say, two group means) and then works out, given the variation in the scores and the number of scores in each group, the likelihood that a difference of that size would have occurred by chance. The results obtained allow you to determine whether the difference observed can be considered large enough to conclude that the groups are meaningfully different.

When using statistics to explore differences between groups we are moving from describing the data that we have collected to making more substantial claims about whether the difference implies that the groups themselves are different. This is the difference between describing a sample (the data that you have collected) and making inferences about the population from which the sample comes, based on observations about the sample (extrapolating to the wider group of people, similar to those sampled, but not included in the sample; see Chapter 10).

PAUSE FOR REFLECTION

If a counselling service is interested in looking at how well the therapy they offer works with different clients, they will probably already be collecting data on those clients in the form of demographic information and outcome measures. Can you think how you could use t-tests and this data to answer service-relevant questions?

Comment

One particular area which is of interest to clinicians is why clients drop out of therapy. If counsellors in a service have noticed that young people seem to drop out of therapy, it would be relatively simple to run a t-test to examine the number of sessions attended by clients below 25 years of age (say) with those over that age. If the t-test shows a difference, it might be possible to then use this information to gain management support for interventions to address this issue.

Issues and assumptions in using t-tests

It is only appropriate to use t-tests when you are looking at differences between two groups. For more than two groups, ANOVA (which was introduced briefly in the previous chapter) should be used (the particular type depends on what exactly is being investigated), and for more than two dependent variables (i.e. the things you are looking at, say, age and number of counselling sessions attended), MANOVA, regression or factor analysis should be used (see Chapter 10). Furthermore, your data need to meet a number of requirements in order for use of the t-test to be appropriate (see Information box 11.1). Fortunately, the assumptions are straightforward to check. The first two assumptions can be checked just by knowing the data, the other two need to be explicitly tested before you can run a t-test.

As a general rule of thumb, larger samples usually conform to these assumptions more easily than small samples. If these conditions are violated, it may mean that you draw incorrect conclusions from your analysis. If your data doesn't meet these requirements, a less powerful test, such as the Mann-Whitney u-test (non-parametric test), should be used (the concept of statistical power is discussed further below).

Information box 11.1   Assumptions to be checked before using an independent samples t-test

1. Independence of scores

This means that the data (numbers) you have are independent from each other (i.e. not systematically related to each other – see Chapter 10) so that if you are comparing group A with group B, group A's score should not influence or be related to group B's score (e.g. if people knew which condition they were in and discussed the research with participants in another condition, their scores would not be independent). If the data are related, then a t-test may still be appropriate but you would need to use a repeated measures (or matched pairs) t-test.

2. Data must be interval data

See Information box 10.6 in Chapter 10.

3. Data must be normally distributed

The assumption is that the data you have collected (the dependent variable, e.g. the number of counselling sessions attended) is normally distributed (see Information box 10.5 in Chapter 10). Many statistical programmes (such as SPSS, Excel or R) will allow you to test whether the data you have collected follows a normal distribution.

4. Variation between groups must be homogeneous (similar)

T-tests require that the variations in scores for Group A to be similar in distribution to the variations in scores for Group B (known as the assumption of homogeneity of variance – see Information box 10.4 in Chapter 10 for a reminder about what variance is). Of course, the average of those scores may be different (which is what the t-test examines), but the distribution (spread) must be similar. Again, many statistical programs can test this for you. Furthermore, in programs such as SPSS and Excel, this can be taken into account when running the analysis.

Sample size, effect size and power

There are two more key issues that should be understood before running a t-test: these are the concepts of effect size and power. The likelihood of achieving statistically significant results is in part dependent on the size of the sample of data you collect. For example, while a certain therapeutic technique may improve client well-being, if the sample is too small there will not be enough statistical power for a t-test to be statistically significant. This will force you to conclude that any mean difference you see could have occurred by chance. The concept of power is similar to that of a lens (say a telescope or magnifying glass). More powerful lenses are likely to see things that are small, which may be missed with a less powerful lens. In the same way, when your data have more power, you are more likely to be able to detect effects and patterns in the data than if your data are less powerful. One of the key contributors to power is sample size. Therefore, we can consider studies with larger samples as being more powerful and more likely to detect an effect. Smaller studies, conversely, are less powerful.

So what do you do if you have a smaller sample size (as is not uncommon in counselling and psychotherapy)? A simple solution is to measure *effect size*, which is not dependent on sample size. In Chapter 10 we have shown with an example how an effect size (Cohen's *d*) is calculated – it is the difference between the average scores by group (the difference in means) in relation to the estimated overall variation (pooled standard deviation, which is written as SD). Effect sizes can also be calculated online, where lots of effect size and power calculators exist.

The score of the effect size can vary from zero, which indicates no difference between the means, to infinity – the bigger the number, the larger the effect

'I don't think it means that kind of tea ...'

size. As mentioned in Chapter 10, Cohen (1992) suggested that 0.2 can be considered a small effect size, 0.5 a medium effect size and 0.8 a large effect size. Cohen's d is independent of sample size and therefore allows us to add extra information to results. For example, if your t-test demonstrates a non-significant finding (so you cannot infer a real difference in the population), you can still report the size of the effect demonstrated. This would therefore warrant further research in a larger sample. Furthermore, two studies with different sample sizes may demonstrate different levels of significance but the same size of effect.

Types and uses of t-test in counselling research

Single sample t-test

A single-sample (or one-sample) t-test tests the hypothesis that the mean of the population from which the sample was drawn is equal to a specified value. This type of t-test is not often used when looking at counselling/psychotherapy data but could be used, for example, if you wanted to compare scores of clients (e.g. on depression) to a known value (e.g. an average depression score for a comparable group). The example below will help you to understand how this might work.

Two-sample t-tests – paired and independent samples

Two-sample t-tests are encountered much more frequently when working with counselling or psychotherapy data, as we are often interested in comparing treatments.

It could be that your data can logically be paired with other data in the sample, whether this is because one person was measured or assessed at two time-points (repeated measures as with pre/post outcome measurement) or because the two sets of data have some other factors in common (e.g. two siblings completed the measures). If this is the case, then a *paired samples* (also sometimes called repeated measures) *t-test* is the test to use. Alternatively, there may be no common factor which links measurements, in which case an *independent samples* (or unrelated) *t-test* is appropriate. An example here would be if you compared outcome using the CORE-OM measure between one sample of people receiving counselling approach A and a different sample receiving counselling approach B.

Two-tailed and one-tailed tests

In a two-tailed test, the hypothesis states that there is a difference between two conditions, but does not specify the direction of that difference (which one is higher). Two-tailed tests should generally be used unless there is convincing theoretical and empirical evidence (such as previous research) that the difference is likely to be in a particular direction, in which case a one-tailed test can be used (see examples in Information box 11.2 below).

Hypothesising and null hypothesis significance testing

In quantitative research, we often form a *hypothesis* (an idea about what might or might not be true) and then set out to support or negate that hypothesis using available data and *null hypothesis significance testing* (NHST). So, for example, we might be working with two groups of students at final exam time and be interested in their anxiety levels, measured using the Generalised Anxiety Disorder Assessment (GAD-7). We measure the scores of all students to provide a baseline assessment. One of our hypothetical groups of students attends a six-week mindfulness training course while the others receive no intervention. We might hypothesise that those students who receive some training in the use of mindfulness techniques will be able to control their anxiety symptoms better and thus have lower GAD-7 scores after six weeks. We could look at their pre-post scores and say 'It looks like I'm right, the "mindful" students' GAD-7 scores have reduced compared with the other group', but it would be far better to have a way of showing that this difference is *statistically significant* (see the discussion of this concept in Chapter 10).

Information box 11.2   Setting up a two-sample hypothesis

There are three basic forms of hypothesis but in each case the null hypothesis will be that there is no difference between groups *(the means of the two groups are equal) and with our statistical test we set out to reject this null hypothesis:*

1. The mean of one sample is larger than the other. *For example, you might hypothesise that people who eat more than 200g of chocolate per day would, on average, weigh more than people who ate less than 50g of chocolate per day.* In this context, use a one-tailed t-test.
2. The mean of one sample is smaller than the other. *So you might hypothesise that the post-treatment scores on an outcome measure of a group of clients attending a counselling service would be lower than the pre-treatment scores.* In this context too, use a one-tailed t-test.
3. The means of the two samples differ, but you do not have a clear idea of which has the higher mean. *You might want to look at the pre-post PHQ-9 score change for two groups of clients receiving different interventions but have no clear idea of which group will have the highest mean.* In this context, use a two-tailed test.

We start with a *null hypothesis*. If you are working with a single data sample (i.e. you only have data on students who did the mindfulness intervention), the hypothesis you form will simply be that the mean of the sample is equal to a specific value (e.g. the level of anxiety of students at final exam time as found in previous research). You can then decide whether you are interested in the direction of the difference of the sample mean from the hypothetical value (a one-sided test) or just in whether there is a difference (a two-sided test). However, you are more likely to come across the situation where the means of two samples are compared. This is rather more complex as there are a variety of potential hypotheses, which are described in more detail in Information box 11.2.

Once the null hypothesis has been established, you need to use your data to test and see whether or not it provides evidence that supports or refutes your hypothesis. And, as described in Information box 11.2, setting up your hypothesis enables you to establish whether you need to use a one-tailed or a two-tailed t-test. For our two samples of students, there is an increasing body of evidence suggesting that mindfulness can help with anxiety, so we could establish a null hypothesis that there is no difference between groups but use a one-tailed test as we would expect the mindful group to have greater reductions in pre-post GAD-7 score.

Activity 11.1

Which types of t-test would be appropriate in the following situations?

1. 100 students complete a CORE-Outcome Measure (CORE-OM) at the start and end of a time-limited block of counselling sessions.
2. A counselling service randomly allocates all clients who attend to one of two different treatments, either cognitive behavioural therapy (CBT) or interpersonal psychotherapy (IPT).
3. A sample of people completes a Patient Health Questionnaire (PHQ-9). You want to know whether the sample's mean score is above or below the PHQ-9 clinical cut-off (10 is generally used as a cut-off).

What would your null hypothesis be in each case? Would you use a one-tailed or a two-tailed test? (Answers to these questions can be found in the footnote on page 158.)

How to run a t-test with Excel (or online spreadsheet)

To calculate a t-test to compare outcome scores between an experimental and a control group (independent samples t-test), the following, rather unwieldy, equation is used:

$$t = \frac{\bar{X}_e - \bar{X}_c}{\sqrt{\left(\frac{\left[\sum X_e^2 - \frac{(\sum X_e)^2}{N_e}\right] + \left[\sum X_c^2 - \frac{(\sum X_c)^2}{N_c}\right]}{N_e + N_c - 2}\right)\left(\frac{1}{N_e} + \frac{1}{N_c}\right)}}$$

Key:

X_e, X_c = scores in experimental/control groups, respectively

X_e^2, X_c^2 = squares of scores in experimental/control groups, respectively

N_e, N_c = number of cases in experimental/control groups, respectively

= mean score in experimental/control groups, respectively

$\sum X_e$ = sum of all scores for experimental group (column 1)

$\sum X_e^2$ = sum of all squared scores for control group (column 2)

$\sum X_c$ = sum of all squared scores for control group (column 3)

$\sum X_c^2$ = sum of all squared scores for control group (column 4)

It is good to have an idea of the 'ingredients' that are used to calculate a t-test. However, we will spare you from running it by hand as it is rather a cumbersome process! Luckily, it is far more likely nowadays that you will use computer software of some kind to conduct t-tests and other statistical analyses. We will now take you step by step through the process of conducting a t-test using Excel using the scores from a fictional experimental and control group (Table 11.1).

1. First enter the scores for the experimental and control group from Table 11.1 into Excel, as shown in Figure 11.1, *Step 1*. It is easiest if you put your data in two columns next to each other. We have also added a column with the participant numbers and a row with information about the data.
2. Next choose an empty cell (we have chosen cell E7, see Figure 11.1, *Step 2*). In the empty cell type = (equals sign). Then type 'TTEST'. This should generate the following formula:

   = TTEST (array1, array2, tails, type).

If this does not work for whatever reason, you can get to the same place by clicking on 'Formulas' in the bar at the top of the screen, selecting 'More Functions', then 'Statistics' and finally scrolling down until you get to TTEST and selecting that. This will bring up a box for array 1, array 2, tails and type that you can then fill in as in the instructions below.

In all cases the null hypothesis is that the means are not different. 1. is one-tailed but 2. and 3. are two-tailed as you do not know which group is higher. 1. paired t-test; 2. independent samples t-test; 3. single sample t-test.

Table 11.1 *Scores for a fictional experimental and control group*

	Column 1	Column 2	Column 3	Column 4
	Experimental group scores (X_e)	**Square of Experimental group scores ($X_e{}^2$)**	**Control group scores (X_c)**	**Square of Control group scores ($X_c{}^2$)**
	8	64	6	36
	12	144	5	25
	7	49	7	49
	15	225	7	49
	13	169	5	25
	8	64	3	9
	9	81	6	36
	12	144	2	4
	13	169	4	16
	10	100	7	49
Sum	$\sum X_e = 107$	$\sum X_e{}^2 = 1209$	$\sum X_c = 52$	$\sum X_e{}^2 = 298$
Mean = sum/N	$\dfrac{\sum X_e}{N_e} =$		$\dfrac{\sum X_c}{N_c} =$	
	$107/10 = 10.7$		$52/10 = 5.2$	

- **Array1** should be replaced with your first set of data (in this case, the Experimental Group data). To do this, highlight all the cells for the Experimental Group data (B2:B11 in the case below, see Figure 11.1, *Step 2*), then type a comma. [Note that you highlight the cells by dragging your cursor across them while holding down the right mouse button.]
- **Array2** should be replaced with your second set of data (in this case, Control Group data, cells C2:C11, see Figure 11.1, *Step 3*). Again, type a comma.
- **Tails** is used to indicate whether you are using a one-tailed (i.e. predicted, directional) or two-tailed (non-predicted) hypothesis. Use **1** to indicate one-tailed and **2** to indicate two-tailed. We shall use a two-tailed hypothesis in this case as I am not sure of the direction in which any difference might lie, so we input the number '2', followed by another comma.
- **Type** tells Excel what type of t-test you would like to conduct. Input **1** for a paired sample (when the same participants are used at different time points); input **2** for a two-sample t-test where the variances are the same (independent t-test with equal variances) or **3** for a two-sample t-test where the variances are unequal (independent t-test with unequal variance). You can use Excel to find out if the variances are equal, but if you are unsure use the unequal variance option as this is a stricter test (so less likely to yield false positive results). We are using an independent samples t-test so we will enter number 2.

3. Close the brackets and click enter.

Our final formula is

=TTEST(B2:B11, C2:C11, 2, 2)

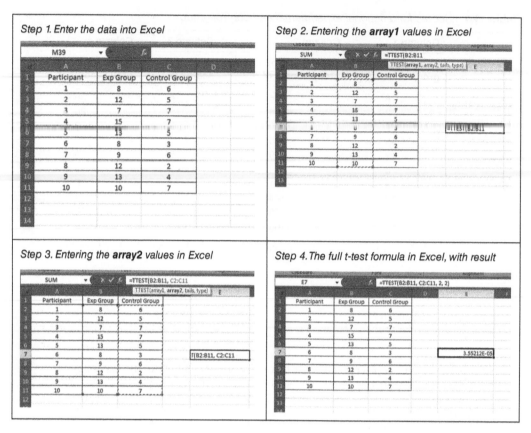

Figure 11.1 *t-test with Excel*

This tells Excel that the first set of data is in column B2 to B11, the second set is in column C2 to C11, it is a two-tailed test and it is an independent samples t-test.

4. The cell (in this case E7) now contains the probability value that the two samples are significantly different from each other. In psychology, it is conventional to use 0.05 as the critical value. Any value *less than* 0.05 indicates a significant difference in scores (see above and Chapter 10, information box 10.7). In this case, the score says 3.55212E-05. This can be confusing. What the E-05 means is that the number is very small and that you should move the decimal point five places to the left. The actual probability value is therefore 0.0000355212, which is much smaller than 0.05. This means that the two group scores are significantly different from each other and that we therefore infer that the experimental group is having a significant effect on the outcome.

It works in the same way if you only have one sample and want to see whether there is a difference before and after therapy (pre-post change). The only difference is that you enter your Time 1 and Time 2 scores into Excel, input **1** for **Tails** to indicate one-tailed (you will probably expect that the therapy has an effect) and input **1** for **Type** as you want to run a paired sample t-test in this case.

Reporting and understanding t-test results

There are conventions to follow when reporting t-test results in order to enable readers to understand more about your sample and the results obtained. Information box 11.3 provides guidelines on these conventions.

Information box 11.3   How do I report a t-test and what information should I include?

When writing up the results of a t-test you need to include a minimum amount of information for readers about the number of people involved in the study, the t-value that the t-test generates, the statistical significance of the result as well as some indication of the averages of the groups examined (sample mean scores) and variation in scores (standard deviation). As mentioned above, it is also increasingly common to include measures of effect size, such as Cohen's d. To ensure that information is easily understood and digested, common ways of reporting results have been agreed upon. In psychology, we generally use the guidelines of the American Psychological Association's manual (APA, 2009) when writing up t-test results.

   For example:

An independent samples t-test was used to investigate whether clients at two counselling centres differed in their initial severity of depression. Initial levels of depression for two randomly selected cohorts of clients attending the two centres were measured using the Beck Depression Inventory. The results demonstrated a significant difference in the levels of depression across the two centres, t(78) = –3.636, p <.001, Cohen's d = .81. Clients in Centre A had significantly lower levels of depression (mean = 27.3, SD = 5.12) than those at Centre B (mean =31.77, SD = 5.85). This indicates that clients presenting themselves at Counselling Centre B have statistically significantly more severe levels of depression than those at Counselling Centre A. This difference is reinforced by the effect size for the difference between levels of depression at the two centres which was large.

So, you know now how you should report your own t-test results, but you may still be a little unclear as to how to interpret the results you read in other publications. The example in Information box 11.4 guides you through exactly how to go about this.

Information box 11.4   Example – Interpreting t-test results from a published paper

A recent paper by Cavanagh et al. (2013) examined the impact of online mindfulness training on perceived stress and anxiety as measured by the PHQ4. They compared the online mindfulness intervention with a waiting list control. They used repeated measures (within subject) t-tests since data was recorded for the same clients at two time-points (before and after the waiting list/control) and reported the following results:

> [Results] showed that while scores for the waiting list group remained unchanged, $(t(49) = 0.07, p = 0.94, d = 0.01...)$, a significant decrease in anxiety and depression was found for the intervention group $(t(53) = 3.00, p = 0.004, d = 0.24$ (Cavanagh et al. 2013, p. 575).

We can glean much information from the above, concise results. First, the degrees of freedom (df) (i.e. the first number in brackets after t) enables us to deduce sample size in each group: a repeated measures t-test has n-1 degrees of freedom, which means that the waiting list control group had 50 participants and the mindfulness training group had 54 participants. The results indicate that the waiting list control group's scores were not significantly different between time 1 and time 2: the t-value is very low (0.07) and the probability of this result occurring by chance is quite high ($p = 0.94$ means that there is a 94% likelihood that any differences between the time 1 and time 2 scores are just down to chance – the scores are essentially no different between the two time points). The Cohen's d score of 0.01 is almost zero, which again shows there is no real effect.

Compare these results with the mindfulness intervention group. The t value of 3.00 is unlikely to indicate that there is no difference between the groups. In fact, the probability of finding a difference between the time 1 and time 2 scores of the magnitude they did, if there wasn't really a difference, is .04%, which means that we are 99.6% confident that the differences found reflect a real difference in scores. Moreover, Cohen's d is .24, which informs us that the mindfulness training had a small (but significant) effect. The mean pre- and post-treatment PHQ-4 scores thus provide evidence to support the theory that online mindfulness training reduces anxiety and depression.

Conclusion

We hope that you now have an understanding of t-tests and of their value when working with data. In this chapter we have seen that t-tests enable us to state with some specified degree of certainty whether differences in scores for two groups, or between one group and a specified value, are statistically significant, i.e. whether the observed differences are likely to be simply due to random variations which are always present in data. We have also shown you that it is really rather easy to do a t-test using commonly available computer software.

Suggestions for further reading

One of the best ways to understand how t-tests can be used in counselling and psychotherapy research is to read examples of their use. As has already been stated, t-tests are very widely used and there are almost countless examples. We have provided a few in the chapter but here are some more, focused on: mindfulness training (Aggs & Bambling, 2010); chronic fatigue syndrome (Thomas & Smith, 2007); the long-term effects of primary care counselling practices (Davis, Corrin-Pendry & Savill, 2008), internet-mediated counselling (Skinner & Latchford, 2006), separation anxiety (Kirsten et al., 2008), school counselling (Cooper, 2009), and emotional support towards visual impairment (Barr et al., 2012). *Full reference details are listed in the Reference section at the end of this book.*

If you want more information about t-tests from a bona fide statistics book, try: Chapter 9, Comparing Two Means, in Field, A. (2013). *Discovering Statistics Using IBM SPSS* (4th edition) (pp. 357–379). London: Sage.

TWELVE

Qualitative methods
Dr Linda Finlay

Introduction

In their quest to describe and interpret personal/social experience, qualitative researchers revel in being explorers, embarking with an open mind about where their research journey will take them. Aware that difficult terrain lies ahead where they may become 'bogged down' in the data or have to negotiate a 'swamp' of analysis, they relish the prospect of adventure and the opening up of new, unexpected vistas (Finlay & Evans, 2009).

As qualitative researchers prepare to set forth, they must first make sense of the baffling range of research methodologies and methods available (Cresswell, 1998). Like therapists, they must choose between competing practice and theoretical traditions.

This chapter aims to give you an overview of this diversity. The next section discusses the range of methodologies available and uses two exemplar studies to illustrate some of the differences between them. These exemplars are then used to illustrate subsequent sections, which focus on gathering and analysing data and discussing how to present research. A concluding section outlines some ways to evaluate qualitative research.

Qualitative aims and methodologies

Qualitative researchers study individuals and social worlds in their natural setting. They want to explore people's stories. The focus is on attempting to make sense of phenomena in terms of the social meanings people bring (Denzin & Lincoln, 1994).

Qualitative research begins not with hypotheses to be tested or causal relationships to be established but rather with open research questions. A qualitative study cannot answer questions such as 'Why do women develop eating disorders?' Instead it might ask 'How do women with anorexia make sense of why they have developed the condition?'

Rich, textured description is valued, along with a focus on the 'hows' and the 'whats' rather than the 'whys' or 'how manys'. For instance, researchers might choose a research question which asks *'How* are mental health problems repre-sented in the media?' or *'How* do therapists experience ruptures in therapy?' or *'What* is it like to experience a traumatic relationship break-up?' It is important to avoid questions which contain an implicit hypothesis: for instance, asking 'What are the perceived benefits to victims of domestic abuse of self-help groups?' contains the presupposition that such groups are helpful. It is best to have a narrowly focused, open research question.

Qualitative researchers understand that the lived world is too chaotic to be represented in unambiguous, clear-cut ways or cause-and-effect terms. Complexity and ambivalence are celebrated. The researcher's own role and the research context are understood to be part of that complexity. Unlike quantita-tive researchers, who seek to be objective and to minimise their impact, qualita-tive researchers recognise they are part of what is being studied. They acknowledge the impact on the research of their own background, values, moti-vations and reactions (see section on reflexivity below).

PAUSE FOR REFLECTION

As you read this chapter, I invite you to reflect on the similarities *and* differences between qualitative research and therapy.

Counsellors and psychotherapists are often drawn to qualitative research because its processes can be likened to therapy and its results often resonate with us (McLeod, 2001; Sanders & Wilkins, 2010). At first sight, the differences seem profound: research aims to produce knowledge rather than enable indi-vidual awareness or change. But there are similarities, too. Both are concerned with mutual discovery, exploring meanings and understanding how the world is experienced by another. Both involve a relational 'process' which calls to be engaged and examined. Both attend to ethics and to promoting collaborative, empowering relationships (see also Chapter 8). Many of the familiar skills, val-ues and qualities of counsellors/psychotherapists are transferable to the research arena, among them interviewing skills, the use of intuitive interpretation, and the capacity for warmth, openness and empathy. A competent therapist equipped with some qualitative research knowledge is likely to make a compe-tent qualitative researcher (Finlay & Evans, 2009).

Multiple methodologies and methods

The terms 'methodology' and 'method' are often confused. *Methodology*, as you saw in Chapters 6 and 7, refers to the *overarching approach* and includes both philosophy and methods, while the term *method* refers specifically to *procedures* of gathering and analysing data.

Pick up any qualitative research book and different methodologies and variations will come tumbling out (Cresswell, 1998; McLeod, 2001; Wertz et al., 2011). The debate between the variations is how they espouse different understandings of 'reality' and the nature of knowledge (see Chapter 6). These can be placed on a continuum (see Table 12.1). At one end, much grounded theory is located in 'post-positivism', while phenomenologists usually prefer 'constructivism-interpretivism'. At the other end, discourse analysts embrace a 'critical' epistemology.

Information box 12.1 indicates some links between methodologies and methods. This is my personal 'map' – different qualitative researchers view the terrain differently. Be aware also that there are different versions of each methodology (see Table 12.1) and, in practice, the categories may blend. For instance, some grounded theory studies are akin to phenomenological ones given a focus on lived experience.

Information box 12.1　Major methodologies and their methods

Exploring lived experience

(Auto)Biography – *In-depth analysis of individual/s life stories culled from interviews and/or documentary sources; data are analysed and presented as a historical narrative.*

Heuristic research – *Reflective search to discover meanings of experiences; data are usually collected through interviewing co-researchers and through researcher self-reflection; analysis is presented through themes and various creative modes.*

Phenomenology – *Descriptive study of the 'lifeworld' (human experience); data (often collected through interview or written accounts) are analysed thematically, narratively or existentially.*

Case study research – *In-depth analysis of an individual's (or group's) subjective world. Data are gathered from interviews (and/or transcripts from therapy sessions). Theoretical frameworks such as 'psychoanalysis' offer an analytical lens.*

Investigating social settings and culture

Action research – *Researcher aims to improve the quality or performance of a group/organisation as part of the research process; data (gathered variously, e.g. interviews, focus groups and questionnaires) are analysed both qualitatively and quantitatively. 'Participatory action research' (PAR) involves greater co-researcher participation.*

Documentary content analysis – *Researcher analyses historical documents and/ or cultural artefacts to discover what they reveal about a particular time/place.*

Ethnography – *Researcher immerses his/herself in a cultural context as a partici- pant-observer aiming to understand local rules, practices and shared knowledge ('auto-ethnography' is a variant where an autobiographical element is figural).*

Grounded theory – *Researcher aims to build inductively from data collected (interviews and observation primarily) to theorise about a process or aspect of the social world. Analysis involves presenting key emergent categories and/or presenting a model/theory.*

Examining social action/interaction and language

Conversation analysis – *Researcher engages in fine-grained analysis of nat- urally occurring dialogue (or interviews) to identify patterns and sequences underlying interactions.*

Discourse analysis – *The analysis of language in use (talk and text) and how meanings are socially constructed; text is created from naturally occurring discourse or formal interview.*

Ethnomethology – *The study of everyday practices in order to identify 'taken-for-granted' rules behind interactions; data are collected from natu- rally occurring conversation or text, and critical observations are made.*

Narrative research – *Exploration of people's stories (gained from interviews) in terms of how narrative identity is developed, performed and constructed. Findings analyse the stories.*

After choosing a methodology, researchers must settle on their *methods*. Data can be collected via interview, focus groups, participant-observation, written accounts or even through sustained researcher reflection. The resulting data is then analysed thematically, through narratives, or in other creative ways. These are discussed in more detail below and in the next section. See Table 12.1 which indicates some of the links between methods normally engaged in a few of the key methodologies mentioned in Information box 12.1.

How do you choose between so many competing methodologies, and differ- ent methods of data collection and analysis? What is it that you want to research? What accords with your values? Are you more comfortable with a well-defined approach or do you favour a more fluid, artful project? Practicalities, too, need to be considered. What resources are available? If you are new to qualitative research, you might be better off starting with a basic, general *the- matic analysis* (see Chapter 13). This tends to be philosophically-neutral and can be used within different theoretical frameworks and data collection methods.

Table 12.1 Different methodologies and versions (adapted from Braun & Clarke, 2013)

Method	Aims/ Epistemological commitment	Variations	Recommended type/ amount of data (N=)	Data analysis/ presentation
Thematic analysis (TA)	A philosophically neutral method for identifying themes/patterns across data; probably the most widely used qualitative method of data analysis, but not 'branded' as a specific method until recently.	**Inductive TA** **Theoretical TA** **Experiential TA** **Critical/Constructionist TA**	Interviews (N = 1–10), focus groups (N = 2–4), textual (N = 10–30), naturalistic (N = 1–50)	Thematic categories
Phenomenology	Constructivist/interpretivist exploration of lived experience. Aims to explicate the 'lifeworld', including sense of self, embodiment and relationships; lived time and space. Approach depends on variant.	**Descriptive** – fine-grained description; post-positivist **Hermeneutic** – more philosophically grounded **IPA** – idiographic, interpretative TA **Heuristic** – includes personal reflection **Dialogal** – reflexive, collaborative	Interviews, diaries, etc. N = 3 N = 1–6 N = 1–6 N = 1–10 N = 6–9 group of researchers plus participants	Thematic, narrative or creative presentations
Grounded theory (GT)	Developed by Glaser and Strauss in the 1960s and has evolved considerably, with different varieties of GT. Focuses on building theory from data.	**Positivist** **Post-positivist** **Constructivist**	Interviews (N = 1–10), focus groups (N = 2–4), textual (N = 10–30), naturalistic (N = 1–50)	Themes, categories and/or a model/theory
Narrative analysis (NA)	Argues 'everything is narrative', that people make sense of their experiences through telling stories. NA analyses stories using various analytic strategies – usually constructivist/interpretivist in orientation.	**Thematic** – focus on stories **Structural** – focus on nature of narrative **Dialogal/performance** – focus on production and context of narrative	Interviews, diaries, etc (N = 1–3)	Narrative presented creatively as stories and/or themes
Discourse analysis (DA)	Argues 'everything is discourse'. DA is concerned with understanding discourses underlying particular accounts and how accounts of objects/ events are constructed. Critical, emancipatory and post-structuralist epistemologies.	**Post-structuralist** (e.g. Foucault) **Discursive Psychology** **Conversation analysis**	Interviews (N = 1–10), focus groups (N = 2–4), textual (N = 10–30), naturalistic (N = 1–50)	Thematic or critical analysis

Hope and Harry contemplate qualitative methodologies ...

PAUSE FOR REFLECTION

Review the list in Information box 12.1 on methodologies, Table 12.1 on analysis methods and Table 12.2 on data collection (below). Which of these different methodologies would interest you most if you were going to undertake a qualitative study?

Comment

Many trainees feel drawn to phenomenologically-oriented research, with its exploration of individuals' embodied experience. This may explain why there are many published IPA studies (see below) in counselling and psychotherapy (Finlay, 2011).

Two exemplar studies

The following exemplars aim to show something of the potential of qualitative research. They demonstrate two commonly employed methodologies: 'grounded theory' and Interpretative Phenomenological Analysis ('IPA', a version of hermeneutic phenomenology), representing much recently published research conducted by therapists.

Exemplar 1 – Anne Thériault and Nicola Gazzola (2008, see also 2006) interviewed 12 experienced therapists to investigate therapists' feelings of incompetence. They had noticed that while such feelings are commonly experienced, there has been little research into the topic. Using grounded theory methodology (Strauss & Corbin, 1998), the authors describe a relationship between four main categories: intensity of self-doubt; sources of feelings of incompetence; mediating factors; and consequences.

Discussing their emerging model (see Figure 12.1), the researchers argue that even experienced therapists continue to have doubts at levels one or two, routinely questioning whether they are 'right' or whether they are being 'effective'. However, such doubts were not found to contaminate their self-judgement and seemed to be better contained with experience. Despite this, experience was not always found to be a helpful buffer: self-doubt stemming from personal historical wounds remained potent despite experience, with therapists observing that they could be regressed to previous levels of vulnerability under certain circumstances. Also, therapists' self-expectations were raised with experience, making them somewhat vulnerable to feelings of incompetence.

Exemplar 2 – John Rhodes and Jonathan Smith (2010) explore what it is like to be depressed in a study which aims to capture the complexity of the experience from the point of view of the sufferer. Using IPA (Smith, Flowers & Larkin, 2009), they present a case study of one man diagnosed with reactive depression.

Their semi-structured interview revealed how the depression occurred in the context of the man's work and financial difficulties. The authors note how his sense of vulnerability sat uncomfortably with his experience of conventional masculinity. Becoming depressed involved a painful eruption of old negative memories plus a catastrophic view of the present and future. The experience of depression in this case is so extreme that it is reported as if the person or self is dying – highly valued life projects and the man's sense of self were destroyed. The authors stress the importance of putting aside stereotypes of depression as a general 'thing' and exploring what it means for the specific individual concerned.

PAUSE FOR REFLECTION

Both grounded theory and IPA take an inductive, iterative approach to analysing data. For instance, interview transcripts will be examined line by line to identify emergent themes. Both methodologies also aim for a systematic, rigorous, scientific approach.

Their difference lies in their focus: grounded theory seeks to *categorise* behaviours; IPA seeks to *describe* lived experience. Grounded theory studies also tend to use more participants, so there is less engagement with each individual transcript and idiographic aspects (see Table 12.1).

Activity 12.1   Identifying methodologies and methods

Spend 10 minutes examining exemplars 1 and 2 above.

1. *Referring to Information box 12.1, can you identify their chosen 'methodologies' and 'methods'?*
2. *What challenges do you think would you be likely to face doing these studies?*

Comment

One challenge might be to stay in the role of researcher rather than therapist. Contact with research participants is more boundaried and focused than in therapy, and often short-lived – you may only have an hour or so of conversation with them (as in exemplar 2). However, the processes of contracting, dialoguing and developing a relationship may well mirror those occurring in therapy.

Doing the research: data gathering and analysis

Recruiting participants and ethics

The process of recruiting participants needs extra attention in qualitative research. Consider research which asks for volunteers. Often only those who have a strong view about the topic apply, which is probably not a 'representative' sample. Also, for some sensitive topics, people may be reluctant to come forward and it can be hard to recruit participants.

When thinking about sample size (N), it is important to remember that 'more' is not necessarily better: don't fall into that quantitative trap! Interviewing 25 people may result in more superficial results than those gained by interviewing three people well. An in-depth relational interview lasting just one hour along with extensive researcher reflection can offer profound insights. The number of participants also tends to vary according to the methodology selected (see Table 12.1 for guidelines for what is usually required with varying research designs). You also may be constrained by external factors, such as course stipulations or the requirements of journals where you hope to publish your findings.

Before approaching participants, consider key ethical issues around consent, confidentiality, care and risk assessment. First, the question of how participants will be briefed to give their *informed consent* is a particular issue in qualitative research as often both are engaged in an exploration and don't know where the research will lead. Beyond seeking consent at the beginning of research, you need to build in a series of negotiation points, checking with the participant if s/he is prepared to go on, and to ensure an adequate *debrief*. Information about the nature and course of the research needs to be given in a non-coercive manner where participants are allowed to change their mind and withdraw (or not answer certain questions) at any point.

Exemplar 1 provides some insights into ensuring *confidentiality* as part of the wider requirement to protect participants' rights and safety (see Chapter 8).

Exemplar 1 – Thériault and Gazzola (2006, p. 317) discuss how they approached the ethical issues involved in conducting their study:

> Because of the highly sensitive nature of the information disclosed during the interviews, special precautions were adopted. The possibility, however remote, that the therapists and clients discussed in their vignettes could be identified was a particular concern. To guard against this, all demographic and descriptive information about therapists was minimized and kept at a group level. In order to protect the participants' privacy, pseudonyms were used and any information that would make them susceptible to identification was omitted or deliberately made vague.

Many of the issues therapists routinely confront concerning *care* for their clients also apply to the field of qualitative research, given studies can deal with sensitive, difficult areas of human experience. Beyond the ethical concerns of seeking to do no harm, qualitative researchers may well aim to 'empower', 'witness' and 'give voice' to their participants. They are mindful that research which encourages participants to reflect on themselves and the social world around them may evoke strong emotional responses, both on the part of participants and of themselves. There is also a power dimension at play which demands recognition and management. A key question to ask is: 'Whose interests are served by our research?' (Finlay & Ballinger, 2006).

Risk assessment within qualitative research is complicated, raising questions about what constitutes 'harm' and how to debrief participants to ensure they are left richer for the experience. If a participant gets upset during an interview, does that constitute 'harm'? Some participants welcome the opportunity to talk at a deep personal level. For them, getting upset may not be a problem. Engaging in an in-depth process may actually be affirming and transformational. At the very least, participants may appreciate opportunities to talk about, and make sense of, their experience.

Every research encounter brings up context-specific ethical challenges and uncertainties. Probably the best a qualitative researcher can do is to be sensitive to the ethical implications *throughout* the research and to handle them as conscientiously as possible.

Data gathering

The choice of methods of data collection and analysis generally follows from the choice of methodology. Grounded theory and phenomenological research (as in exemplars 1 and 2) tend to rely on face-to-face interview data, though other methods can be used as well. See Table 12.2 which contrasts interactive, textual and naturalistic methods.

Whichever data gathering methods are chosen, the challenge lies in being able to carry them off skilfully, rigorously and sensitively. Often, the most productive qualitative research encounter is one where the researcher relates to participants in a natural, empathic and genuinely human way.

As interviews are the most common mode of data collection, it is worth thinking about what constitutes a good interview. As a therapist, you have the advantage of having been trained to listen and help others express themselves. The downside of your training is that in your role of researcher you may be so worried about not being a therapist that you become curiously flat, stiff, distanced or disengaged (McLeod, 1999). For this reason, it might be helpful to conduct a pilot interview before you begin your actual project.

Table 12.2 *Data Collection Methods*

Interactive (researcher interacts with participants to generate data)	• Interviews (semi-structured/unstructured; email, Skype, phone or face-to-face)
	• Focus groups
	• Web blogs
Textual (participants write/record responses)	• Qualitative surveys/questionnaires
	• Researcher-directed diaries (text or audio-visual)
	• Vignettes/story-stem completion
Naturalistic (data-in-the world independent of research)	• Media (e.g. newspapers, magazines, radio/TV, film, web pages, online forums)
	• Literature (e.g. novels, academic textbooks, self-help books, dictionaries)
	• Parliamentary debates (e.g. Hansard, BBC TV)
	• Documents (e.g. health promotion leaflets, policy documents)
	• Institutional interaction (e.g. audio-visual recordings of professional–patient interaction or therapy)
	• Mundane interaction (recordings of telephone calls, family dinner-time, etc.)

Information box 12.2   Four key tips for carrying out effective research interviews

1. *Prepare your environment and participant carefully in advance. Participants need to feel reasonably safe and comfortable, and that includes feeling at ease with any recording equipment.*
2. *Ask open, singular questions rather than closed, leading or multiple ones. Sometimes participants just need a place to start. You might begin with basic demographic questions about the person's age, gender and occupation and/or ask them simply to tell the story of their experience.*
3. *Listen responsively. The aim is to dialogue and to tune into what the person is saying rather than be thinking about your next question. Questions such as 'what feelings did that provoke in you?' could help the person respond in greater depth. Be spontaneous and follow your intuition rather than sticking rigidly to pre-prepared questions and protocols. At the same time, be wary of not stepping into a therapist role in terms of making emotional connections or offering interpretations.*
4. *Allow time at the end of the interview to debrief the participant. The process of being witnessed can have powerful impact and you need to take this into account. As McLeod (1999, p. 125) notes: 'One of the hallmarks of a good qualitative interview lies in the extent to which the informant learns or gains from the experience.'*

(See King & Horrocks (2010) for more on 'how to' interview.)

Data analysis

Most qualitative researchers would agree that difficulties encountered during the early stages of research pale into insignificance when compared with the challenge of analysing the huge amount of descriptive data invariably generated by qualitative procedures. It is all too easy for researchers to feel overwhelmed as they work through the minutiae of the data.

Exemplar 1 – Thériault and Gazzola (2008) used grounded theory method to make sense of their data. This involved engaging in iterative stages of coding and categorising. The first stage was a close reading of the text. Then, slowly, general emergent themes were organised into basic categories. Next, the process of 'axial coding' was engaged. Here, themes were clustered and refined into major categories and subcategories.

With qualitative analysis, the task is to describe the important patterns within the data. It is often said that findings 'emerge from data', but the notion that they are self-evident is simplistic. Meanings, being implicit, have to be searched for, and then painstakingly shaped up in successive iterations. Both semantic content and language (verbal and non-verbal) need to be examined, with key phrases or explanations which the participants used highlighted. These then need to be coded with a word or phrase which captures the sense of the content.

Exemplar 2 – The researchers engaged in a close reading of the interview transcript and written notes while simultaneously attempting an interpretation via use of a 'double hermeneutic' (whereby participants make sense of their experiences while researchers make sense of the participants' sense-making). Then the notes were transformed into multiple themes which were eventually clustered into core themes. Each was illustrated with carefully chosen, evocative quotes from their participant 'Paul'. To give you a taste of the writing, here is an extract from one theme entitled *'The horror of depression'* (NB the '[...]' denotes missed out words):

> At several points Paul described his state of being depressed as if he was in a pit or hole [...]
>
> P: 'It's not like a well of bricks [...] I had a [...] conjured vision of erm *Silence of the Lambs* with err Buffalo Bill [...] and it was that sort of hole [...] But it is a feeling of hopelessness, I get tremendous, tremendous fears sometimes ... very scary. Cos that image to me is one of no escape [...] I didn't think, well, you know, gonna get saved here [...] a rope's gonna come down. Cos' my hands are tied anyway, err, no no no no no way way out.'
>
> We would suggest that this image vividly captures a number of central features of Paul's experience of depression. At one level he is completely helpless, his 'hands tied', 'gagged', with 'no escape' [...] In an anxious tone, he says that he will not let the water rise, but this is not said with confidence; it comes across more as a desperate plea, rec-reating his futile attempts to stop it rising. So there is also an implicit suggestion of a slow agonizing death as the water rises and drowns him [...]. The image also suggests being abandoned: in the earth, forgotten, un-mourned and not ceremoniously 'buried' by others. He will be alone [...]. Part of depression seems to crucially involve a sense of utter loneliness. And this loneliness at the point of death is perhaps one of our deepest terrors. ... The metaphor of the hole emphasizes the notion and feeling of no escape, loss of normal living experience, and ideas of imminent death. (Rhodes & Smith, 2010, pp. 403–404, 406)

PAUSE FOR REFLECTION

Notice how the authors have drawn on metaphors to evoke the presence and 'alive-ness' of Paul's experience? They also discuss Paul's own use of metaphors to express and constitute his implicit experience and how those images seemed to say more than he necessarily intended.

Reflexivity

As part of the process of engaging critically with data, qualitative researchers usu-ally examine the key role they have played in the construction and production of the findings by engaging in a process known as *reflexivity* (Finlay & Gough, 2003). This requires them to critically *self*-reflect on the ways in which their social background, assumptions, positioning, behaviour, presence and power relations impact on the data collection/analysis. Reflexivity involves a continuing self-awareness of the research dynamics and claims being made. How this is achieved varies.

In the following example, Scott (1995, cited in Johnson & Scott, 1997) studied 17 families moving through the child protection system. She writes of the strong emotions aroused in her, which came as a surprise as she was an experienced practitioner. As researcher, she felt helpless witnessing the distress she could not alleviate, plus an unease with the inherent 'voyeurism' of her research:

> What caused me the most anguish was not the abuse itself, but witnessing children and their parents ... suffering at the hands of professionals... This led to me developing a strong identification with the vulnerability of clients... [The] negative feelings ... led me to see ... the hostility I observed being expressed between different professions ... Interagency conflict [seems to be] ... related to displacement of hostility. (Scott, cited in Johnson & Scott, 1997, pp. 35–7)

PAUSE FOR REFLECTION

Imagine you were going to carry out a research project on the experience of perceptions of 'helpful and unhelpful aspects of therapy'. Reflect on your own assumptions and experience about this topic. How might these influence the research (both the process and the outcomes)?

Now take another subject – the experience of 'traumatic abortion'. Would your personal views about abortions be relevant? How might they impact the research?

In an example of reflexive writing taken from my own research, I show how 'embodied reflective writing' enabled me to be open to the data and tune into a participant's experience while simultaneously protecting myself from getting lost in the trauma of my research topic (the experience of having a traumatic abortion).

> The interview made a profound impact on me. I had anticipated finding Eve's experience ... painful to hear. What I had not expected were certain disturbing images which haunt me still. Through these I caught the edge of a deep and abiding trauma. As I faced Eve in the interview and later dwelt with the data, I was aware of a continuing, lurking impulse to flee, cut off and deny. ... Transcription has been hard ... I'm on my third day ...I keep needing to stop. I recognize my sense of feeling disturbed, a fuzzy but tight spiralling anxious grip in my stomach ... I tune into my felt-sense:

> I have that fuzzy feeling ... I am finding it difficult to breathe – breathing shallowly. ... There are some tears there; aloneness; an unspeakable horror. My tummy tightens some more ... [and says] 'I need to hold on; I need to hold in; I need to not cry, not speak'.

I reflect then on these words. I wonder to what extent they reflect Eve's experience and how she had to hold on to her emotions and push down her words. (Finlay, 2014, pp. 12–13)

Many qualitative researchers argue that researchers should celebrate their subjectivity and seize it as an opportunity for further insight. But constraints apply. Reflexivity should not descend into self-indulgent wallowing where the focus shifts away from the participants and towards the researcher (Finlay & Gough, 2003). Once again, therapists have something of an advantage here, since they are used to engaging reflexivity and to using this awareness positively in therapy.

Analysing therapy talk

Strange to say, not much research in counselling and psychotherapy appears to be based on directly analysing what actually happens in therapy sessions. The benefits of rigorous empirical exploration of the talk that occurs between clients and their therapists would appear self-evident. Information box 12.3 presents some approaches that have been developed to be used with transcripts of therapy sessions. Whatever method is used, the promise of a rigorous empirical approach to analysing therapy talk is enticing.

Information box 12.3   Analysing therapy talk

Georgia Lepper and Nick Riding (2006) describe how various qualitative methods (e.g. grounded theory, conversation analysis, and narrative analysis) have been used to examine talk in sessions.

The book also describes formal coding systems which use researcher-created scales and categories to assess talk between a counsellor and client. One example is the Core Conflictual Relationship Theme (CCRT), a method developed by leading psychotherapy researchers Luborsky and Crits-Christoph (1998), which is based on psychodynamic ideas about transference. The aim is to use the coding system to identify a client's main relationship conflict in terms of what the client wishes for, how they experience the response of others and what that then means to them. The analysis focuses on early and late sessions and makes it possible to systematically examine whether counselling appears to have led to any shifts in core relational conflicts.

Presenting the findings

After the analysis stage, the next challenge is how to present the findings (see also Chapter 16). Qualitative findings are often complex, layered and messy, reflecting people's ambivalent life experiences and diverse social worlds. What is the best way to portray participants' experiences and/or discourses in all their complexity?

Three key steps need to be kept in mind. First, you need to *marshal your evidence*, e.g. by selecting the interview extracts which best illustrate your point. Second, you need to *present the material clearly in ways that carry impact*, perhaps by the inclusion of a diagram or a particularly powerful extract from the data. Third, it's essential to *make your argument as strongly as possible* e.g. by including academic references to buttress your case.

Exemplar 1 – The authors pull their findings together in a diagram that offers a clear representation of relational trends between the major categories (see Figure 12.1).

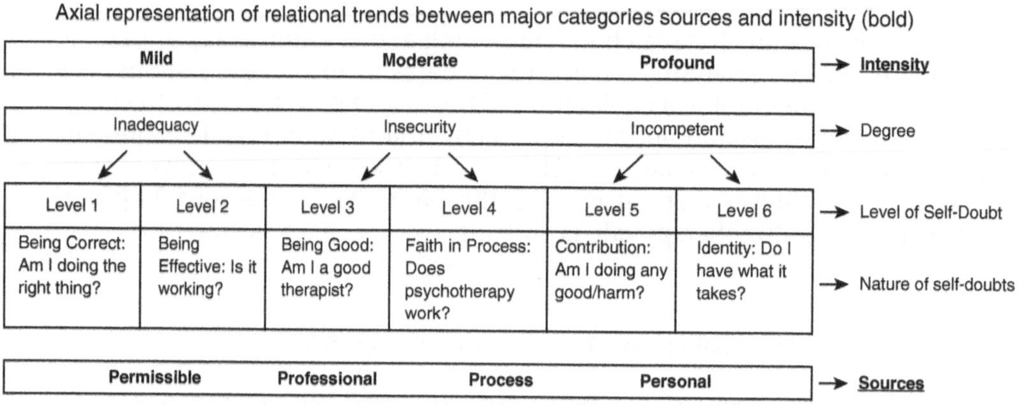

Axial representation of relational trends between major categories sources and intensity (bold)

Figure 12.1 *Therapists' feelings of incompetence (from Thériault & Gazzola, 2008)*
Note: Arrows represent the tendency towards increased intensity from left to right

Many phenomenologists, 'animated by the desire to do justice to human existence' (Halling, 2002, p. 20), seek to restore a poetic heart to academic writing. To this end they draw on all sorts of images, myths and creative forms. Some phenomenological research, for instance, makes use of artwork rather than written findings. As Braud and Anderson (1998, p. xxvii) playfully suggest, 'We need an imaginative, even outlandish, science to envision the potential of human experience ... not just tidy reports'.

Speedy (2005) draws on poetry to explore her use of narrative therapy. The poem below was written by a client, Hyatt, a lonely Afro-Caribbean woman studying in Britain who had a complicated relationship with food, her body and anorexia nervosa. The poem's focus on 'bones' is a poignant symbolic recognition of how Hyatt's flesh had at times been stretched thinly across her bones. But for her, these prominent 'bones' were life-affirming rather than a cause for concern. Their feel reminded her of a shared ancestral bone structure with her much-loved family at home.

The cruel inroads
of patriarchy
(and other animals)
into friendships, companionships
and secret alliances with much-loved brothers

brought you vividly
back in touch with that time
of being so lonely
lonely down to the whites of
your bones

yet now it seems those bones
those same authority-troubling bones
those 'alone bones'
were the very bones that kept you
safe and calm
and in touch with your ways. (Speedy, 2005, p. 293)

Evaluation

The examples offered throughout this chapter indicate the potential richness, depth and power of qualitative work. At the same time, qualitative findings are invariably limited, partial, tentative and emergent, not least because qualitative work often involves interpretation of implicit meanings. In a field where subjectivity plays such a central role, how is it possible to judge the value and veracity of qualitative findings?

Activity 12.2 Validating qualitative research

In the Rhodes and Smith (2010) study, the analysis was discussed with the second author, who offered a validating 'independent audit' (2010, p. 401). In other studies, researchers may invite participants to take part in engaging in the analysis and even to corroborate the research – a process called 'participant validation'.
  Take 10 minutes to reflect on the following questions:

1. *Do these kinds of approaches to validation enhance the credibility of research for you?*
2. *If a second person disagrees with the analysis, does this mean it must be 'wrong'?*
3. *While participant validation is often presented as being an ethical option, when might it be less ethical?*

(Continued)

(Continued)

Comment

If research is explicitly 'interpretive', then it would not be surprising if another person came up with different interpretations. In such cases, it would be important for the researchers involved to be reflexive and transparent about their process.

Ashworth (1993) supports participant validation on moral-political grounds but warns against taking participants' responses too seriously or at face value – after all, it may be in their interest to protect their 'socially presented selves'. Participant validation may be used to increase the transparency of the research and foster a sense of collaboration between participants and researchers. However, the process can be problematic. Participants may have 'moved on' from how they were at the time of their interview, in which case it would not be appropriate to pull them back. Also, there are occasions when participants may feel overly objectified by an academic representation of their words.

Qualitative research differs from quantitative investigation in the lesser importance it attaches to traditional positivist criteria such as reliability, validity and generalisability. Whereas quantitative researchers value reliable measures to allow studies to be replicated (see Chapter 10), qualitative researchers argue that research situations, by their very nature, cannot be repeated. They also have less concern for the statistical significance of findings or the generalisability of findings to wider populations. Instead their concern is to explore the uniqueness of people's accounts and capture underlying meanings. For them, the questions at stake are: 'has the social world been evoked in a credible or resonant way?' and 'can the findings be usefully applied more widely?'

PAUSE FOR REFLECTION

If qualitative researchers reject traditional quantitative criteria of evaluation, how can the quality of their research be judged? When you read accounts of research, what makes an article stand out as 'good' research for you?

New and different criteria, responsive to qualitative research ideals, are necessary to ensure the integrity and value of the research (Finlay & Ballinger, 2006). Different researchers (e.g. see Elliott, Fischer & Rennie, 1999; Lincoln & Guba, 1985; Tracy, 2010) suggest various criteria. In brief, research is judged to be *trustworthy* when the processes involved in it are presented transparently and attention is paid to rigour and credibility.

The two exemplar studies were selected for this chapter in part because they represent clear, trustworthy examples of research evidence offering relevant understandings for the therapy world. In **Exemplar 1**, Thériault and Gazzola offer the following critique, one which reveals their 'post-positivist' leanings in its concern to demonstrate scientific credentials:

> Although theoretical saturation was reached, it may have been preferable to include a larger sample base in the final analysis. [...] Another potential limitation is the sample procedure. Several therapists were familiar to the interviewer and were deliberately selected because of their capacity for self-disclosure and insight. On the positive side, the relationship with the interviewer allowed therapists to expose personal and professional vulnerabilities. (2006, p. 327)

In **Exemplar 2**, the authors focus on wider applications, invoking criteria of transferability and professional relevance:

> Our analysis of this single case suggests several implications for working with depression. First, that when we approach someone with 'depression' we should attempt to bracket, to put aside, our assumptions, our stereotypes of depression as a general 'thing', and explore with the person their unique experiences. ... Our case study also points to the importance of aims, purposes, and projects constituting a person's way of living. ... It was obvious in the interview to Paul that he could not just go back to his old way of living. (Rhodes & Smith, 2010, p. 408)

Yardley (2008) usefully suggests four broad principles for assessing the quality of qualitative research: (1) *Sensitivity to context* relates to the awareness shown by the researcher regarding the topic of investigation and the interactional nature of the data collection; (2) *Commitment and rigour* refers to the extent the researcher makes credible interpretations and ensures analysis is convincing, thorough and systematic; (3) *Transparency and coherence* refers to the extent the process of the research (namely the selection of participants, the design of interview schedules and the steps taken for analysis) is dependable and open to external audit – does it hang together in a logical way as fitting the methodology?; and (4) *Impact and importance* asks whether findings are useful, resonant, interesting and can be applied more widely.

As a phenomenologist, I value both science and art. I celebrate qualitative research for its potential to evoke the rich ambiguity of human experience. I like research that wields emotional power and that, by challenging taken-for-granted assumptions, reveals something fresh and new. Like any explorer, I revel in discovery. I hope you too can share this excitement and feel ready and open to explore what lies ahead.

Activity 12.3   Evaluating qualitative research

Take 10 minutes to write notes evaluating the two exemplar studies. How would you evaluate them using Yardley's criteria? With reference to the above quotation from Thériault and Gazzola (2006), do you think the fact that they knew some of their participants is a strength or a limitation of the research? Regarding the Rhodes and Smith (2010) study, what value do you think there is in hearing one person's story, given that one person's experience may not generalise to the wider population?

Comment

Qualitative researchers vary in the extent to which they seek to embrace research as 'science' or 'art'. Grounded theorists prioritise being scientifically systematic and rigorous. Issues such as sample size and sampling procedure are more important for them than they would be for other qualitative research-ers. Phenomenologists tend to prize artistic flourishes while varying in their concern for rigour. IPA values both prizing systematic analysis and experiential resonance.

Suggestions for further reading

Finlay, L. & Evans, K. (Eds) (2009). *Relational-centred Research for Psychotherapists: Exploring meanings and experience.* Chichester: Wiley.
    The authors use practical examples to explain their version of relational-centred research which mirrors psychotherapy processes.

McLeod, J. (2011). *Qualitative Research in Counselling and Psychotherapy* (2nd edition). London: Sage.
    McLeod introduces a range of qualitative methods and research examples, discussing their use in the therapy field.

Smith, J.A. (Ed.) (2008). *Qualitative Psychology: A practical guide to research methods* (2nd edition). London: Sage.
    Covering the main qualitative approaches in psychological research, this book pro-vides useful practical guidance on how to employ qualitative methods.

THIRTEEN

How to use thematic analysis with interview data

Dr Virginia Braun (University of Auckland), Dr Victoria Clarke and Dr Nicola Rance (both UWE Bristol)

Introduction

This chapter introduces you to thematic analysis (TA), one of the many methods of analysis for qualitative research. TA is an ideal method for researchers new to qualitative research because it is one of the most accessible qualitative analytic methods and it involves procedures that are common to most forms of qualitative analysis (another accessible method is Interpretative Phenomenological Analysis (IPA); Smith, Flowers & Larkin, 2009). It also offers great flexibility to the qualitative researcher, as we discuss further below.

Qualitative research, like all research, begins with a research question. In contrast to quantitative research, in which the research question is determined at the *start* of the research process, qualitative research questions are fluid and flexible; they evolve and the focus of research can expand, contract, or even change altogether, as the research progresses. To illustrate the procedures of TA we draw on a qualitative study, conducted by Nicola, guided by the following open and exploratory research question: 'How do women with a self- or formally-diagnosed history of anorexia nervosa (AN) make sense of their experiences of eating disorder (ED) treatment/therapy?' Information box 13.1 provides a brief overview of Nicola's interview study with 12 women participants. Her interest in this question was informed by her professional practice as an ED therapist and her research with ED counsellors (Rance, Moller & Douglas, 2010).

Activity 13.1 Reflecting on the research topic

Identify and make notes on your assumptions about, reactions to and experiences of this topic. How might these shape the research process if you were doing research on this topic?

**Information box 13.1   Example of a TA study – Lived experiences of
AN treatment/therapy (Rance, Moller & Clarke, 2012)**

*In light of the poor success rates (Bulik, Berkman, Brownley, Sedway & Lohr,
2007; Keel & Brown, 2010) and high levels of drop-out in the treatment of AN
(Surgenor, Maguire & Beumont, 2004; Wallier et al., 2009), this qualitative interview study was designed to explore the thoughts and feelings of women who
had received treatment for their ED (regarding the rationale for such a study,
see also Information box 9.1 in Chapter 9). Twelve women with a formal or self-
diagnosed history of AN, who saw themselves as recovered or on the road to
recovery, and who had received counselling from at least one female therapist,
took part. The women's ages ranged from 18 to 50 years (mean 31.5); the duration of their ED ranged from 2 to 28 years (mean 13.3). The interview guide
included a range of questions (possible prompts are roman):*

- *Can you tell me a bit about your ED history?*

  o *When do you think your ED began?*
  o *Why do you think you developed an ED?*
  o *How long did your ED last?*
  o *How do you see yourself now?*

- *When and how did you access help?*
- *Why did you decide to access help?*
- *What sort of help did you access?*

  o *Did you see a counsellor/psychotherapist/psychologist/psychiatrist?*
  o *Did they work in the NHS/private practice/voluntary organisation?*
  o *Did you specifically ask for a female counsellor or was it coincidental?*

- *Can you tell me a bit about your experiences of therapy/counselling?*

  o *Do you think it helped you?*
  o *If so, in what ways?*

*Interviews lasted between one and 1¾ hours. The results revealed the partici-
pants' dissatisfaction with the treatment(s) they had experienced and suggested
that they perceived the treatment system as overly focused on, and driven by,
food and weight. Furthermore, it appeared that what the women really wanted
was to be seen and treated as a 'whole person' and to have a 'real' relationship
with their therapist.*

Qualitative research often involves the collection of people's experiences, views
and opinions *in their own words* (see Chapter 12). The most common way of gathering people's words as data is the qualitative interview, in which the researcher

asks a series of planned questions (based on an 'interview guide') and unplanned/ spontaneous questions (responsive to the participant), and the participant answers in their own words (see Braun & Clarke, 2013, for a detailed discussion of qualitative interviews). In Nicola's study, as is typical in qualitative interview research more generally, the interviews were audio-recorded and prepared for analysis through a process of transcription. Transcription involves translating the speech and sounds from the audio-recording into a written record of the interview (Activity 13.2, below, provides a sample of Nicola's transcript). Although this sounds relatively straightforward – and in some ways it is – transcription requires us to make choices about how to translate between spoken and written language (see Sandelowski, 1994). To aid the transcription process researchers have developed various transcription notation systems (for a notation system suitable for TA research, see Braun & Clarke, 2013).

Introduction to TA: Identifying patterns across your qualitative data set

Just as quantitative data require systematic analysis to identify key trends in, and features of, the data, qualitative (interview) data require systematic analysis, albeit based on quite different premises (see Chapter 12). The most common strategy for analysing qualitative data is to identify recurrent features or patterns across the data set. At their essence, pattern-based approaches focus on what people say (and sometimes *why* they say it). Other qualitative approaches are also interested in *how* peoples say things (e.g. narrative or discursive approaches, see Riessman, 2007; Wetherell, Taylor & Yates, 2001). In this chapter, we introduce you to one method for identifying and interpreting patterns in what people say in data – TA. There are lots of different versions of TA (e.g. Boyatzis, 1998; Guest, MacQueen & Namey, 2012; Joffe, 2011). The approach we draw on was developed by Virginia and Victoria (Braun & Clarke, 2006, 2012, 2013). In our approach, TA can produce analyses that range from quite basic descriptive accounts of the surface or semantic meaning of data to complex conceptual interrogations of the underlying or latent meanings in data (see Table 13.1).

One of the hallmarks of TA is its flexibility. Most qualitative analytic approaches are best thought of as methodologies, meaning they offer theoretically-informed frameworks for conducting research (see Chapter 12). In contrast, TA is (uniquely) *just* a method. A method is a *technique* for collecting or analysing data (see Chapter 7). An approach like IPA tells you what theoretical framework – phenomenology – should underpin your research, the types of research questions you can ask (about lived experience), how ideally you should collect data (interviews), as well as specifying an array of analytic procedures. Imagine you popped into your local deli to buy a loved one a gift hamper – IPA is like a ready-made hamper, where the deli has made all the choices for you. TA, in contrast, is like a hamper you assemble yourself. Because TA is just a method, and therefore flexible, you decide what type of research question you will ask, how you will collect your data, the theoretical framework that will inform your data analysis, and what form of TA you will use. TA can be used to address most types of qualitative research question (see Table 13.2), it works with most types of qualitative data, including interview data, and it can be used across the spectrum of theoretical approaches used in qualitative research, and in variations from inductive to deductive, semantic to latent (see Table 13.1).

One of the advantages of TA is that it is theoretically flexible. This means it can be used within different frameworks to answer quite different research questions. And there are different *ways* TA can be approached, as illustrated in Table 13.1.

More inductive, semantic and realist approaches tend to cluster together; so too do more deductive, latent and constructionist ones. In reality, the separation isn't always rigid. What *is* important is that the analysis is theoretically coherent and consistent.

Let's explore these different choices in relation to Nicola's study (see Information box 13.1). The research question was an experience-type question; data were collected using interviews; the ontological framework was critical realism and the broad theoretical (or epistemological) framework was contextualism (Henwood & Pidgeon, 1994), an approach that assumes meaning is related to the context in which it is produced. TA was used inductively, and coding and analysis were primarily at the semantic level. These choices reflect that the aim of the research was to identify patterns in what women said about their experiences of AN treatment/therapy and to stay close to how the participants made sense of their experiences. In some ways this approach to qualitative research and therapeutic practice are

Table 13.1 *Definitions of some key terms in TA*

Analyses can be more Inductive or more Deductive

Inductive	Analysis driven by, and reflective of, the content of the data.	Deductive	Analysis guided by pre-existing theoretical concepts or analytic ideas separate from the data themselves.

Analyses can be more Semantic or more Latent

Semantic	Analysis captures meanings that are explicitly stated in the data, so that words themselves are taken at face value.	Latent	Analysis captures meanings not explicitly stated in the data, including the ideas, assumptions or concepts that underpin what is explicitly stated.

Analyses can be more Essentialist or more Constructionist

Essentialist	Analyses that assume that there are fixed qualities 'inside' people (essences), such as personality, that result in the experiences and interpretations that people report.	Constructionist	Analysis conducted within a framework that doesn't assume an essence, or a single reality but rather theorises multiple realities, produced (constructed) through language, representation and other social processes. These are still, however, experienced as true and real by people.

Table 13.2 Suitable and unsuitable research questions for TA studies

Type of question	Examples of unsuitable types of question	Examples of potential suitable alternative questions	Examples of TA studies exploring this type of question
How do particular groups (of clients/therapists) experience and/or conceptualise therapy?	Assessing whether computer-delivered CBT is a cost-effective treatment for anxiety and depression – including measurement of before and after depression scores (McCrone et al., 2004). *Unsuitable because:* no concrete way of 'measuring' depression/the effectiveness of treatment in TA.	Could explore clients' expectations of CBT (*before* therapy) and/or their experiences and views of CBT (after therapy), or therapists' views on CBT training or their experiences of implementing CBT.	How do trainee counselling/clinical psychologists and counsellors perceive personal therapy? (Moller, Timms & Alilovic, 2009) What do clients perceive as a hindering experience in counselling? (Paulson, Everall & Stuart, 2001)
What are the characteristics and needs of a particular client group?	What is the prevalence of psychological distress, and what factors predict psychological distress, in men with prostate cancer? (Balderson & Towell, 2003) *Unsuitable because:* No concrete and comparable way of measuring distress and the relationship between variables in TA.	Could explore how such men make sense of their illness and the ways in which they experience it as distressing.	What are the mental health needs of forced migrants living in London? (Palmer & Ward, 2007) Exploring the experiences and needs of mothers who become homeless (Tischler, Rademeyer & Vostanis, 2007).
How do particular groups engage with therapy (or not)?	How successful are oncologists in identifying patient distress and need for counselling? Including use of scales measuring patient distress/oncologists' assessment of patient distress (Söllner et al., 2001). *Unsuitable because:* no concrete way of measuring levels of distress in TA.	Could explore oncologists' perceptions of patient distress and need for counselling, and patients' perceptions of their needs (and discuss the themes generated from each group).	Exploring stigmatising beliefs about depression and help-seeking (Barney, Griffiths, Christensen & Jorm, 2009). Why do drug and alcohol service users drop out of group therapy? (Monahan, 2010)

similar. Both acknowledge that people make sense of things in their own way and so can view the same event quite differently, and that how people make sense of things is influenced by a range of factors, so their understanding is *contextual*. Furthermore, as a researcher/therapist it is possible to take two perspectives simultaneously: to try to step into your participant's/client's shoes and view the world through their eyes, which is about staying close to the participant's worldview, or analysing data *semantically*, on the surface; and to view the participant's/client's position in the world from your – somewhat removed – standpoint, which means you might see things that the participant/client doesn't. In therapy this is sometimes referred to as stepping into the supervisor perspective. In TA, this would be a *latent* – beyond the surface – analysis.

Because TA is like a 'select your own items' gift hamper, using it requires you to make choices. Recognising this helps you to reflect on the *active* role you play in the research process and in the generation of results – a process known as personal reflexivity (see Chapter 12 and Wilkinson, 1988). This is another reason why TA is a good starter analytic method for counsellors and psychotherapists: right from the start, it invites you to be *reflexive*, an important component of both qualitative research and being a good practitioner. We encourage you to keep a *research journal* where you reflect on your role in shaping the research throughout the research process (see Braun & Clarke, 2013).

PAUSE FOR REFLECTION

How would you feel about embarking on a TA study? What particular fears or anxieties, if any, would this stir up for you?

Doing TA

We now outline (and illustrate) the different phases of TA, following our approach (Braun & Clarke, 2006). Information box 13.2 provides a brief overview of six phases of this approach. Remember that although this seems very clear and linear, analysis is more of a recursive process, so there is often a bit of back-and-forth between the different phases.

Information box 13.2   Braun & Clarke's (2006) six-phase approach to TA

1. Familiarisation with the data: *reading and re-reading the data.*
2. Coding: *generating succinct labels that identify important features of the data relevant to answering the research question; after coding the entire data set, collating codes and relevant data extracts.*

---

3. Searching for themes: *examining the codes and collated data to identify significant broader patterns of meaning; collating data relevant to each candidate theme.*
4. Reviewing themes: *checking the candidate themes against the data set, to determine that they tell a convincing story that answers the research question. Themes may be refined, split, combined, or discarded.*
5. Defining and naming themes: *developing a detailed analysis of each theme; choosing an informative name for each theme.*
6. Writing up: *weaving together the analytic narrative and data extracts; contextualising the analysis in relation to existing literature.*

Familiarisation (1) and coding (2)

The first phase of TA is common across qualitative research: it is about becoming intimately engaged with your data. This involves immersing yourself in the data through focused and repeated reading of them, so you know their content thoroughly (transcribing interview data can also facilitate data immersion). But it is not a mindless process – you want to keep your analytic mind engaged, by treating the data *as data*. That involves thinking about how the data might address your research question, starting to notice patterns in the data, or even thinking about what assumptions or ideas are being articulated in the data (see Braun & Clarke, 2012). It is really helpful to make notes of things that strike you as interesting in the data, or any initial analytic ideas you've had in your research journal. Think of these as notes to yourself, to ensure that you don't forget any early analytic ideas – at this stage, the process of noting is not systematic or thorough.

Where it does become a thorough and systematic process is when you begin coding. Coding is the process of systematically working through your entire data set, noting ideas, concepts and points of interest relevant to answering your research question. In practice, it involves tagging a segment of data with a *code*. A code is a label (a brief phrase) which provides a succinct summary of something of analytic interest in the data. The code needs to capture the essence of what is in the tagged data segment, so that it is meaningful without reading the data (because in the next phase you will develop themes from the codes and coded data). Some codes might be fairly *descriptive* and simply summarise the content of the data (*semantic* codes). In Table 13.3, which provides an example of coded data from Nicola's research, the codes are descriptive, summarising key aspects of Claire's commentary. If we took away the data, you would still have a good sense of the sorts of things that Claire was saying about treatment from just the codes. Other codes can be *interpretative*, and offer some *analytic* interpretation of the content of the data (*latent* codes). In the extract in Table 13.3, more interpretative codes might identify Claire as emotionally conflicted or ambivalent, or as experiencing no sense of entitlement to treatment.

Table 13.3 *An example of coded data from Nicola's interview with 'Claire'*

Transcript	Codes
Claire: I feel very lucky to have actually got the, you know been offered the place because, th- always with eating disorders there's this, there's this thing like, "am I, really entitled to this, d do I need this level of support", you know you feel desperate for it but then you feel so guilty and thinking "well, maybe, maybe I can't gain any weight because maybe, once my weight starts to go up they will kick me off the programme" and, it it's	Feels lucky to be getting treatment Belief that people with an ED question their entitlement to help Desperately wants help Feels guilty for wanting help Worried that gaining weight will lead to treatment being withdrawn
Int: Mm-hmm. Claire: so dependent on, on this [weight]	Belief that treatment provision is dependent on weight

When doing coding, you systematically code the entire data set, trying to stay consistent in how you code the data. If your familiarisation phase has been thorough, you will be better prepared for this. But the deep, analytic focus on the data for coding means that analytic ideas *inevitably* develop as you code. Therefore, it is important not just to go through the data set once, but to go back and check for consistency, and recode the data as necessary. A key difference between our approach to TA and other approaches is that we see coding as organic, and coding *evolves* as it progresses (data are not coded using a predetermined 'coding framework' or 'codebook', as in Boyatzis, 1998; Guest, MacQueen & Namey, 2012; Joffe, 2011). The boundaries of codes can expand or contract, very similar codes, with lots of overlap, can be merged together. Larger, more complex, codes can be split into two or more codes. Keep your research question in mind when coding but code inclusively. Coding can help you to refine and focus your research question – there may be a 'flip-flop' (Henwood & Pidgeon, 1994) between your research question and your coding, with each informing how the other is honed.

In practical terms, coding can be done manually (on hard copy using paper, pens, highlighters, file cards, etc.) or electronically, either in a word-processing program, or using software specifically designed to assist qualitative analysis, such as NVivo or ATLAS-ti (these are collectively referred to as computer-assisted qualitative data analysis software or CAQDAS; see Silver & Fielding, 2008). Once you've finished coding, you need to collate the coded data. How you do this depends on how you have done your coding. If working manually, you might cut and paste and collate the data relevant to each code (keeping note of where it is from) on a separate file card. If using a CAQDAS program, your coded data can be collated by the program.

Activity 13.2   Coding exercise

Have a go at coding this segment of data from Nicola's interview with Sarah (keep in mind the research question). First, try coding it in a descriptive way, then try coding it in an interpretative way. What different things do you see in the data?

Sarah: .... it gets so competitive and you do get jealous of other clients and
Int: Mm-hmm.
Sarah: especially ones that you know, with eating disorder specialists because you do you do you think, "oh they're comparing me and
Int: Mmm.
Sarah: (pause) she looks sicker than me so obviously she's sicker than me and that's not fair and (pause) cos they're going to take her more seriously than me and" (pause) that's, cos as well specially with, eating disorders, anorexics are always prioritised over bulimics, because of the BMI
Int: Yeah.
Sarah: your weight is always (pause) to get help you have to, an unhealthy weight (pause) and that especially with St Thomas'* you will always get prioritised, my admission date got put, just kept, being, put, back and back because someone with a BMI of thirteen came in (long pause) and they took priority (pause) or someone with a BMI, twelve came in and they got priority

Transcription symbols:

Underlining = emphasis on a particular word

Brackets = pauses

Quotation marks = reported thoughts or speech of self or others

* Hospital name anonymised

Searching for (3) and reviewing (4) themes

TA involves the identification and interpretation of *patterns* – conceptualised as themes – across the data set. A theme 'captures something important about the data in relation to the research question, and represents some level of patterned response or meaning within the data set' (Braun & Clarke, 2006, p. 82). A theme identifies a *broader* level of meaning than a code, so lots of different codes will usually be combined to create each potential theme. In practical terms, the search for themes involves initially identifying clusters of similar meaning across your codes. There are three important questions to keep in mind in this process:

1. Is this potential theme centrally relevant to answering my research question? There are many potential themes in data. The ones you develop should individually, and collectively, provide the richest account of meaning in the data, relevant to your question.
2. Is this potential theme evident across more than one or two of my data items ('data item' refers to each individual piece of data you have, such as an interview, or a magazine article; your data items combine to form your data set)? Although themes may sometimes be important, even if not evident across a substantial proportion of data items (see Braun & Clarke, 2006; Buetow, 2010), overall TA is concerned with *patterned* meaning, and so it is important that themes are evident *across* different data items.
3. Can I easily identify a central organising concept for this potential theme? A central organising concept is a clear core idea that underpins a theme, the essence of what the theme is about (Braun & Clarke, 2013). It is about ensuring themes are internally coherent, and also distinct from each other. Don't worry if this isn't apparent right away – the central organising concept for each theme might only become apparent through the revision of (candidate) themes.

Keeping these questions in mind, cluster codes together to form larger patterns. Not all your codes will contribute to themes – some data, and some codes, will be irrelevant to the developing analysis and/or to answering your research question. At this point, the analysis is all very provisional, so it is best to think of the larger patterns as *candidate* themes, and not get too attached to them – the process of analysis means your themes will likely evolve, with some even being discarded!

In developing themes, you need also to go back to the data associated with each code, and then the whole data set, to review whether or not the candidate themes map on to the coded data, and the data set. You also want to determine that there are rich and diverse data to support each theme. This involves a thorough re-reading of the data in light of your developing analysis. This process of looking at codes, coded data and the whole data set, and developing the 'shape' of each theme, is a recursive one. Throughout the review process, you need to keep your research question in mind.

At this stage, you also need to work out the overall 'structure' of your analysis – your different themes, and how they relate together. You want to make sure the different themes 'fit well together', capturing distinct but related aspects of the data (Braun & Clarke, 2012). This usually means certain potential themes are discarded. In Nicola's research, discarded potential themes included 'you have all the answers just fix me', 'obsession with weight', 'not trusting others' and 'not trusting self' during the process of analysis.

Using a visual mapping process – developing thematic maps – can be really helpful at this stage. Figure 13.1 provides the final thematic map from Nicola's research. In it, you can see there is a central point that the analysis coheres around, three different branches off this, and then another layer of branching off each of these three main branches. This nicely illustrates the different 'levels' of themes you can work with. At the 'top' level there are *overarching* themes, which correspond to Nicola's central point in Figure 13.1. An overarching theme is effectively an umbrella concept under which different themes might be developed. Then there are themes themselves. As noted, these are organised around a central organising concept, and the analysis of a theme describes and illustrates the ways that concept plays out in the data. Finally, there are *subthemes*. Subthemes – if they are used – cluster underneath themes. A subtheme shares the same central organising concept as the theme it sits beneath, but develops a distinct aspect or element of it. A few subthemes can be useful when there are notable aspects of a theme that are worth highlighting. Too many subthemes and the analysis is likely be unnecessarily complex and lack coherence.

This brings us to the important question of 'how many themes (and subthemes) should an analysis have?' This is a tricky one to answer. Sometimes, an analysis may focus on only one theme, and develop it in a lot of detail, with a few subthemes. Other times, the analysis may present an *overview* of themes in

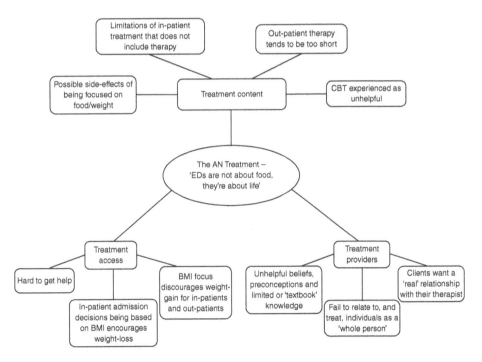

Figure 13.1 *A worked example of a thematic map*

the data set. In that case, we generally think two themes is probably the minimum, and six about the maximum. But it depends, again, on things like length of the analysis, as well as its purpose. The more themes, the fewer subthemes you are likely to have.

Defining and naming themes (5) and writing up (6)

As your analysis develops, you work on refining the focus, scope and clarity of each theme and the depth of your analytic interpretation. In our approach, 'writing' is a separate phase, and 'writing up' the whole analytic report *is* the last thing that you do. But writing is an integral part of the development of analysis in TA and in much qualitative research. Therefore, the process of 'defining and naming' themes also involves considerable writing – you can't really do TA (or other qualitative analysis) without it!

This is the point where you tell 'the story' of your analysis. You select the data quotations that you will present in your write up, and situate these within an analytic narrative (your story of the data) that tells the reader what was in the data, why this is interesting and important, and, overall, how it relates to your research question. As part of this, it can be a helpful exercise to write a 'theme definition' for each theme (see Information box 13.3 for one from Nicola's research). This exercise helps check there *is* a clear, central organising concept for each theme (and that this is different for each theme), and that your overall analytic 'story' is clear. Another thing to decide is what to call your themes. Names are important because they provide the reader with a skeleton structure of your analysis. Names can range from simple descriptive titles (as in Nicola's themes and subthemes; see Figure 13.1) to the use of a brief data quotation – sometimes with a brief subtitle – that captures the essence of the theme (as in Nicola's overarching theme; see Figure 13.1).

Information box 13.3   A theme definition

The theme 'treatment access' describes the women's belief that the treatment system (in their experience) is both difficult to access and potentially iatrogenic due to its focus on body mass index (BMI) as a means of deciding who should receive treatment and when it should be withdrawn. More specifically, the theme presents their sense that BMI-based admission decisions can incentivise weight loss and – as a result of the additional weight that had to be lost in order to gain admission – increase the amount of weight (and thus duration of in-patient stay) that would have to be gained to reach a healthy weight at which discharge would occur; and that BMI-based discharge decisions are not only prioritising physical rather than psychological readiness, but also discourage weight-gain when in treatment.

Writing involves combing data quotations and analytic narrative, to build a convincing, evidenced and interpretative story of your data that answers your research question. There are two different ways of using quotations in TA: (a) in an illustrative fashion, where they provide illustrative examples of your narrative points, and you don't say anything specific about the content of each quotation; or (b) analytically, where your narrative says something particular about the specific features of each quotation. Sometimes analysis combines both (see Braun & Clarke, 2013). Regardless, the quotations selected should be clear and compelling, and drawn from across the data set. And make sure you don't simply paraphrase the content of the data! Your analysis also needs to be situated in relation to existing scholarly literature.

Avoiding common problems with TA

Reading the instructions before starting the work is a good idea ...

Starting to do qualitative analysis can be a frustrating and mind-boggling experience – not unlike putting up a tent when you have never done it before, and have no idea what it should look like. And there are lots of ways TA can be done badly – which you might not even realise. Table 13.4 provides a quick checklist of criteria to ensure the process and outcome of a TA are thorough, plausible and of high quality. When presenting an analysis, typically, you want a balance of at least 50:50 data:analytic narrative (point 10 in Table 13.4), or even 40:60, and you need to make sure you actually tell the reader what sense *you* make of the data, and how the data *answer* your research question (point 9). So a *key* requirement is that you actually present an *analysis* of the data. Don't just reiterate in your analytic narrative what has been said by a participant (pesky paraphrasing!), but tell the reader what is interesting about it, and why it is relevant for answering your research question (point 7). The other main problems we see with TA are inconsistency and 'passivity'. Given there are lots of different ways to do TA, make sure that when you write up, you are explicit about what approach(es) you have taken (point 12), and make sure that the language and claims that you make about the data are consistent with the approach(es) to TA you say you have taken (points 13 and 14; see Table 13.1). Finally, don't treat themes as something you passively *uncovered* in the data! As a researcher, you work to identify salient patterns through the knowledge and perspectives you bring to the data. Own this position, and don't talk about 'themes emerging' as if you sat back and watched while your themes climbed, ready-formed, from your data set (point 15).

Table 13.4   *A 15-point checklist for a good TA (Braun & Clarke, 2006)*

Process	No.	Criteria
Transcription	1	The data have been transcribed to an appropriate level of detail, and the transcripts have been checked against the tapes for 'accuracy'
Coding	2	Each data item has been given equal attention in the coding process
	3	Themes have not been generated from a few vivid examples (an anecdotal approach), but instead the coding process has been thorough, inclusive and comprehensive
	4	All relevant extracts for each theme have been collated
	5	Themes have been checked against each other and back to the original data set
	6	Themes are internally coherent, consistent and distinctive
Analysis	7	Data have been analysed – interpreted, made sense of – rather than just paraphrased or described
	8	Analysis and data match each other – the extracts illustrate the analytic claims
	9	Analysis tells a convincing and well-organised story about the data and topic
	10	A good balance between analytic narrative and illustrative extracts is provided
Overall	11	Enough time has been allocated to complete all phases of the analysis adequately, without rushing a phase or giving it a once-over-lightly
Written report	12	The assumptions about, and specific approach to, thematic analysis are clearly explicated
	13	There is a good fit between what you claim you do, and what you show you have done – i.e. described method and reported analysis are consistent
	14	The language and concepts used in the report are consistent with the epistemological position of the analysis
	15	The researcher is positioned as active in the research process; themes do not just 'emerge'

Conclusion

TA is an excellent method to begin qualitative research for counsellors and psychotherapists. Once you have built confidence and skills, you can progress to more sophisticated implementations of TA, or explore other analytic methods, such as IPA (Smith, Flowers & Larkin, 2009), grounded theory (Charmaz, 2006), or discourse analysis (Coyle, 2006). Once you're experienced with qualitative research, we recommend you choose the method that best suits your research purpose. We wish you well on your qualitative analytic journey!

Suggestions for further reading

For a more detailed discussion of TA as an approach, see: Braun, V. & Clarke, V. (2006) Using thematic analysis in psychology. *Qualitative Research in Psychology, 3(2)*, 77–101.

For a detailed worked example of doing TA, using interview data, see: Braun, V. & Clarke, V. (2012) Thematic analysis. In Cooper, H. (Ed.), *APA Handbook of Research Methods in Psychology: Vol. 2. Research designs* (pp. 57–91). Washington, DC: American Psychological Association.

For an in-depth discussion of conducting, designing and transcribing qualitative interviews and a comprehensive worked example of a TA of focus group data, see: Braun, V. & Clarke, V. (2013) *Successful Qualitative Research: A practical guide for beginners*. London: Sage.

This book is accompanied by an extensive website, which includes examples of research materials for interview research and data sets for practising transcription, coding and analysis: www.sagepub.com/braunandclarke

Braun and Clarke's TA website includes answers to FAQs about TA: www.psych. auckland.ac.nz/thematicanalysis

FOURTEEN
Case study methodologies
Julia McLeod, Mhairi Thurston &
Dr John McLeod (all University of Abertay, Dundee)

Introduction

When thinking about research into the process and outcomes of counselling and psychotherapy, it is important to appreciate that research-based knowledge (the 'literature') is made up of a wide range of different types of research that complement each other. Taken together, the many and varied forms of research that have been carried out constitute a web or mosaic of knowledge. To be able to make use of research evidence, it is therefore necessary to understand the distinctive contribution made by different types of study.

Case study research occupies a somewhat ambiguous position within the domain of counselling and psychotherapy research as a whole. On the one hand, therapists work with 'cases', and as a result, case-based knowledge has an immediate relevance for practice. On the other hand, it is clearly not a good idea to base general conclusions on evidence from a single case. In addition, it is not a straightforward matter to know whether the findings from analysis of a single case are reliable and valid – there are many ways that sources of bias can creep in. The aim of this chapter is to provide an overview of the arguments and methodological strategies that have been developed in recent years, by researchers in many countries, to support the use of *systematic* single-case research within the field of counselling and psychotherapy. In this context, the concept of a 'systematic' approach to case study research refers to the emergence of a set of methodological principles that have the potential to lead to credible and robust case-based knowledge that can claim equal status with other forms of inquiry, such as randomised controlled trials (see Chapters 1 and 6) or qualitative analysis of interviews (see Chapters 12 and 13).

Beyond its contribution to the evidence base for counselling and psychotherapy, case study research also holds a unique relationship to therapy training. On most courses, therapy trainees are required to submit one or more case reports, and sometimes also an in-depth analysis of a segment of a case (often described as a 'process report'). Although very few of these student cases are ever published or otherwise disseminated, the fact that trainees need to engage with the issue of 'what makes a good case report?' opens up some potentially valuable points of connection between training, research and practice. For example: Do trainees write more satisfying and meaningful case reports if they know about principles of systematic case study inquiry and read research-informed cases? Is it possible for trainees to use their assignment case reports as the basis for published articles that are available in the literature? When students learn about principles of systematic case research, during their training, do they become more discerning readers and consumers of research-based cases throughout their careers? We return to these questions at various points throughout this chapter.

For reasons of space and clarity, this chapter is only concerned with case study research into the delivery of therapy. In other words, a 'case' is defined as an episode of therapy, from start to finish, received by an individual, couple, family or group. Case study methodology can also be applied in research into therapy organisations, or the development of therapy in different countries. Further information and examples relating to case studies of organisations can be found in McLeod (2011).

Harry: 'But I thought we were doing a single case study?'

Why case study research is necessary

Quite often, both students and more experienced researchers who hope to undertake case study research, find themselves needing to justify what they are planning to do.

Critics of case study methodology often complain that 'it is impossible to generalise from a single case' or that 'cases are only useful for teaching purposes and are not a valid form of research'. There are five basic reasons why case study research constitutes a necessary and important element of any general strategy for the advancement of research-based knowledge in counselling and psychotherapy.

1. *The issue of logical levels.* From a philosophical perspective, thinkers such as Bertrand Russell have demonstrated that the attributes of a set are not necessarily exhibited in individual members of a set (and vice versa). For example, in relation to therapy research, a controlled outcome study might find that, over a sample of clients, Therapy X is more effective than Therapy Y for clients with a particular problem. However, it may also be true that the client who benefitted most in the study was a person who received Therapy Y, and the one who did least well was someone who received Therapy X. From the perspective of aggregated data, therefore, Therapy X comes out best, but from a case-based perspective, Therapy Y comes out best. It seems obvious that a balanced and comprehensive evaluation of the effectiveness of psychotherapy for this disorder needs to take account of findings from both aggregate and single case analyses. Further discussion of this issue, and a real-life research example, can be found in Eells (2010).

2. *The development of theory.* Scientific progress is not based in the accumulation of facts, but on the development of powerful theories that take account of complex phenomena, and that can be used to anticipate or guide future action. Case study evidence contributes to theory development in two ways. First, while a single observation or case example is not sufficient to substantiate the validity of a theory, it is sufficient to refute that theory. Medical science has a long-established tradition of using published accounts of unusual or anomalous cases to raise questions about existing knowledge, and drive the research agenda forward. Second, the meaning of the concepts and propositions within a theory, and the linkages between these concepts, can be tested and elaborated by a process through which a theory is tested against a case, revised as necessary, then tested against a further case (Stiles, 2007).

3. *Sensitivity to important aspects of therapy.* Case studies represent a methodology that is particularly sensitive to aspects of the therapy process that are hard to investigate using other methods: the relationship between therapeutic processes and the social and organisational context within which therapy takes place; the complex interplay between a wide range of potentially relevant processes and factors; the unfolding of a change process over time. While it is certainly possible to study these aspects of therapy using aggregate data, they become much more visible and salient when richly-described single case data are available.

4. *Key role within broader programmes of research.* Research that is of practical value usually arises from programmes of research that use different methodologies to explore different aspects of a problem. One of the central questions that has been the focus of massive research effort within the world of counselling and psychotherapy has been the issue of what therapy approach is most relevant for specific disorders such as depression, PTSD, etc. At some point, the research community (and the public) wants to see evidence that a form of therapy has been effective with a large sample of clients. There

are practical and ethical barriers to collecting large-scale data on new forms of therapy. It is feasible, however, to begin by carrying out single case analyses, or a series of cases, that report on the effectiveness of a new intervention for a particular disorder. At a later stage in many therapy research programmes, it may become apparent that there are some clients who do not gain from a therapy approach that is nevertheless beneficial for the majority of a sample of clients. In this situation, detailed analysis of single cases can be used to identify what is going wrong in these poor-outcome therapies.

5. *Overcoming the gap between research and practice.* There is little point in doing therapy research unless, at some stage, it makes a difference to practice. However, practitioners are busy people whose clinical work involves making decisions that draw on many different sources of information. There is evidence that practitioners tend to disregard findings from large-scale studies, or recommendations of research-informed clinical guidelines, as being too divorced from the reality of their everyday practice (see Chapter 1). On the other hand, there is evidence that practitioners are more likely to change their practice on the basis of credible and rigorous case examples (Stewart & Chabless, 2010).

A key point here, which needs to be emphasised, is that the arguments summarised in this section are not based on any assumption that case studies provide better evidence than other types of research (however 'better' might be defined), or that case studies represent the only type of research that therapists need to do. Instead, the position that is adopted is that all forms of research are valuable, each in their own way, and that an absence or neglect of case study evidence has the effect of weakening the therapy evidence base as a whole.

PAUSE FOR REFLECTION

How useful have case studies been in shaping your own understanding of counselling and psychotherapy? Which cases have your read that have made a particular impact on you? What was it about these cases that made them particularly memorable?

The history of case study research

In the early years of the emergence of counselling and psychotherapy as a discipline, the advancement of theory and practice was largely conducted through the documentation and discussion of clinical case studies. A clinical case study can be defined as a case report written by a therapist on the basis of his or her clinical notes. The published output of Freud, Jung and other pioneers of psychotherapy consisted largely of clinical case studies. New theoretical ideas and clinical methods were presented in clinical case reports that were then subjected to critical discussion. It is important to appreciate that, during that era, no other methods of inquiry were available. Psychological tests only started to become available from the 1920s. Psychological experiments on human beings, or survey questionnaires, did not emerge until the 1930s. The medical training received by Freud, Jung and many of their colleagues had made them aware of how clinical case studies could be used to generate knowledge, so this was what they did when they began to work as psychotherapists.

Clinical case studies have been highly effective in creating a knowledge base for psychoanalysis and psychodynamic therapy. It is not hard to trace the evolution of psychoanalytic ideas through a rich thread of case evidence that gradually opened up new ways of thinking about the process of therapy. But, at the same time, the increasing sophistication of psychological research as a whole (and research in allied areas such as education and sociology) began to make it painfully obvious that traditional clinical case studies were associated with numerous methodological limitations. For example, how accurately can a therapist observe and record the therapy process? How objective can a therapist be, when identifying themes and patterns in the clinical notes that they have taken? It does not need a great deal of reflection to come to the conclusion that there is a strong tendency, within traditional clinical case studies, for therapist-authors to find what they expect to find. Moreover, there is no possibility of an independent check on whether this is happening. A therapist may be a superb observer of what happens with his or her clients, or be trapped within a hall of mirrors – there is no way of knowing.

Alongside a growing scepticism around the reliability of the clinical case study method, those conducting research into counselling and psychotherapy research were gradually accumulating a vast armoury of research tools that were not available to Freud and those around him – questionnaires, rating scales, projective techniques, video and audio recorders, rigorous methods for analysing quantitative and qualitative data, and so on. Over the past 30 years, these research instruments have begun to be integrated into single-case research, in an effort to construct a methodology for systematic and rigorous case study inquiry.

The development of systematic methods of therapy case study research can be divided into four broad phases:

- *'N=1' or 'single subject' research designs.* From the 1960s, behaviour therapists and then CBT therapists adopted a technique of time-series analysis to track session-by-session (or even hour-by-hour) change in the frequency and intensity of target symptoms exhibited by individual clients. This type of case study research has made a major contribution to the success of CBT as an evidence-based approach, because it has enabled CBT practitioners to document and evaluate the effectiveness of new interventions, in preparation for carrying out large-scale studies. Further information on this form of case study research can be found in Morley (2007).
- *'Research-informed' case studies.* Researchers began to conduct case studies that made use of multiple sources of information, such as session recordings, questionnaires completed by the client and therapist, and follow-up interviews. Some of these analyses were carried out on cases selected from larger data sets, thus allowing detailed exploration of the differences between good-outcome and poor-outcome cases. The availability of a range of sources of data, and the capacity to locate the case within a wider clinical population, made it possible to be more confident in the reliability and validity of the findings of each case analysis. An early pioneer of this way of doing case study was Hans Strupp, one of the leading figures in research into psychodynamic psychotherapy (see, for example, Strupp, 1980).

- *'Pragmatic' case studies.* Although each specific case study that is carried out has the potential to provide useful insights, the scientific and practical yield of case study research is much increased when it becomes possible to examine themes and trends that occur over a series of case analyses of a particular therapeutic approach, or that have looked at different models of therapy applied to a particular disorder. It is clear that a great deal of potentially valuable case study information, in the form of examples of everyday therapeutic practice, is never recorded and disseminated and is therefore lost to the cumulative knowledge base for therapy theory and practice. In the 1990s, Dan Fishman and others argued that it would be useful to build up a large database of 'pragmatic' case studies, in which therapists reported on their work in a rigorous and comprehensive manner. Pragmatic case studies can be regarded as a form of 'enhanced' clinical case study. Examples of pragmatic case studies can be found in two journals: *Pragmatic Case Studies in Psychotherapy* (an online journal) and *Clinical Case Studies*.
- *'Adjudicated' case studies.* The most recent development within the domain of systematic case study research in counselling and psychotherapy has focused on the way in which case data are analysed. When a lone researcher analyses complex material, there is a risk that he or she will focus on patterns and themes that reflect their own existing assumptions or theoretical model, and disregard other findings that may be of potential significance. One way of addressing this issue is to use a team of researchers, who independently analyse the case material and meet up to compare their conclusions and arrive at an agreed interpretation of the case. It is possible to gain even more insight into a case by adopting a 'quasi-judicial' procedure, as used in courts of law, in which different researchers construct opposing interpretations of the case, using agreed rules of evidence, and then subject their analyses to expert external judges. This kind of process has the effect of forcing researchers to consider a case from different perspectives. Further discussion of the rationale for this approach is available in Elliott (2001, 2002) and Stephen and Elliott (2011). The adjudicated case study provides a highly appropriate basis for a student research study, which is why it is presented in further detail in Chapter 15. It is an approach that is flexible, and can be used with whatever data are available. In addition, the adjudication process provides an opportunity to work in a supportive team environment, and develop skills in critical analysis of different types of research evidence.

The impact of these developments in the direction of greater methodological rigour has been a steady year-on-year growth in the number of systematic case studies that are published within the counselling and psychotherapy literature.

Ethical issues

Case study research is a highly ethically sensitive form of inquiry. When information is collected from a sample of people, it is relatively easy to safeguard the identity of research participants. In quantitative research the responses of any single individual are aggregated into an overall score for the group. Even when in-depth interviews are conducted on a sample of 6–12 informants, only brief quotations are used from individual participants to illustrate themes or categories that refer to the sample as a whole. By contrast, in a case report, even if the age, occupation and even gender of the client are altered, the basic life story remains.

Activity 14.1   Reading case studies

To gain an appreciation of the strengths and limitations of case study research, it is necessary to read different types of case study article and reflect on what they have to offer. The studies listed below represent contrasting styles of case study inquiry. All of them are available online and are readily accessible.

- *The case of Irvina (Kuenzli, 2009). Cross-cultural Gestalt Therapy with a young woman who was angry and suicidal – a good quality clinical case study that offers a vivid, fascinating and closely-observed account of the process of therapy, but based solely on the therapist's notes and memories.*
- *The case of Grace (Pass, 2012). An example of a 'pragmatic' case study, which examines in great detail the use of psychodynamic therapy and expressive writing with a woman who had experienced severe trauma.*
- *The case of Peter (Widdowson, 2012b). An 'adjudicated' case study of Transactional Analysis psychotherapy with a depressed man. Multiple sources of evidence were analysed to determine the extent to which the client experienced a good or poor outcome, and whether client change could be attributed to the action of therapy rather than other factors.*
- *The case of Lily (Kasper et al., 2008). The client in this case study was a woman with difficulties around anxiety and forming relationships, who received interpersonal therapy. The case analysis drew on multiple sources of evidence to generate a model of the role of therapist–client immediacy as a factor in the process of therapy.*

Comment

As you read each study, consider the following questions:

- *To what extent, and in what ways, does this study make a contribution to the overall evidence base for the effectiveness of therapy?*
- *To what extent, and in what ways, does this study provide knowledge and information that will help me to be a better therapist?*
- *How credible is the case report I am reading? Is it possible to construct a plausible alternative interpretation of what happened in the case? What additional information or validity procedures might have enhanced my confidence in the validity of what I was reading?*

It is usually possible to anonymise case studies so that general readers will not be able to identify the subject of the case, but it is virtually impossible to write up a case in a way that will prevent friends and family members from realising who is being described. The risk of personal exposure is heightened in situations where case reports are published on the internet. As well as the issue of confidentiality, it is possible that a client may be disturbed by reading what a researcher, or their therapist, has written about them, even when they have given consent for their case to be analysed. There are also important ethical issues associated with the process of seeking consent to carry out a case study. For example, if a client is asked for consent once therapy has commenced, or at the end of therapy, it may be hard for them to refuse, because of a wish to please their therapist. On the other hand, seeking consent before therapy has commenced can never be sufficient in itself because at that point the client will have no idea about the kind of material that will be generated over the course of therapy.

It is important to avoid reaching a position in which ethical issues prevent case studies from being carried out. A detailed account of strategies that can be used to address the ethical challenges of case study research is available in McLeod (2010b). A broader discussion of ethical issues in counselling and psychotherapy research can be found in Chapter 8 as well as in McLeod (2013, Chapter 5).

PAUSE FOR REFLECTION

Imagine that you are a client who has arrived at a first appointment with a therapist. If you have had personal experience of being a client, cast your mind back to your first meeting with your therapist. How would you feel if your therapist explained that he or she might wish, at some point in the future, to write up their work with you and publish it in a book, and now wanted you to sign a form to give your approval to this possibility?

Guiding principles for systematic case studies

As a result of the growth in interest in recent years in case study research in counselling and psychotherapy, there exists an extensive literature on the methodological challenges associated with this sort of investigation, and its relevance for policy and practice (Aveline, 2005; Fishman, 1999; McLeod, 2010b; Midgley, 2006). This is an area of methodology that is still in a process of development and innovation, and it is inevitable that useful new ideas about how to carry out good-quality case study research will continue to emerge. Nevertheless, at this point in time it is possible to identify a number of methodological principles for which there exists a broad level of agreement.

1. *Careful attention to ethical issues.* It is essential to be willing to consider all aspects of the potential impact on the client of the decision to participate in a case study project. To ensure that a sufficient degree of attention has been given to the client's well-being, it is always necessary to make use of independent external consultation on ethical procedures (e.g. through university ethics committees). It is also necessary to continue to obtain consent all the way through the inquiry process, and to be willing to 'lose' cases through client withdrawal. The test of an ethical consent procedure is that it creates a space where the person can say 'no'. Ambiguous ethical procedures create situations where participants (clients and therapists) do not wholly trust what is happening, and hold back on important information, and where researchers feel conflicted and guilty about publishing their findings.

2. *Creating as rich a data set as possible, based on multiple sources of information.* There are many different types of data that can be used in case study research, such as questionnaires, transcripts, therapist notes, and interviews (McLeod, 2010b; McLeod & Cooper, 2011). Multiple sources of information create the possibility of 'triangulation' – demonstrating that different observations lead to the same conclusions. The principle of corroboration of evidence is a basic feature of good practice in areas such as the law, journalism and historical research.

3. *Collecting data that allow points of connection between 'this' case and the wider clinical (or non-clinical) population.* The ready availability of brief measures such as the CORE outcome scale makes it possible to make reliable statements about the similarity between the client being studied in a case and other clients (see Chapter 10 for more on CORE). This makes it possible for readers of case studies to think about the similarities and differences between the findings of a specific case study and their own work with clients.

4. *Providing information about the context in which therapy was carried out.* Sensitivity to context represents one of the distinctive strengths of all case study research. Defining the boundaries of a 'case' is never a straightforward matter. For example, in therapy research with multiple participants, it is generally necessary to focus on a limited number of variables, usually restricted to outcome measures and information about what happens in the therapy room. The potential links between what happens in therapy and the broader context within which the therapy has taken place are rarely explored. By contrast, in a case study, the amount of space that is available to describe a single case means that it is possible to include detailed information about such contextual factors as the organisational and cultural setting within which therapy occurred, the process through which the client decided to seek help at that particular service, the physical environment, the experience and working conditions of the therapist, and so on. This kind of information helps to bring a case to life for readers, and allows them to make connections between the case and their own practice.

5. *Telling the story.* One of the distinctive advantages of case study methodology, compared to other forms of research, is that it creates the possibility of presenting findings and conclusions in a way that is memorable and engages the interest of the reader or audience. To achieve the objectives, it is necessary to tell the story of the case in a coherent manner. Being able to offer a coherent account of what happened in a case is a primary test of the adequacy of the analysis that has been carried out on the case materials – an incoherent case narrative suggests that the author has not developed a clear enough understanding of the case. In writing the story of the case, it is also important to provide sufficient detail for the reader so that they can make up their own mind about the credibility of the account that is being offered. Readers

tend to be suspicious of case narratives that do not incorporate the client's perception and evaluation of what happened.

6. *Using a systematic approach to analysing case-based information.* A case study in which the author does not explain how he or she made sense of the complex data that were collected is not likely to be regarded as credible. Readers will have more confidence in the conclusions of a case if they can follow, at least in principle, a 'paper-trail' or 'audit-trail' that leads from data to conclusions. There are several strategies that can be applied to the analysis of case data. One essential strategy is to carry out some form of time-series analysis. This can involve identifying stages within the therapy, turning points, change events and trends. A deeper level of time-series analysis looks for potential causal linkages between events in therapy and outcomes. For example, a long gap in therapy over a vacation may be associated with a dip in ratings of the therapeutic alliance. Plausibility of such analysis can draw on triangulation – for instance, the idea that the vacation undermined the growing trust between therapist and client gains more plausibility if the client said something to this effect in a follow-up interview, or the therapist mentioned it in her notes. Plausibility is also enhanced through a process of critical examination of alternative interpretations of the data. It is important to be critical and scholarly, rather than using a case study to 'sell' yourself or your approach to therapy. The use of *multiple analysts*, rather than depending on a single perspective on the data, represents another invaluable analytic strategy.

7. *Using a standard format for writing up the case.* It makes it much easier for future scholars to include your case report in literature reviews if a case study is written in a standard format. It also makes it easier for readers to find their way round the case, rather than having to go looking for information. Journals such as *Pragmatic Case Studies in Psychotherapy* and *Clinical Case Studies* have developed guidelines that have proved to be appropriate to case study reports from many different forms of therapy and client group (see Information box 14.1).

Information box 14.1   Headings used in writing up a pragmatic case study

Case context

The client

Guiding conception with research and clinical experience support

Assessment of the client's problems, goals, strengths and history

Formulation and treatment plan

Course of therapy

Therapy monitoring and use of feedback information

Concluding evaluation of the process and outcome of therapy

References

Appendices

This list of methodological principles represents a broad-brush summary of some of the key ideas that have been shown to be useful in relation to doing good quality case study research. A more comprehensive appreciation of how these principles can be applied in practice can be gained by reading published recent examples of therapy case study research (see Activity 14.1).

PAUSE FOR REFLECTION

If you are a student on a counselling or psychotherapy training programme, you will almost certainly be required to write some kind of case study. A written case report that reflects your way of working with clients is also a requirement for some professional accreditation schemes. As a practitioner, you will need to present information on your cases as part of your regular clinical supervision, perhaps including a 'case formulation' or treatment plan. Take a few moments to reflect on how the principles of systematic case inquiry might help you to approach these professional tasks in a more satisfying, meaningful and effective manner.

Types of research question that case studies can answer

There are four broad categories of research question that can be addressed using case study methodology:

- *Outcome questions*: How effective has therapy been in this case? To what extent can changes that have been observed in the client be attributed to therapy? To what extent is this approach to therapy potentially relevant for this group of clients?
- *Theory-building questions*: How can the process of therapy in this case be understood in theoretical terms? How can the data in this case be used to test and refine an existing theoretical model?
- *Pragmatic questions*: What strategies and methods did the therapist use in this case that contributed to the eventual outcome? How were therapeutic methods adapted and modified to address the needs of this specific client? What are the principles of good practice that can be derived from this case?
- *Experiential or narrative questions*: What was it like to be the client or therapist in this case? What is the story of what happened, from the client's or therapist's point of view?

If sufficiently rich data are collected on a case, it is possible to carry out multiple analyses that focus on each of these four types of research question. However, within the usual word length of a journal article, it is only possible to do justice to one of these questions, with perhaps some acknowledgement of one further question as a minor theme within the paper. Any attempt to incorporate all four of these questions within a single article of 6–8,000 words is likely to lead to a report that is not sufficiently detailed in any one area to be convincing to readers. Further discussion of these research questions, and examples, can be found in McLeod (2010b).

Selecting cases for research

A great deal of effort and commitment is required to produce a credible case study report. It is therefore important to make a careful and informed choice around which case or cases to select for analysis. The choice of case depends on what is possible in the specific research context, and on the aims of the research. It may be that a case is interesting because it represents a typical example of a particular kind of therapy. Alternatively, a case may be interesting because it is non-typical (e.g. a good-outcome or poor-outcome case, or an example of a form of therapy that has never been used before with a particular client group). A case may be worth studying because it exhibits unusual or unexpected features, such as a good outcome despite a poor client–therapist alliance. At the same time, it is necessary to avoid the trap of waiting for the 'perfect' case to come along. In most areas of counselling practice, there are no more than a handful of published systematic case studies currently available, so almost any carefully reported case will be likely to make a valuable contribution to knowledge. It is also important to avoid any tendency to characterise a case in overly simplistic terms. For example, 'good-outcome' cases will almost certainly include some areas in which the client was disappointed, and 'poor-outcome' cases will include some evidence of client learning and change.

As stressed in this chapter, there are significant ethical issues that need to be taken into account when planning a case study investigation, particularly when the therapist is the primary investigator or is a member of the research team. It is not ethically sound to allow the aims of a case study project to determine what happens in therapy. For example, if a therapist is aiming to complete a case study that analyses the role of metaphor in therapy, he or she may pay more attention to metaphor in his or her work with a client than is actually warranted by the needs of the therapy itself. It is important, therefore, to create research contexts in which therapy proceeds as usual, and then cases are selected for intensive analysis only *after* therapy has been completed. It is also important to collect data on more cases than are needed. For instance, if a student aims to base their research project on the analysis of a single case drawn from his or her own client load, it is good ethical practice to recruit three or four clients into the project, thus enabling the researcher to accept with relative equanimity the possibility that some clients may withdraw their consent at some stage. By contrast, if the fate of a student's research project depends on the cooperation of a single client, there is a risk that this individual may be subjected to undue pressure to give consent.

Conclusion

Systematic case study research can be used to explore a range of questions in the field of counselling and psychotherapy. The disadvantages of case study methodology are that a case study can take a long time to complete (e.g. if ethical consent is obtained at the start of therapy, the study will require at least as long as the total length of therapy), and can involve significant ethical challenges. In addition, it is essential to define the research question so that it is clear that unsustainable claims for generalisability are not being made. However, the advantages of case study methodology are that it allows research to be carried out that is relevant to practice, it involves a research process that supports personal and professional development, and it can create opportunities for using diverse research tools (e.g. analysis of transcripts, questionnaires, interviews, etc.).

Systematic case study research in counselling and psychotherapy represents a form of inquiry that is highly relevant to the ongoing personal and professional development of both trainees and experienced practitioners, as well making a distinctive contribution to the evidence base as a whole. In order to be considered as a valid and reliable example of research knowledge, it is essential that a case study should be carried out in a systematic way, drawing on methodological principles that have been developed in recent years. These methodological principles reflect a general assumption within all areas of inquiry in social science that the process of data collection and analysis should be open to external scrutiny. In order to carry out worthwhile case study research, it is important for prospective case study researchers to become connoisseurs of case study methodology by reading different types of published case report. As in any area of research, it is necessary to design a case study in a way that achieves the best possible balance between the research question being pursued, the access to information that is possible within the specific research context, and the resources of the researcher. Research design always involves making compromises. There are no currently published examples of therapy case study research that do everything right. It is only by careful reflection on the methodological choices made by different researchers, and the implications of these choices for the quality and plausibility of the final research product, that new researchers can become sensitive to the range of options that are open to them.

Suggestions for further reading

Fishman, D.B. (1999). *The Case for a Pragmatic Psychology.* New York: New York Universities Press.

This book represented a turning point in relation to the acceptance of case study methodology in the field of counselling and psychotherapy research. It clearly and carefully explains why case study has a vital role to play within the domain of therapy research as a whole.

Flyvbjerg, B. (2006). Five misunderstandings about case-study research. *Qualitative Inquiry, 12,* 219–245.

A classic paper that debunks popular myths about the limitations of case study research. It is not a therapy paper, but it draws on examples from several social science disciplines.

McLeod, J. (2010b). *Case Study Research in Counselling and Psychotherapy*. London: Sage.
Further discussion, examples and references in relation to all of the topics discussed in this chapter.

FIFTEEN

How to use case study methodology with single client therapy data

Mhairi Thurston, Julia McLeod & Dr John McLeod (all University of Abertay, Dundee)

Introduction

A significant development in the field of counselling and psychotherapy research has been a resurgence of interest in the use of case study methods. This initiative has been made possible by the identification of a set of methodological principles designed to maximise the rigour and credibility of this form of inquiry (see Chapter 14, and McLeod, 2010b). One of the key ideas within this set of principles has been the concept of 'adjudication'. Therapy case study researchers have looked to the operation of the legal system for a model of how to arrive at reasoned conclusions in relation to individual cases. In a courtroom trial, prosecution and defence teams present alternative interpretations of a case, and have an opportunity to offer rebuttals to the arguments put forward by their adversaries. In the light of these arguments, a final judgement on the case is made by a jury or panel of judges. The proceedings of such a trial follow a predetermined structure and are bound by rules of evidence. In essence, some version of this framework has increasingly been adopted by therapy researchers seeking to arrive at credible and practically useful understandings of evidence from therapy cases. This is a good starter method for those wishing to conduct case study research. Thus, the aim of this chapter is to provide therapy trainees and practitioners with a set of instructions of how to use a 'quasi-judicial' or 'adjudicational' methodology for doing case study research.

Background: The development of adjudicational methods

It is important to understand the scientific rationale for the adjudicational method. The academic discipline of philosophy of science is concerned with the issue of elucidating the basis on which reliable scientific knowledge is produced. There is a broad consensus within that field that knowledge does not emerge from the accumulation of 'facts'. Rather, new understandings arise from a process of dialogue, within which theories or propositions are formulated and then subjected to critical test. The well-known philosopher of science, Sir Karl Popper, characterised advances in understanding as comprising a cyclical process of 'conjectures' and 'refutations'. This is basically what happens in adjudicational research. A 'case' consists of a complex array of information that can be interpreted in different ways. When one specific interpretation of the data is subjected to critical test (an attempted refutation), it forces the person presenting that interpretation to reflect more deeply on their interpretation. What emerges is a better interpretation (or theory) from which unnecessary or unsubstantiated ideas have been eliminated, and whose core ideas have been further refined. The activity of arriving at a comprehensive and plausible interpretation of the meaning of a phenomenon is known as 'hermeneutics'. Scientific rules of evidence can be regarded as a system for interpreting phenomena in the natural world. The rules of evidence that have evolved in law, literary criticism, theology and historical research can be regarded as systems for interpreting phenomena in the cultural world. Further discussion of the philosophical basis for research in counselling and psychotherapy can be found in McLeod (2010b, 2011, 2013).

PAUSE FOR REFLECTION

What do you feel about introducing a quasi-judicial methodology into counselling and psychotherapy research? What might be the advantages and disadvantages of this approach, compared to more widely used methods for investigating the process and outcome of counselling and psychotherapy?

Historically, research in psychology and psychotherapy has been dominated by the methods and procedures of the natural sciences. It has taken some time for the potential value of interpretative approaches from other disciplines, such as law, to be recognised. The earliest example of the use of an adjudicational approach within psychology was the research into personality conducted by Henry Murray and his colleagues at Harvard University in the 1920s and 1930s. In that programme of research, a team of researchers considered alternative interpretations of the personality structure of an individual person before arriving at an agreed analysis. This set of ideas, or model, was then tested against a subsequent case. Over the course of a series of cases, a comprehensive model of personality was established. It was only in the 1990s that this type of approach began to be applied in research in counselling and psychotherapy. The most influential example of adjudicated single case therapy research is the hermeneutic single case efficacy design (HSCED) approach developed by Robert Elliott (2002). The HSCED protocol was devised primarily to analyse the extent to which a case can be judged to be a 'good' or 'poor' outcome. Information about the case is interpreted from an 'affirmative' position (the client improved over the course of therapy and these gains can be attributed to the action of therapy) and a 'sceptic' position (the client did not improve, or any observed gains can be attributed to factors other than therapy). The affirmative and sceptic briefs are then subjected to adjudication by independent external judges. The case of 'George' (Elliott et al., 2000) is the most fully described HSCED study that is currently available and represents a major landmark in therapy research.

Information box 15.1   Deepening your understanding of an adjudicational/dialogical approach to research

This chapter focuses on the practicalities of designing and completing an adjudicated case study. This is a relatively new methodology, which is still evolving as groups of researchers try out different ways of collecting and analysing case data in different settings. Further discussion of adjudicational procedures in case study research can be found in Bohart et al. (2011) and Stephen and Elliott (2011). Also relevant is the method of dialogical understanding used by Halling, Leifer and Rowe (2006).

Stages in adjudicated case study research

Information box 15.2   Stages in the process of conducting an adjudicated single case study

1. *Identifying the aims of the research and research questions.*
2. *Defining the types of information that can be collected in order to produce evidence that is relevant to the research questions.*
3. *Negotiating access to an appropriate case or cases.*
4. *Developing ethical procedures for obtaining informed consent and ensuring the confidentiality, safety and well-being of participants.*
5. *Data collection and the assemblage of a 'case book'.*
6. *Designing and implementing a procedure for systematic data analysis based on the construction of alternative or competing interpretations of the data. Implementing these procedures in relation to the material in the case book.*
7. *Dialogue between proponents of alternative interpretations.*
8. *External adjudication: case book and account of alternative interpretations sent to independent judges.*
9. *Writing the case study.*

The following sections offer a step-by-step guide to using the adjudicational single case method. This is illustrated with the case of Silvia, which is an example of an investigation that is well within the scope of counselling and psychotherapy students, trainees and practitioners. Although carried out in a university setting, it made use of research tools that are readily available on the internet, and did not involve any specialist training for those carrying out the analysis.

Information box 15.3   A case of sight loss

With an ageing population, the prevalence of acquired sight loss is rising, and there is growing recognition of the need to provide emotional support for people with sight loss (Royal National Institute of Blind People, 2012). However, at the present time there has been little research into counselling for people who have experienced sight loss. Carrying out a series of case studies represented a research strategy that would make it possible to begin to map out factors that might be important in evaluating future large-scale research, and would allow a preliminary model of practice to be developed.

---

1. Identifying the aims of the research and research questions

Chapter 14 outlines the types of question that can be answered with case studies: outcome, theory-building, pragmatic and experiential or narrative questions. The HSCED methodology developed by Elliott (2002) provides an example of how an adjudicational method can be applied to the investigation of the outcomes of therapy. An adjudicational approach can also be applied in single case research that seeks to develop theory, and is also relevant for therapy case study research that aims to produce comprehensive accounts of how therapy operates in specific contexts ('pragmatic' case studies) or to document the experience of the therapist or client ('narrative' case studies). For the case of Silvia, there were two research questions that were identified as particularly relevant at this stage of the research programme:

- To what extent was counselling helpful for the client?
- What were the specific therapeutic tasks (McLeod & McLeod, 2011) that contributed to outcome?

In relation to the broader literature on case study research in counselling and psychotherapy, these questions focus on *outcome* and *theory-building*. As the research team, we were hoping to obtain some evidence of whether counselling was helpful, and to begin to build a model of practice. In addition, we were aware that there were no published case studies of counselling with a client experiencing sight loss. We were therefore interested, if at all possible, in also using this case study for *narrative* purposes, to tell the client's story.

2. Defining the types of information that can be collected in order to produce evidence that is relevant to the research questions

As discussed in Chapter 14, the aim with case studies is to collect as much information and types of information as practically and ethically possible. In coming up with the research design it is necessary to devise a research protocol that collects information about the process and outcome of counselling that is relevant to the research questions, and which also allows for an adequate degree of cross-source triangulation to be possible. Lots of different types of data are potentially useful, including readily available data sources such as referral information, therapist notes of sessions, transcripts of audio-recordings of sessions, and any service evaluation questionnaires that a counselling service routinely uses. It is also possible, however, to purposively add into a counselling engagement additional data collection methods and opportunities. Examples might be questionnaires focused on particular symptoms or aspects of client experience (e.g. therapeutic alliance) or interviews with clients. In principle, any data collection method suitable for counselling and psychotherapy research can be utilised (see Chapter 7 as well as Chapters 10 and 12). For the case of Silvia, we made use of a range of quantitative and qualitative data collection tools that are typical of the kinds of instruments that have been utilised in systematic case study research in recent years (Table 15.1).

3. Choosing a case – negotiating access to a case

The selection of a case for systematic analysis will depend on a number of factors, including availability (see Chapter 14, Selecting cases for research, and McLeod, 2010b). One idea is to use existing research to guide choices about good potential case study clients. However, as in the case of Silvia, if there is a lack of research, this may not be possible. Alternatively, the exact focus of the research can be dictated by which cases are available. For example, the therapy case study by Råbu, Halvorsen and Haavind (2011) emerged from an initial intention to use case study methodology to explore the process of the client–therapist relationship. One of the cases that was available for study included a fascinating process during early sessions that incorporated a number of theoretically-interesting implications. These researchers therefore narrowed the focus of their case analysis to pay special attention to what happened in the early sessions of that particular case. Since students may have limited access to potential case study clients this can be a good strategy to adopt.

For the case of Silvia, the process of selecting an appropriate case began with thinking about who might be a good 'case' and what the best counselling setting might be. The impact of sight loss on well-being is complex and depends on a number of factors, such as the age of onset of vision problems, the rapidity with which problems develop, the pre-existing coping strategies of the person, and the amount of social support that is available (see Nyman, Dibb, Victor & Gosney, 2012). These

Table 15.1 *Data collection methods used in case of Silvia*

Method	When data collected	Information collected
Clinical Outcomes in Routine Evaluation (Evans et al., 2000)	34-item questionnaire given before and after counselling	Self-reported psychological functioning
	10-item questionnaire given at all other sessions	
Goals/Target Complaints Rating (Deane, Spicer & Todd, 1997)	Every session, at start	Client identifies their three main problems/issues and how severe they think these are (on a 1–10 scale)
Working Alliance Inventory – short form (Hatcher & Gillaspy, 2006)	Every session, at end	12-item questionnaire – client view of the therapeutic alliance.
Helpful Aspects of Therapy form (Llewelyn, 1988)	End of every session	Client description of the most helpful and most hindering events that took place during the session.
Client Pre-Counselling Interview	Semi-structured interview, before beginning of counselling	Focused on reasons for seeking counselling and description of problems as well as relevant background information and feelings about taking part in research.
Change Interview (Elliott, Slatick & Urman, 2001)	Semi-structured interview, after end of counselling	Focused on what client identifies as changes that have occurred as a result of counselling. The interview explores the extent to which these outcomes might have occurred in the absence of therapy. It also identifies helpful and hindering aspects of the therapy from the client perspective.
Session recordings	Transcriptions of each therapy session	
Structured therapist session notes	Written after each session	Weekly therapist record of the themes and issues addressed in therapy, helpful factors and events, and overall progress.

varied factors suggested that different clients might have quite different issues and thus experiences in counselling. We therefore decided to conduct a case series, beginning with the first case that became available, and gradually building a model of practice on a case-by-case basis. In the case of Silvia, it also seemed likely that the outcomes of counselling might well be influenced by counsellor characteristics (such as depth of personal knowledge and experience around sight loss), as well as aspects of the therapeutic contract, such as the number of sessions and the mode of therapy (e.g. telephone counselling versus face-to-face counselling). On pragmatic grounds, it seemed sensible to begin with a case of brief counselling that could be completed and analysed relatively quickly.

Silvia (all names and identifying information have been changed to ensure confidentiality), a 70-year-old woman, was the first client to be recruited to the project. She received six sessions of counselling from Mhairi Thurston. Silvia had no experience of vision impairment until the sudden loss of sight following a routine medical procedure. She had no previous experience of counselling and responded to an advertisement for the current study following encouragement by a friend.

4. Developing ethical procedures for obtaining informed consent

As discussed in Chapter 14, it is critical to carefully think through ethical issues in case study research. In the case of Silvia, the ethical procedures used in the study were approved by the researchers' University Research Ethics Committee. Silvia was provided with information about the project before agreeing to enter counselling, in both written form and at a meeting, and signed a consent form. Further verbal consent was obtained at every session, concerning the use of audio-recording. At the end of therapy Silvia was provided with a draft copy of the report and was able to stipulate any changes or omissions that she felt might be necessary for accuracy or to maintain her anonymity. She was free to withdraw from the study at any stage, without any consequences for her ongoing counselling. The information provided to Silvia included the name and contact details of an independent person within the university whom she could consult if she was unhappy about any aspect of her involvement in the study. These ethical procedures were designed to create a situation in which everyone could participate fully in the study in the knowledge that their contribution would be treated with respect and sensitivity.

PAUSE FOR REFLECTION

How do you imagine that a client, such as Silvia, might react to being asked to read a copy of a case report based on their own experience of being a client? How might a researcher ensure that the well-being of the client was maintained throughout this procedure?

5. Data collection and the assemblage of a 'case book'

In the case study of Silvia, data was collected by two research assistants and the counsellor. One person met with Silvia at the beginning and end of sessions, to read aloud the scales that needed to be completed, and note her responses. Another person conducted the Change Interview, and the counsellor carried out the pre-counselling interview and was responsible for the recordings. In other circumstances, most of the data can be collected by the counsellor, as part of routine practice. However, it is valuable to use the end-of-therapy Change Interview to give the client an opportunity to talk about their experience in therapy to someone other than their counsellor because this makes it easier for the client to be forthcoming. In this project, the counsellor looked at the questionnaires completed by the client, and used that information to facilitate a process of collaborative working. This strategy was consistent with the counsellor's normal practice. Again, in other circumstances it might be appropriate to apply a greater degree of separation between data collection and the process of counselling. There are many other examples, and a full discussion of this issue, in McLeod (2010b).

All of the information collected on the case was assembled into a case book, which functioned as the basis for the analysis phase of the project. A set of case books was printed. For ethical reasons, each one had an identifying number that enabled its use to be tracked and to ensure that it was returned and shredded at the end of the analysis.

6. Designing and implementing a procedure for systematic data analysis

The adjudicational structure used in the case described in this chapter is based on the method of hermeneutic single case efficacy design (HSCED) research developed by Elliott (2002), and within the HSCED tradition itself the sceptic-affirmative process has been organised in different ways within different projects. As with the present study, Widdowson (2012b) used groups of therapy trainees as members of the sceptic and affirmative groups. By contrast, Elliott et al. (2000) used experienced researchers, working together over an extended period of time, to generate sceptic and affirmative arguments. The HSCED study by Stephen, Elliott and Macleod (2011) was based on sceptic and affirmative interpretations developed by a single researcher. Alternative adjudicational methodologies are described by Bohart et al. (2011), Jackson, Chui and Hill (2011) and Miller (2011). There are also several case study reports that are based on open discussion of case data within a small research team (see, for example, Råbu, Halvorsen and Haavind, 2011). The 'Ward' method offers a useful structure within which this type of open dialogue can be organised (Schielke, Fishman, Osatuke & Stiles, 2009). A case study project by Robinson (2011) incorporated the use of a lay member in the external panel of judges. A key point here is that there are many ways in which processes of dialogue and adjudication can be facilitated. The adjudicational structure that is used in any particular study will depend on the aims of the project and the resources that are available. It is important to recognise that judicial systems in different countries can operate in very different ways. The basic underlying principles in all humane systems of justice are that a case is scrutinised from a variety of perspectives, and that participants present reasoned arguments based on shared ideas around what counts as relevant evidence.

Information box 15.4   Suggestions for student researchers

One way to maintain the benefits of having multiple perspectives while engaging in a process that is still eminently doable for student researchers is to create four-person research case study groups. For each case, there is an identified key researcher, someone arguing the affirmative reading of the case, a sceptic and a judge, and these roles rotate so that a student who is researcher for one case may be judge for another.

---

7. Dialogue between proponents of alternative interpretations

The key task here is to develop affirmative and sceptic arguments about the case, with both arguments being evidenced with material from the case book. It is possible for largish groups of people to be involved in this stage, as in the example of Silvia below, but, as discussed, other models are also possible. It can be useful for the sceptic judge(s) to reference a list taken from Elliott (2002) of potential issues to which they might pay particular attention (e.g. the client might present a positive account of therapy because she had been trying to please the therapist and/or interviewer). It is also important to treat the output of the group (e.g. flip charts) as part of the data for analysis.

In the case of Silvia, 22 students on a postgraduate Diploma in Counselling course were given the case book and asked to generate either 'affirmative' arguments (that the client had benefited from counselling), or sceptic arguments (the client had not benefited, or any apparent gains were due to non-therapy factors). Once the case for the affirmative and sceptic had been presented, each side was given time to develop rebuttals in order to provide a detailed and balanced argument. Each group was also invited to identify, discuss and report on helpful and hindering aspects of the therapy.

8. External adjudication

The next step is for the nominated judge(s) to review the rich case record and the interpretations of the affirmative and sceptic groups. This does not have to be done by someone external to the research (i.e. it could be done by the researcher), but independent and, if possible, multiple judges offer additional validation of the study findings and can bring a range of discipline and relevant expertise to the case. In the case of Silvia, the judges were: a university lecturer in counselling, with expertise in long-term health conditions and in case study methodology; a narrative researcher with expertise in the field of sight loss; a counselling practitioner with expertise in the pluralistic approach; and a senior social science researcher who was not a counsellor. The judges were asked to examine the evidence and to report on their level of confidence regarding whether this case was a good outcome case or a poor outcome case, and their views on the factors that contributed to outcome. The judges communicated only with the leader of the project (MT) and did not meet as a group.

9. Writing up the study

The process of writing up a case study involves condensing a large amount of information into a typically short word limit (e.g. of an academic piece of work or research paper results section). It is useful to have fellow researchers review drafts of the write-up and it is ethically recommended for the client to read and comment on a final draft. In the case of Silvia, this process led to a published research paper (Thurston, Thurston & McLeod, 2012) as well as presentations at a counselling conference and at national meetings on provision of service for individuals with sight loss.

Observations from the case of Silvia

Evidence of the value of the use of multiple participants during the sceptic–affirmative dialogue comes from the experience of one member of the research team who has been involved in many case study projects. Although very familiar with the material in the case book, this individual found that students with no prior background in case study analysis were generating plausible interpretations of the data that had never occurred to him.

A further observation around the process of analysis concerns the central role of the Change Interview (or some other form of post-therapy interview) in the interpretation of the case. When confronted by the extensive material available to them in the case book, readers are inevitably drawn to the Change Interview transcript because it provides a summary of the case in the client's own words. An obvious starting point for triangulation is to compare the statements made by the client in the interview with (a) statements made in other sections of the interview, and (b) data from other sources. It is therefore essential for the person carrying out the Change Interview to be aware of how other members of the research team might want to use that information at a later stage. For example, it is extremely valuable if the interviewer can push the client as hard as they can on the existence of potentially negative aspects of the therapy, and on the relevance of extra-therapeutic influences and changes that are reported.

A final observation relates to the use of therapy transcript material. At this time, most of the adjudicated case studies that have been published have not made use of session transcript data. In the Silvia case, transcripts of all sessions were included in the case book. We found that this information was useful for members of the sceptic and affirmative teams, even if they did not have sufficient time to analyse it in detail. Even a relatively rapid scan of a session transcript can be effective as a means of either verifying that a particular reading of a case is consistent with what seemed to be happening in sessions, or alerting the reader to potential anomalies that require further consideration. The availability of a transcript is particularly important in studies that have a predominantly theory-building focus (see, for example McLeod, 2013).

Conclusion

There are many benefits to a single case design ...

The basic data for systematic case study inquiry already exists in many clinical settings – what needs to be added may be no more than ethical consent and a follow-up interview. This type of research does not have to be time consuming. The case study described in this chapter was completed and published within a nine-month period. Participation in the analysis of systematic case study data is an interesting and stimulating activity, which can be regarded as part of a commitment to ongoing personal and professional development, and can be incorporated into training (Stinckens, Elliott & Leijssen, 2009). Moreover, adjudicated case study methodology is a flexible approach that can be adapted for different research questions or to reflect the values of the researcher. Given that there are many areas of contemporary counselling and psychotherapy for which no detailed, systematically-analysed case examples exist, this method represents a massive opportunity to simply look at, document, and reflect on what we do, in addition to having the potential to produce evidence that is grounded in practice while addressing important theoretical questions and issues around effectiveness.

Case-based research has, in addition, the potential to make a valuable and distinctive contribution to the evidence base that is used to inform counselling and psychotherapy practice. Research designs, such as randomised controlled trials, that aggregate information from multiple cases play a vital role within the research literature by verifying the existence of general causal factors, such as the efficacy of a particular form of intervention for a particular client population. Systematic case study designs, such as HSCED, play a complementary role within the literature, in four main ways. First, case study research makes it possible to provide preliminary evidence about the effectiveness of an approach to therapy, prior to exposing that approach to a large-scale study. Second, in-depth case studies can be used to examine what happens in poor outcome cases, in ways that enable the ongoing development of innovations in theory and practice. Third, the kind of mixed-method case study described in this chapter allows the researcher to examine the impact, at a micro level, of specific elements of therapy. Finally, the narrative detail that is provided in a case study report represents a form of research-based knowledge that is accessible and credible to practitioners.

Suggestions for further reading

Elliott, R. (2002). Hermeneutic single case efficacy design. *Psychotherapy Research*, *12*, 1–20.
   One of the key contributions to the development of adjudicational single case research.

Elliott, R., Partyka, R., Wagner, J., Alperin, R., Dobrenski, R., Messer, S.B., Watson, J.C. & Castonguay, L.G. (2000). An adjudicated hermeneutic single case efficacy design study of experiential therapy for panic/phobia. *Psychotherapy Research, 19*, 543–557.

A powerful example of the potential of adjudicational research.

Jackson, J.L., Chui, H.T. & Hill, C.E. (2011). The modification of consensual qualitative research for case study research: An introduction to CQR-C. In C.E. Hill (Ed.), *Consensual Qualitative Research: A practical resource for investigating social science phenomena* (pp. 822–844). Washington, DC: American Psychological Association.

Clear, step-by-step guidelines for conducting a systematic case study investigation form of adjudicated analysis.

PART IV
Completing the research journey

SIXTEEN

Dissemination of research

Dr Andrew Reeves (University of Liverpool)

Introduction

The purpose of this chapter is to help you to think about your research process differently. That is, to challenge the assumption that research begins with a question and ends with a perfectly-bound dissertation or thesis. While both of these two aspects may well be important stages of the research process, it is the assertion of this chapter that research can run the risk of becoming meaningless unless steps are taken to actively disseminate the outcomes of your study. It is therefore the process of successful dissemination that should mark the end of your research journey.

As we know, to *disseminate* is simply defined as the process of passing on information to a relevant audience: nothing complicated or contentious about that. Theoretically, we might all agree that dissemination is, in principle, a good idea. Sadly, however, the world of counselling and psychotherapy research is littered with interesting, relevant, well-written, engaging, challenging, sometimes startling and occasionally profound examples of research that never see the light of day. While dissertations and theses are officially in the public domain, in reality they populate unfashionable academic library bookshelves, or lurk unseen in dark corners of online databases, rarely read, never thought about and always on the edge of becoming completely irrelevant – after all that hard work. Yet we have the potential to make a much greater contribution to the world of counselling and psychotherapy.

It is my intention to consider the process of dissemination of research findings – the final stage of the research process – in some detail and hopefully to encourage you to integrate dissemination into your own approach to research. I will outline why you should consider talking about *your* research and look at the process of dissemination in the context of other stages of the research process. I will then look at specific ways in which we might share our research outcomes and the particular tasks and challenges in undertaking such steps. I will also consider how you might support yourself during this stage and offer particular working 'hints and tips' which might facilitate the process. Using myself as a 'case example', I will outline the ways in which I have disseminated my own research findings, before drawing all the points together.

Why talk about your research?

There are good reasons why this book contains a chapter about disseminating research findings. Placing dissemination of outcomes as an integral part of the research process has many potential benefits. See Information box 16.1 for more information.

Information box 16.1   The benefits of dissemination

Personal

- *Helping to further place your work in the public domain and increasing its profile or visibility.*
- *Providing new career or other professional opportunities for the researcher(s).*

For the study

- *Providing more opportunity for feedback and critical evaluation, thus helping to enhance the validity of the findings.*
- *Creating opportunities for new perspectives, which can bring new ideas and develop research questions further, leading to new research ideas.*
- *Promoting collaboration between researchers who might not otherwise be aware of your work.*
- *Ensuring that existing research, otherwise unknown to the researcher, is highlighted.*
- *Enhancing the possible implications for practice.*

For the discipline

- *Contributing to a growing evidence-base for counselling and psychotherapy (see Chapter 1 on practice-based evidence).*

Regardless of modality, the process of research *and* the dissemination of research findings have been integral in developing our current understanding of what we do and why we do it. For example, person-centred therapy would not be as it is practised today without the extensive writings of its founder, Carl Rogers (Rogers, 1951, 1961, 1978, 1980), and subsequent theorists, academics, practitioners and researchers who have taken those beginning ideas and nurtured them into something new. The same is true for almost all theories and modalities. The impact such research has on the development of the profession cannot be overstated. I hope, therefore, that the case for talking about your research findings and ensuring that as many people as possible know of the work you have undertaken, despite it being an exposing and therefore 'risky' endeavour, is beginning to be made.

Dissemination: The forgotten stage

As we have seen in Chapter 1, research can be undertaken for a number of reasons. Sometimes through curiosity, at other times because of auditing a service or particular types of intervention, and often because it is part of an academic programme where you have been required to undertake a piece of research and write it up. Particularly in the latter example, the sense of profound satisfaction when the dissertation or thesis is finally printed out, bound and handed to the tutor is almost palpable (I must confess to not experiencing the same degree of satisfaction when 'submission' is electronic, but perhaps that is just me). Seeing the piece of work in its entirety and being able to put behind us the hours of work and preparation with a sense of a job well done is not to be understated. However, herein lies a problem.

It is a mistake to imagine that the task of research has now been completed, for there is one very important final stage: that of disseminating your research findings. Having written that last sentence I can almost sense the collective groan and rolling of eyes. After all, who is ever going to want to read someone else's research anyway, and don't I think you have better things to be doing with your time?! The thought of finding that extra energy and motivation to do *more* work is really the last thing you will want to hear. However, research without dissemination is ultimately an incomplete process: like a tick without a tock; or breathing in without then breathing out. Walking away from research without taking steps to inform others about what you have found is, in many ways, like stealing the potential for knowledge from them. Put it this way, if there was something we thought about a client's distress, or some insight we had had during the therapeutic process, it is highly unlikely we would keep it to ourselves. Instead, we would find an appropriate way of sharing that insight or knowledge with the client, for not doing so would potentially deprive them of something important, even profound.

PAUSE FOR REFLECTION

Consider your thinking and emotional responses to the prospect of talking to others about your research. What are the positives of doing so, and the negatives? What factors might inform your responses (e.g. previous experiences of sharing your work) and how might you address these issues positively?

This chapter argues that dissemination needs to be thought of as the last stage of research. It is helpful, therefore, to factor this into our thinking right at the very beginning, when contemplating the stages of research.

Most of the research stages shown in Figure 16.1 will have been discussed, in varying ways, in previous chapters. Dissemination of research is the point at which research will really come alive: when we begin to actually tell people about it. We share our outcomes so that further discussion can be prompted, our study can be opened to further critical reflection (which may undermine its authority, but may also enhance its validity), and to prompt the potential for further research and inquiry. In doing so, we actively participate in the cascading development of knowledge and understanding. Hence, dissemination should be seen and understood as a way of creating an ongoing research and feedback loop rather than a discrete stage in a research process.

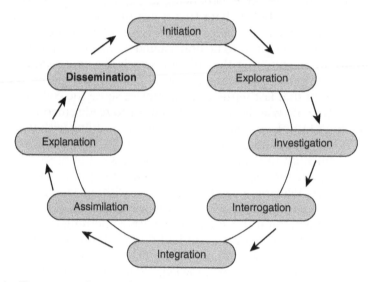

Figure 16.1 *The stages of research*

Sharing your research with others: Forms of dissemination

Most people, wrongly, consider that the 'proper' way to disseminate research is through the publication of a paper in an academic journal. While this may be one of the most common ways of communicating research, it is not the only way. In fact, there are many ways of disseminating research, particularly in a field like counselling and psychotherapy where there are different 'types' of audience. For example, different interested groups are outlined in Information box 16.2.

Information box 16.2   Potential consumers of counselling and psychotherapy research

- *Academics interested in the development of theory based on research*
- *Academic-practitioners who embed research into the delivery of counselling and psychotherapy in a university-based research clinic*
- *Practitioner-researchers who work primarily as therapists in therapy settings but integrate research into their work*
- *Practitioners who may not identify themselves as researchers, but critically consume research to inform their practice*
- *Practitioners who are entirely new to research but are 'interested'*
- *Allied professionals interested in the application of counselling and psychotherapy principles into their own work (e.g. social work, nursing, teaching, psychology, psychiatry, etc.)*
- *Commissioners of services who utilise research to ensure decisions are based on a sound evidence-base*
- *Managers of settings in which counselling and psychotherapy are delivered*
- *Current and potential clients of counselling and psychotherapy looking to make informed choices about therapy*
- *The media and other outlets looking for relevant news in mental health*
- *Potentially everyone else*

Looking at the list in Information box 16.2 demonstrates the diversity in the potential audience and how each might require something different in the delivery of information. For example, those looking for detail regarding research method and outcome might look towards an academic paper in a peer-reviewed journal, while practitioners with little experience in research might be interested in the implications for practice and how 'outcomes' relate to what they do with clients. Clients themselves might be interested in which particular types of therapy are indicated for certain types of problem or difficulty, while commissioners might instead look for a meta-analysis of outcomes (the integration of several studies) in the development of an evidence-base. With this in mind, it is helpful to consider different ways of disseminating research. Some alternatives are indicated in Information box 16.3.

Word limitations prevent a detailed discussion of all the options above in this chapter, and neither is it possible to indicate which one is more difficult than the other as that will depend on your personal style of working and particular anxieties. Some may find writing relatively easy, but presenting may be more challenging, or vice versa. Instead, then, I will focus on three of the more common methods of communicating research findings: *presenting a poster* or a *paper at a research conference* and *publishing a paper in a peer-reviewed journal*.

Information box 16.3   Ways of disseminating research findings

- Presenting a poster at a research conference
- Presenting a paper at a research conference
- Presentation at practitioner conferences
- Articles in peer-reviewed academic journals
- Articles in practitioner magazines
- Articles in mainstream newspapers and magazines
- Keynote talks at relevant events
- Publication of a book
- Publication of practitioner guidance
- Development and production of a training DVD
- Development and delivery of a one-day training workshop
- Talking to mainstream media

Presenting a poster or paper at a research conference

There are a number of conferences both in the UK and internationally that focus on counselling and psychotherapy research: for example, the British Association for Counselling and Psychotherapy's (BACP) annual research conference, the Society for Psychotherapy Research's (SPR) research conferences, which take place in the UK and internationally, and the British Association for the Person-Centred Approach (BAPCA), among others. There are two primary ways of disseminating your research findings at a conference: by poster or paper presentation. Both require you to submit an abstract to the conference organisers for consideration. Some conferences will accept most abstracts, while others seek peer-reviewed abstracts. It is essential that you follow any instructions for the preparation of abstracts as failing to do so will be the quickest and most effective way of having your abstract rejected.

A *poster presentation* is what it says: the researcher(s) prepare a large poster, usually of A1 size, which includes the information outlined in Information box 16.4.

Information box 16.4   Typical content of a poster presentation

- Title of paper
- Summary of research intention
- Brief background information
- Method
- Summary of findings
- Key points and implications for practice
- List of references
- Relevant images, figures, tables and boxes to summarise key points

Presentation is key in a good poster to ensure it is eye-catching and easy to read. Information has to be accessible and quick to assimilate as conference delegates usually only spend comparatively short periods of time looking at posters in relation to other things they will do. The aim is to interest 'passing traffic', i.e. the people walking past the poster, to engage them so that they want to read more. Some conferences will provide an opportunity for the researcher(s) to talk for a few minutes to all the conference delegates, perhaps following a keynote talk, to further engage interest. Abstracts for posters are usually contained in the 'Abstract book', which is circulated to all delegates and includes abstracts of all accepted posters and papers. While preparing a poster might seem less intimidating than presenting a paper, it requires careful work and close attention to detail. Resources that provide guidance on technical issues (such as what font size and type to use) as well as practical information about how to use PowerPoint to create a poster are listed at the end of this chapter.

What might seem the more immediately scary option – *presenting a paper* at a conference – is typically experienced by those who do it as not being quite as bad as they anticipated it would be. Usually presentations are made to smaller groups in the conference and typically not to all the delegates at once. So, for a conference with 200 delegates, the paper might only be presented to 20–30 people: those who had selected to attend that presentation. Time is often quite tight (typically around 20 minutes, with 10 minutes for questions) and the challenge, therefore, is to cover all material in the time allowed. A common mistake is to over-prepare because of anxiety, with some researcher(s) coming armed with PowerPoint presentations containing 30 slides or more. They then rush through the slides, talking a great deal, but saying very little. The key is to prepare for the time allowed. If using computer presentations, only very few slides are needed; I would suggest a slide for each of the following information:

1. The *title* of the research and details of the researchers (names, affiliations)
2. The *aims and objectives* of the research, in simple and accessible terms
3. Information about *method*, including participants, data collection, means of analysis (where appropriate)
4. Summary of key *findings*, in simple and accessible terms
5. *Limitations* of the research
6. Summary of *implications for practice*, or for further research
7. *Contact information* of the key researcher, for following up contact, and details of where the paper is available

The list above allows for seven slides. Assuming that you talk to each slide for two minutes, your presentation will take 14 minutes, although obviously more will be said for slides 2, 3 and 4. This approach allows for a comfortable 20 minutes of presentation, leaving sufficient time for questions and discussion. Good programs to use are Microsoft PowerPoint or Apple Keynote because they provide simple templates that allow you to deliver material clearly. It is worth noting that I have been attending such conferences for many years and almost entirely have experienced questions and comments as encouraging, supportive and constructively challenging. While I cannot guarantee that this will be your experience, it is likely.

Some researcher(s) will make a copy of their full paper available for circulation, while others may not have written it as a full paper but will, instead, prepare a summary of the research or hand-outs of the slides used. If the paper has been published in a peer-reviewed journal (or elsewhere), it is helpful to provide a full reference so that delegates can obtain a copy. I would advise against circulating photocopies of published papers, as there are usually copyright issues to attend to. Again, further resources on successful conference presentations can be found in the suggestions for further reading at the end of this chapter.

Some anxieties

For many people the thought of presenting their work publicly is a challenging prospect. Public speaking can often raise anxiety and make you fearful of doing it badly. Keeping the message simple is important here, as well as not over-preparing (e.g. including too many presentation slides, which then causes the presenter to rush). A number of useful tips for public speaking are summarised in Information box 16.5.

The nightmare of all presenters ...

Information box 16.5 Tips for public speaking

- *Know your topic*
- *Get organised*
- *Practise, and then practise some more*
- *Breathe calmly*
- *Focus on your material and not the audience*
- *Don't be afraid of moments of silence*
- *Recognise your success*
- *Get support*
- *Don't rush; take your time*

(from Flavin-Hall, 2013)

PAUSE FOR REFLECTION

In your view what might be the relative advantages and disadvantages of presenting a poster rather than a paper at a conference? For example, having to speak in front of a large audience versus summarising complex research into a poster format?

Publishing a paper in a peer-reviewed journal

For this section, I intend to put my 'Editor hat' on and talk about the process of submitting papers that has been informed by my work over the last six years on *Counselling and Psychotherapy Research (CPR)*, BACP's research journal. I will take this position because I obviously know that process well, and know it is reflective of many peer-reviewed journals. It is important to begin with a consideration of how to write a research paper for a journal. It is essential in the first instance to read the 'instructions for authors', which are usually outlined on a journal's website. These will detail word length, document format, the process of submission, reference style, how to manage boxes, tables and figures, and issues about copyright, for example. Many papers will be rejected simply because the author did not follow these basic rules. Different types of research (e.g. systematic reviews, case studies) might require different structures in the paper (see Chapter 4 for more detail on typical sections in research papers as well as differences between qualitative and quantitative papers).

A 'peer-reviewed' journal will send the paper out for consideration by two or three peer reviewers. Such people are rarely paid and are academics and practitioners, in the UK and internationally, who have a particular expertise in your area of research, or the methods used. For most journals, and *CPR*, the process is 'double-blind', which means that the author will not know who the peer reviewers are, and the peer reviewers will not know who the authors are as all identifying information will be removed prior to the paper being sent out. I have outlined the typical journey of a paper through the process of consideration as a flow chart (Figure 16.2).

You will notice in Figure 16.2 that I have identified three key stages, marked by a (1), (2) and (3), and I will talk these through briefly. At stage (1) the author(s) will submit their manuscript to the Editor. Sometimes they will have corresponded with the Editor about the relevance of their paper for submission, but that will depend on each Editor's policy. Submission is often (but not always) electronic, i.e. it is sent either as an email attachment or via a dedicated journal website. *CPR* uses Manuscript Central, where authors create a free account and the management of the paper throughout the process takes place within the 'system'. Two versions of the paper are usually required: one that contains all information and another where all identifying information (name, affiliations, self-references, etc.) has been removed in order to facilitate anonymous peer review. The Editor, at this stage, either decides the paper is suitable for peer review or will reject it and inform the authors accordingly. Rejection at this stage is typically because the instructions for authors have not been followed (these MUST be read and followed thoroughly prior to submission), the paper is

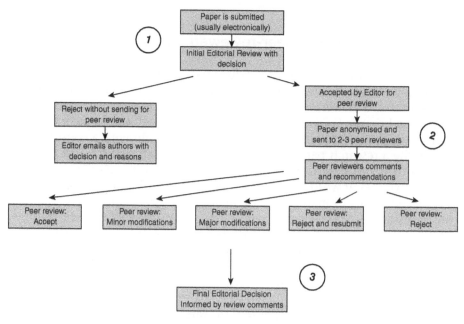

A journey of consideration for a peer-reviewed journal

too long, or the topic is not relevant for the journal. If accepted for peer review, the Editor will identify peer reviewers and will send the paper out. This process can take anywhere from a couple of weeks to a couple of months, and patience is required on behalf of the submitting author(s).

At stage (2) the Editor will receive comments back from the reviewers with one of five recommendations:

- *Accept*: where the paper is worthy of publication and requires no further development. This is unusual as all papers benefit from some additional work.
- *Minor modifications*: the paper is worthy of publication and the modifications are considered minor (e.g. basic editing, typos, minor points of clarification).
- *Major modifications*: the paper is worthy of publication but the modifications are considered major (e.g. it requires the further development of particular arguments, some rewriting, or editing down or increasing word length).
- *Reject and resubmit*: the paper is not worthy for publication in its current form because of major problems (e.g. there are major flaws in the analysis, the outcomes and conclusions are overstated, or the discussion is insufficiently drawn), but is retrievable and worthy of a resubmission (and peer review).
- *Reject*: there are major problems with the paper that are impossible to rectify (e.g. there are ethical problems, an inappropriate use of method, or the quality of data is insufficient).

At this stage (3), the Editor will decide whether or not to concur with the peer review recommendations and will make a final decision. That decision will be emailed to the authors, together with all the peer review comments, and with further details of the 'next stage' if the paper isn't rejected. The Editor's decision is final and while some will be willing to elaborate further on the basis of the decision, few will engage in a lengthy discussion or be open to persuasive emails.

There is no doubt that the peer review process is challenging. Comments often highlight problems with the paper or the research, as well as noting strengths. However, if comments are challenging, it is important to let them 'settle' for a while before responding. Most Editors will take great care in ensuring criticism is constructive and that the authors are enabled to make positive use of peer review comments. From my own experience of submitting, I have received some very negative comments at times, all of which – without exception – have proved beneficial and have helped me to develop my writing or research (once I had suitably recovered from the narcissistic injury, of course). It is important to stress that *all* authors, regardless of their experience, will have papers rejected by journals. Some journals reject up to 80% of all papers submitted, while others reject at least half. Rejection does not necessarily mean your research is poor, but might simply be because you have not followed the journal's conventions, or the focus of your research would be better for another journal.

There will be occasions when peer reviewers do not agree with each other. It is the role of an Editor to help you make sense of potentially contradictory comments so you can respond appropriately. When you resubmit your paper it is helpful to include either a separate Word file detailing the changes you have made, or to use the Word 'track changes' facility. This will help clearly communicate how you have responded to the reviewers' comments.

It may be that you disagree with a point a reviewer has made. It is acceptable to approach the Editor with your concerns, providing a clear rationale for your opinion. The Editor may agree with your point, but may also still require you to complete the amendments. At that stage, depending on how strongly you feel, you may either decide to meet the Editor's request or formally withdraw the paper and submit it to another journal.

There are some key points to remember when submitting your work to a journal that, if overlooked, will almost certainly lead to disappointment. These are outlined in Information box 16.6.

Information box 16.6   Key considerations when selecting a journal and submitting to it

- *Be clear about what it is you want to say, and to whom*
- *Think carefully about your intended audience (e.g. people interested in methodology, or research focus, or practice)*
- *What particular aspects will be of interest to the journal (i.e. it is highly unlikely you will be able to do justice to an 80,000-word doctorate in a 4,000-word article – which aspects will be the focus?)*
- *Research the journal: is it the right journal for your work, with the readership you are targeting?*
- *Read the aims and scope of the journal*
- *Look at previously published articles in the journal to see style, tone, approach, emphasis*
- *Look on the journal website for more information*
- *Does the journal have an 'impact factor' (a measure of the influence of the journal calculated in terms of the number of times articles in that journal have been cited elsewhere)*
- *Read the Instructions for Authors carefully... and follow them to the letter*
- *Oh, and did I mention to read the Instructions for Authors??*

Following peer review, if a paper is accepted, it will almost certainly go through several incarnations as it is developed and edited. Do not be alarmed, frustrated or downhearted by this; you will almost certainly be happier with the final version than the first. Then, once this process has been completed, it is sent to the publishers for formal typesetting and copyediting (where you will have opportunity to correct 'page proofs') before appearing online first, and then in print. *CPR* uses the Taylor & Francis (publishers) FirstOnline facility, where papers are published online in the same form as they will appear in print, and are fully citable by others. The print issue will then eventually land on your doorstep and you will congratulate yourself on a job well done.

Making it happen: Ways and means

Having considered the importance of communicating your research outcomes with others, and the different ways this might be achieved, it is important to draw breath and reflect on the next steps. Nothing is to be gained by rushing into one course of action without due consideration and thought for what it is you wish to achieve. There are therefore a number of competing demands in how you might approach the next and final step of your research and, by carefully weighing these demands and responding accordingly, you are most likely to make it happen, rather than fall at the first hurdle. Deciding what steps you might take in communicating your outcomes will be partly informed by your capacity in terms of time and energy. It is important to set realistic goals in terms of what you hope to achieve. The checklist of questions in Information box 16.7 might help.

Information box 16.7   What do I want to achieve

- *What do I want to achieve through the process of dissemination?*
- *What aspects of the outcomes do I wish to communicate at this stage?*
- *What is the nature of the audience I am hoping to reach, and how might that best be achieved?*
- *What is a realistic timescale for the process of dissemination?*
- *If there are several aspects to communicate, how might I prioritise them to make the targets achievable?*
- *What other personal and professional demands currently need my attention?*
- *Having identified the goal (i.e. what I wish to communicate, and when), what are the necessary steps?*

Having carefully and honestly answered these questions you are likely to be in a better position to begin taking your findings to a wider audience. In Table 16.1, I have outlined an approach to achieving your goal, using the example of writing a practitioner article (in the second column) to illustrate the points 'in action'.

Table 16.1 Planning a task

Suggested Steps	Example: Writing a Practitioner Article
Outline each individual step on a piece of paper (or using a computer or smartphone). Does not have to be ordered or planned at this stage, just get all steps down, breaking the bigger task down into small steps.	Begin writing Find a colleague/critical friend to read first draft Check for previous relevant articles Email the Editor to see if, in principle, they might be interested Clarify the profile of the desired readership Submit Structure article, defining smaller sections to write Read any 'instructions for authors' regarding format of article, such as length and how to submit Amend following any suggestions Proof read Define focus of research to write about
Prioritise each step according to the order in which each needs to happen, and smaller tasks which you might be able to get out of the way.	1. Define focus of research to write about 2. Clarify the profile of the desired readership 3. Email the Editor to see if, in principle, they might be interested 4. Check for previous relevant articles 5. Read any 'Instructions for Authors' regarding format of article, such as length and how to submit 6. Structure article, defining smaller sections to write 7. Write article 8. Find a colleague/critical friend to read first draft 9. Amend following any suggestions 10. Proof read 11. Submit
Define a timescale within which you intend to work. Writing out a weekly or monthly planner, or using a project management application, allocate each step to a timescale with a due completion date.	Given other work and family priorities, I will allow myself six months to complete the task. 1. Define focus of research to write about *(by end week 1)* 2. Clarify the profile of the readership *(by end week 1)* 3. Email the Editor to see if, in principle, they might be interested *(by end week 2)* 4. Check for previous articles relevant *(within month 1)* 5. Read any 'instructions for authors' regarding format of article, such as length and how to submit *(within month 1)* 6. Structure article, defining smaller sections to write *(by end month 2)* 7. Write article *(by end month 4)* 8. Find a colleague/critical friend to read first draft *(by end month 5)* 9. Amend following any suggestions *(by mid-month 6)* 10. Proof read *(by end month 6)* 11. Submit *(by end month 6)*
Build in regular reviews to ensure steps are being met or, if not, identify why and accommodate timescales and targets accordingly.	Review to happen *end month 1; end month 2; end month 4; end month 5 and end month 6*

Disseminating research: An example from practice

I have talked throughout this chapter of the importance of sharing your research findings with as wide an audience as possible, using a variety of means. Here, I will use my own experience as a practitioner-researcher to look at the ways in which I have publicised my own research. I am not holding my own research as an exemplar of good practice, but it does represent a process that will be familiar to many of you: research from a practice experience conducted as part of a Masters and Doctoral programme.

Counselling suicidal clients

In this section, I will refer back to the stages of research outlined in Figure 16.1.

- *Initiation*: My long-standing client, Isobel, killed herself following a session with me earlier that day. My personal and professional trauma and the sense I made of it in supervision initiated a process of considering my experiences in relation to those of other therapists working with suicidal clients.
- *Exploration*: I began by talking with other counsellors and psychotherapists, reflecting on their experience. I also started looking for general information about working with suicide risk.
- *Investigation*: I developed a research question (*what are the experiences of working with suicidal clients?*, and then later, *how might therapists be trained to incorporate risk assessment into a therapeutic discourse?*) and began formal literature searches to help inform and contextualise my research.
- *Interrogation*: I began to interview therapists about their experiences of working with suicide risk and, based on my own research findings and those of others, developed a training session, which I then evaluated using written and verbal feedback.
- *Integration*: I made use of several methods, including constant comparative analysis, a questionnaire study, a discourse analysis and a thematic analysis to analyse my data and, through this analysis, began to develop research outcomes.
- *Assimilation*: Research findings across all my individual research studies were refined and organised into a new 'whole'. Implications for practice were identified, as were the limitations and the potential for future research.
- *Explanation*: The studies were written up for academic consideration, into a dissertation (for my first study) and then into a thesis for my Doctoral research.
- *Dissemination*: Active steps were taken during the research process, and more particularly after the active stages of assimilation and explanation, to disseminate my research findings to as wide an audience as possible.

Taking the *dissemination* stage and looking at it in more detail, there were different things I wanted to say to different audiences that, in turn, informed the nature and form of dissemination. For example, for research located within an academic frame I wanted to share my process and outcomes with an academic audience, to receive feedback, comment and challenge to both inform and shape the nature of my work. To do this I presented my work on a number of occasions at research conferences and published papers in academic journals. While this was exposing and, quite often, I felt out of my depth, I quickly realised that the cost of putting my work out for scrutiny was far outweighed by the benefit of feedback and the opportunity to develop my work and to talk with others, hearing their ideas.

However, as the research had originally been initiated by experiences in practice, I was equally keen to speak with other practitioners and hear their thoughts. I spoke at several practitioner events and published articles in practitioner magazines, such as the BACP's *Therapy Today*. In such articles, my writing 'voice' was repositioned, in that I explored in more depth the possible implications of my study for practitioners and clients, rather than focusing on methodology and research process. Bringing the process full circle, I remembered the traumatic experience of Isobel's death and how I had felt so ill-prepared as a practitioner for it. One of my 'outcomes' was a fully evaluated one-day training programme, which I have since delivered to more than 7,000 therapists in the UK and internationally. I produced a training DVD (Reeves, Shears & Wheeler, 2010), a practitioner book on the research findings (Reeves, 2010), and co-authored practice guidance (Reeves & Seber, 2010).

My hope is to outline here that research undertaken by a practitioner, which was self-funded and relatively small-scale, still has the potential to reach a wide audience by making use of a variety of dissemination opportunities. That is not to say that all research should be disseminated in the same way. Many of you will prefer particular means, e.g. a 'practitioner route' rather than an 'academic route', or vice versa, or a more practical means (training and DVDs) rather than a written means (articles and books), or vice versa. All ways of disseminating research have value and all attempts at communicating findings to others are better than none at all.

Concluding Thoughts

I hope that, throughout this chapter, I have offered a compelling argument for the active and energetic dissemination of our research findings to a wide and varied audience. I have suggested that research dissemination is an important, albeit too often forgotten or overlooked, aspect of the research journey. By bringing this into your thinking you can consider dissemination options from the early stages of your research and, by the time you reach that stage of your journey, be mentally and organisationally prepared for it.

As I have also outlined, the options for dissemination are varied, with too many researchers thinking only of publication as a means of communicating findings. While this is still an important option to keep in mind (and as someone who has been Editor of a journal I would say that, wouldn't I?), it is by no means the only mechanism for informing the wider world of what you have achieved and of your particular contribution to our understanding of counselling and psychotherapy. More importantly, you need to reflect on the nature of your message, the audience you wish to reach, what it is you want to say and, with all that considered, what types of dissemination would best meet your needs. Having made that decision, I have offered some suggestions for how to tackle the tasks in a realistic and timely manner.

Much is to be achieved by taking the risk in putting your work 'out there' for others to consider. Without doubt, however, the fears of doing so are very real, with the 'impostor syndrome' (where you fear being 'found out' as a bit of a fraud) being an ever present issue for many. Not everyone will agree with what you have to say: some will take issue with the premise of your research; others with your methodological approach; some with your analysis and results or findings; while others again will disagree with the conclusions you have made or how you have drawn these into implications. Some will dismiss what you have to say without really reading or listening to your message. I would like to say that these statements have no truth, but it is important to step into the public domain with a sense of realism.

All that said, however, while some people will disagree, they will generally do so constructively, which will, in turn, further develop the debate. Alongside that, many more will welcome what you have to say and will engage positively and enthusiastically with your message. From my own experience, I have learnt as much from the challenge as I have from the approval, and this has equipped me to be prepared to take the next steps of inquiry and investigation. The future of counselling and psychotherapy depends on its proponents being willing to take risks and push boundaries. Your role in that process awaits.

Suggestions for further reading

Beins, B.C. & Beins, A.M. (2012). *Effective Writing in Psychology: Papers, posters and presentations* (2nd edition). Chichester: Wiley-Blackwell.
Includes chapters on conference and poster presentations as well as broader content about how to write up research.

Braun, V. & Clarke, V. (2013). *Successful Qualitative Research: A practical guide for beginners* (Chapter 13: Writing and communicating qualitative research, pp. 316–323). London: Sage.
Provides detailed guidance and examples on how to give a good presentation or create a successful poster for qualitative researchers.

Feldman, D.B. & Silvia, P.J. (2010). *Public Speaking for Psychologists: A lighthearted guide to research presentations, job talks, and other opportunities to embarrass yourself.* Washington, DC: American Psychological Association.
Includes broad information about public speaking as well as specific chapters on giving a research talk, preparing a poster and speaking to a lay audience.

Marek, P.J., Christopher, A.N. & Koenig, C.S. (2001). *Guidelines for Preparing Posters using PowerPoint™ Presentation Software*. The Office of Teaching Resources in Psychology. Retrieved 29 October 2013 from http://teachpsych.org/resources/Documents/otrp/resources/marek01.pdf

Provides a practical guide (which can be downloaded for free) to creating a poster using widely available software.

SEVENTEEN

Student top tips

Brian Sreenan, Harriet Smith & Charles Frost

Introduction

This chapter aims to fill an important gap in the existing literature. Despite the fact that many counselling training courses now include an element of research, there is currently little written about the counselling student's experience of actually *doing* research. Thus, the aim of this chapter is to give voice to students and provide a 'how to' account of surviving the research experience.

Before we start, it might be useful to introduce ourselves:

My name is Brian Sreenan. I did my Doctorate in Counselling Psychology training at a university in the UK. For my research project I conducted a mixed methods analysis to explore the therapeutic alliance in primary care CBT services (i.e. IAPT services). The focus groups for this book chapter were conducted during my second year of training. It gave me a real insight into the common pitfalls that are present during the research process. Having genuinely followed the 'top tips' outlined by the participants in the focus group, I was able to make my journey a relatively smooth one, saving heaps of time by using referencing managers, learning how to generate automatic contents pages in Word, and establishing SMART mini-goals (to name but a few)! I am grateful to the participants who shared their mistakes and musings during the focus groups. I hope this chapter helps you on your research endeavour.

I'm Charles Frost and I'm in my second year of a Doctorate in Counselling Psychology at another UK university. My thesis is looking at how trainee counselling psychologists perceive the scientist-practitioner model within the profession, so I was already interested in perceptions and experiences of research when I was asked to be involved with this chapter. I find myself more drawn to qualitative research that reflects the lived experience of people and so I enjoyed discovering the views and experiences of our student researchers.

My name is Harriet Smith and I am in my final year of a Doctorate in Counselling Psychology at a third UK university. I was surprised to find such limited information on the student experience of research. Shared stories and meaning making are at the core of my research interests so I was particularly drawn to this project as a way of giving voice to the trainee's experiences.

Since there was very little background literature to draw on, we decided to explore students' experiences by conducting our own research. This research project is described in Information box 17.1.

Information box 17.1   using focus groups to examine the experience of novice researchers

We conducted three focus groups at three academic institutions. The focus groups had seven participants (all female), nine participants (one male, eight female) and eight participants (one male, seven female), respectively. All participants were enrolled on Doctoral-level counselling courses.

Choice of methodology – Focus groups were selected in the hope that the group processes would generate thoughts and opinions from a range of students. One of the strengths of focus group interviews as a research tool is that participants are actively encouraged to participate in a forum which seeks to capture diverse views and outlooks. Because group dynamics can generate excitement and interest in a topic as well as allow participants freedom to be spontaneous (by not having to answer every question), the focus group methodology was chosen to generate a rich account of students' experiences (Wilkinson, 1998). An interview schedule was drawn up according to the guidelines outlined by Brotherson (1994). The interview schedule contained open-ended questions about students' experiences of conducting research (e.g. What is being a student researcher like?) and asked them for their top tips to survive the process (e.g. What advice would you give to people about to start their research?). The focus groups were recorded and transcribed and the authors analysed the transcriptions using thematic analysis (see Chapter 13).

The results of the focus groups have been interesting both in terms of the themes that came to light and in terms of our own reflections on both doing research and being researchers. The three main themes that came out of the focus groups were:

1. Practical tips about the process
2. The importance of support
3. Self-care and knowing your style

We have organised the rest of the chapter around these themes. We hope that the combination of fellow students' top tips and our own personal reflections will inspire and reassure as well as help you to avoid the pitfalls that can be part of being a novice researcher.

The practicalities

Most of the students interviewed in our focus groups had plenty of practical tips that they were keen to share with other counselling student researchers. We have divided them into three sections: *Starting out, Doing the research,* and *Writing it up and getting it finished.*

Starting out

There was lots of advice about how to go about choosing your research topic. The most common was:

- Pick a topic that fits in with your ethos as a counsellor, either in an area of practice that you're interested in or in a particular client group; this will make it easier to stay motivated.
- Be clear about what is achievable. As one student commented: *'... be realistic about what we can achieve, you know it can't take five years, we've only got 2 to 3.'*

To help get you thinking about subject areas that might be of interest to you, Chapter 3 has lots of advice and suggestions on this topic.

Doing the research

The biggest message that trainees wanted to get across about actually doing their research was that everything takes much longer than you might predict. In particular, both ethical approval and participant recruitment can take longer than novice researchers assume. Both are, at least partly, out of the researchers' control, but one student had a top tip when thinking about ethics and recruitment and applying for ethical approval:

- *'Make your recruitment pool as wide as possible, your recruitment process as wide as possible, because it just saves so much agro later. Don't think that "yeah, this is a great idea". It may well be but, just in case, save yourself before you make the mistake!'*

This strategy means that if your original recruitment strategy doesn't work, you can widen it out without having to reapply for ethics clearance.

The other part of the research that swallows up huge amounts of time is transcribing. Students reported their experience that it can take 4–6 hours to transcribe one hour of audio. If you are using a qualitative methodology, our students' advice was also to transcribe as soon as possible after doing your interviews: *'I would say transcribe as soon as possible, after interviews ... because it doesn't get better, just do it as soon as possible, just make yourself do it.'* Students commented that it made transcription easier and more accurate when the interview was fresher in memory. They said that transcribing immediately can also help the researcher refine their questions and iron out any problems. Of course, the same point can be made about entering quantitative data in a timely manner – it is time consuming and boring, but don't put it off!

And, after taking all that time transcribing and data entering, back up your work! This was an essential top tip that was reiterated by many of our students: 'definitely back up your work as well! You know ... back it up everywhere! ... A million times!' There are plenty of free systems available on the web. Or get into the habit of emailing copies of your work to yourself.

A list of technical top tips has been provided in Information box 17.2.

Information box 17.2   Technical top tips collated from focus groups with novice researchers

- *Try using a paper and pencil or mind-mapping software to brainstorm ideas*
- *Use hyperlinks when typing up notes so that you can link back to the papers/ pdfs that you are making notes on*
- *Save all files by date (rather than version number)*
- *Back up, back up, back up! (preferably in different places)*
- *Use referencing management software to ease the work of creating a bibliography (see Chapter 4)*

Writing it up and getting it finished

The main tip for writing up your research was to break it down into manageable chunks and take it one piece at a time: 'Another, kind of, top tip to people is to ... I found, you know, breaking it down, writing an introduction, 8,000 words, this section, this amount.' Our novice researchers reported that this was especially important for qualitative research: 'When I felt a bit overwhelmed was with the analysis. I was like "alright, OK, I've got 10,000 words [to write], what the hell am I going to write"?' Achieving small steps (e.g. writing up one theme at a time) helps you to feel that you are making progress and builds momentum.

The other key piece of advice that our students wanted to impart was about referencing. There are lots of different software packages available to help you manage your referencing and bibliography, and most trainees regarded them as essential. We recommend that you get to grips with your preferred system before you go too far into writing up your research.

These practical tips are important, but it was interesting to discover that our students spent as much time discussing the emotional aspects of the research process as they did the practical. And these aspects comprise the next two themes.

The importance of support

One of the main themes that came from our focus groups was the importance of support. Students at every level of study can find the research process incredibly stressful. Sometimes it is the most stressful aspect of the course, perhaps because, as one student said, *'research is actually quite a lonely process'*. However, our novice researchers reported that when support is present it can make the research process more bearable, less stressful, more manageable, more interesting and even quite an exciting process. But where does this support come from? Our students identified four sources of support: friends and family, student peers, professional peers and the research tutor or supervisor. Each of these will be considered in turn, with their benefits, pitfalls and the advice the students gave to make the most of these sources of support.

The support of others can be critical to a successful research journey ...

Friends and family

It seems that, for some, the support of friends and family comes into its own when it provides the opportunity for *'having people that <u>don't</u> ask you about it, where you can go and talk about something completely different'* – thus giving you an emotional and psychological break from your work. Our participants stressed that it was important to keep a psychological and emotional balance, just as it is to balance the physical inactivity of research with something more active, as mentioned in the Self-care section (below).

Some students, however, did benefit from talking to friends and family about their work. Trying to explain it to someone who doesn't understand can aid your own thinking on your subject matter. As one student advises, *'learn to talk about your research in very simple ways, like when my mam gets on the phone she goes, "Oh well that's interesting that you're doing something on grounded theory, son. What does grounded theory mean?"'*

Student peers

Talking to your fellow students can be somewhat of a double-edged sword. Some students found that hearing other people's anxieties just added to their own: *'I think what I struggled with was hearing different people doing things because I always felt like I was not doing enough.'* Comparing yourself to others seems to be a significant pitfall to watch out for, especially if your peer group spends a lot of time discussing the course: *'It's really hard when you're in a year group of people who love to talk about it. … It's really hard to just focus on what you're doing and to keep focused. I'd have a nervous breakdown if I got too involved with other people's anxieties and stress.'*

Others, however, found comfort in knowing that everyone is in the same situation. There seems to be an element of recognition and normalising that can help to reduce anxiety levels, such as in this student's observation: *'I would say peer connection … even if it's an email, even if it's a text, even if it's just a look that says, "yeah, I'm with you".'* This can become even more important outside term time when the risk of isolation increases, leading one student to suggest: *'Make more time to get together every now and again, even if it's just to rant to people that understand the process, because it's quite hard to explain to someone outside the process why you are so stressed about a piece of work.'*

There's also another advantage to being in the same boat as everyone else, particularly when you are working on similar pieces: *'There were groups of people getting together with the same methodology and they were giving each other deadlines … then you've got a commitment to each other as you've said you're going to do something.'* An example of this for those of you doing qualitative research might be to establish a coding group where each person brings a page or two of data to be coded and the group can discuss potential codes. This is particularly useful at the beginning of the coding process and can help you to see potential codes you may have missed on your own.

Professional peers

Students may feel a real benefit in forging links with other professionals in the field (see Ellie's story below for a detailed example). Going to conferences can be an ideal opportunity to make these links (for more on this, see the section on conference presentations in Chapter 16). Although daunting, presenting your work at a conference is particularly beneficial in terms of: *'getting feedback, it might be positive, it might be challenging, it might be critical, but then it's transformed and … new knowledge is created and it's exciting. That dynamic is really exciting and that, for me, is what gives research its life.'* If it is not possible or practical to go to conferences, consider forging professional links online through networking sites such as Linked-In, Twitter and various counselling research-related blogs.

Supervisor support

Supervision (tutor support) is a critical part of the research process just as it is for the therapeutic process. The supervisor was by far the most discussed source of support for all our students. As one participant bluntly put it: *'The top tip for like anyone would be to get a decent supervisor.'* The supervisor can have a huge influence on your work and some students were concerned by the lack of research experience within the world of counselling courses: *'I think there are very few of our tutors who are actually active researchers and I think that that is a shame and I think that can show at times.'* Arrangements for research supervision vary across courses, institutions and study levels. For Doctoral-level courses, you may have up to three supervisors, with one taking the lead, at Masters level there will usually be one supervisor, whereas at undergraduate level you may even have group supervision. In some institutions you may get to choose your supervisor, in others they may be assigned to you based on your topic or methodology. Find out what the arrangements are for your course and what influence (if any) you can have over the selection of supervisor for your work.

Also, the focus group participants advised that it is important to find out what your institution's guidance is on how much support you are entitled to because this also varies. Once you have your supervisor, make sure your first meeting includes a discussion about how they and you prefer to work together. Based on our experience as chapter authors, and the experience of our participants, questions to consider include:

- How many drafts will the supervisor read and provide feedback on?
- How many times/with what frequency can you meet?
- What type of communication do you and the supervisor prefer – face-to-face, phone or email? How quickly can you expect a response?
- Do you as the student prefer frequent deadlines or more flexibility?
- What level of emotional support is expected/available? Some supervisors may not see this as part of their role.
- Where else is support available within the institution? Some institutions will offer support for researchers at the library, in learning centres or in graduate schools.

It is better to negotiate these issues at the beginning of the relationship than to deal with disappointments and misunderstandings later in the process. Many students initially found it difficult to ask their supervisor for help and stressed the importance of getting over this block: *'You have to have a good working relationship with them and I think you've got to get the most out of them.'* Learning to be assertive about your supervision seemed a key learning point for many people, along with taking responsibility for your learning and (depending on your level of study) *'not expecting to be spoon fed'* by the supervisor. It is vitally important not to avoid your supervisor so *'if you start to hide from them because you're embarrassed, actually go and have a meltdown and 20 minutes later you feel a bit more contained and have a new plan of action.'* If the situation is reversed and you feel like your supervisor is avoiding you, chase them, keep emailing them and one student went so far as to say *'hound them if you have to! Chase them until you've got the help you need.'*

Some students felt that sharing your plan with your supervisor helps to set deadlines and they stressed the importance at each meeting of setting the date for the next meeting in order to keep you on track. One key top tip was that each time you meet with your supervisor, it is good practice to write up brief notes afterwards, including any action points that were agreed. Then email your notes to the supervisor for agreement or comment, keeping a copy for yourself. This can ensure that you both have the same understanding of what was discussed and agreed.

PAUSE FOR REFLECTION   FROM ISOLATION TO CONNECTION – ELLIE'S STORY

Read the following extract and think about what resonates – or not – with you.

I felt totally alone and there was a sense of utter panic. ... My mates didn't want to hear about euthanasia, they didn't want to hear about whether I should use interpretive phenomenological analysis or narrative analysis, they just sort of glazed over and said, 'shall we get drunk tonight?' ... In retrospect I see how desperate I was to connect with other researchers ... someone who would give me guidance ... I was so desperate I went on the internet and found a professor in America who I linked with. ... She wasn't very full-on, she didn't require deadlines, but she had those conversations that were like, 'oh I'm really hacked off, I've been alone reading all this or I've been transcribing and my neck's killing me, I've got a headache, I'm dizzy, I haven't seen my mates, I haven't been to the gym, my life is closing in'. ... I think having that dialogue, meeting other professionals, going to conferences, actually networking with other researchers, is brilliant. I spent a month in Europe with researchers in human medicine who were looking at euthanasia ... and suddenly I wasn't a freak, we were all talking death and assisted suicide and heuristics and phenomenology. ... It was so liberating to do that and to go to a specialist conference for your subject and to actually hear other people talking about their journeys and to see their finished research, it's really motivating and brings you out of that bubble.

What is clear in terms of accessing all these forms of support is the need to talk: *'Pushing yourself to talk to people about it is good.'* In asking for the support you need and are entitled to, however, it may be important to keep a sense of yourself and what you are doing, as one student summed up: *'Ask for help, but take it with a pinch of salt, knowing that your journey might be very different to someone else's.'* In that spirit, remember the tips above may not work for some and that it is important for you to find your own solution.

Self-care and knowing your style

Nearly all the student groups we spoke to were keen to stress the importance of 'self-care' and self-acceptance as well as developing practical techniques and approaches that work for you.

Practical things that help

Some practical things that some of our students found helpful were:

- Make your study environment pleasant – plants, pictures, etc.
- Have boundaries around your work: *'I use behavioural techniques around my desk, I don't do other things at my desk apart from study, don't watch dvds, I don't read books, so when I sit down at that desk it's like my brain fits in to study mode.'*
- *'Make sure you're eating enough and drinking enough, because I think it's really easy for all that stuff to get lost.'*
- Take regular breaks: *'Sometimes I'll study for four hours and then I'm knackered, I can't do anything. Whereas, if I had taken a break every 40 minutes I could have gone for six hours, instead of four hours, and I could do more the next day.'*

Understand what to sacrifice!

A lot of students will have a vast array of commitments, whether these are personal commitments, family commitments, client contact hours to complete, additional coursework, reflective journals... the list goes on and on. Our student participants – and we ourselves – recommend that before the start of the research process it is important to think carefully about all of these commitments and how they will fit with your commitment to completing your research journey. As one student who was nearing the end of her research project reflected: '*I think my biggest struggle was realising that you can't have everything. So I think you have to sit down before final year and think: What's important? What will let me get through this? And it's hard because you have to let go of really good things, but I think that that's the thing about final year.*'

Know how you work

Students in the focus groups stressed that it is really helpful to acknowledge how we tend to work. Some people are 'grazers' – the type of person who works in short bursts by doing a small amount every day – while others are 'bingers' – those who tend to set aside longer periods, maybe a couple of days, to get work done. One is not necessarily better than the other; however, it is really helpful to be aware of how you work. Having this awareness gives us the ability to plan ahead and structure our days, weeks and months so we can get the most amount of work done. As one of the participants in the focus groups commented: '*I'm definitely a binger in that I* [break tasks] *into something small and lock myself away for a couple of days with a very small goal. I'm not someone who can pick it up for half an hour, an hour every day when I get home from work.*'

Along with knowing your working *style*, it is important to be aware of your relationship to deadlines. A lot of students find it useful to plan ahead so they know if they are on course to meet the overall project deadline. But for others who prefer to work at the last minute, too many deadlines just create anxiety: '*Everyone in my group was overrunning on deadlines and writing up research in the summer. And I really needed a break, and with all the academic rigour that had gone on before, the pressure got too much.*' And remember that students can have mini-meltdowns just before they are due to hand in their research. Holding this in mind may help when, at the end of the journey, we question whether there are fundamental flaws in our project: whether our results are too obvious, whether we should have picked a different method of analysis! These uncertainties are all part of the ever-changing research process.

Conclusion

We hope that some of these 'top tips' from your fellow students prove useful during your own research journey. Even though all three of us were already part-way through our own research at the time we carried out the focus groups, we certainly gleaned lots of helpful and encouraging information by talking to other counselling students. We have boiled down the things we thought were most helpful into four of our most cherished top tips – and we hope that our summary of these in Information box 17.3 will prove useful to you too.

Information box 17.3   The four 'breaks'

→ **Break it down – set mini goals!**

Without trying to be too CBT or anything ... set SMART goals (i.e. be Specific, and Measurable, Achievable, Realistic and Time-bound) because setting yourself targets, such as 'I will do the analysis by the end of the week', is a massive goal.

→ **Take breaks!**

→ **Break through the guilt about taking time off!**

'If I take the weekend off, I feel guilty. Even if I know I deserve it, I feel so guilty.' Break through the guilt and give yourself some time off when needed. This is really important and will lead to increased productivity in the long run.

→ **Break the isolation!**

You can consciously do things to break that isolation in order to look after yourself.

Suggestions for further reading

Kasket, E. & Gil-Rodriguez, E. (2011). The identity crisis in trainee counselling psychology research. *Counselling Psychology Review, 26(4),* 20–30.

   A critique of trainee counselling psychology research which argues that there is a lack of ambition in the way in which supervisors and trainees approach Doctoral research. It's worth reading as a primer before thinking about the focus of your research.

Moran, P. (2011). Bridging the gap between research and practice in counselling and psychotherapy training: Learning from trainees. *Counselling and Psychotherapy Research, 11*, 171–178.

Worth reading for the analysis of what research training students would find useful. Send a copy to your course leaders!

Widdowson, M. (2012). Perceptions of psychotherapy trainees of psychotherapy research. *Counselling and Psychotherapy Research, 12(3)*, 178–186.

An interesting paper that looks at how negative perceptions of research among trainees affects engagement. It also asks what it would take to increase enthusiasm for research among counselling and psychotherapy trainees.

EIGHTEEN

Next steps: Building on and using research in training and practice

Dr Peter Stratton (Professor Emeritus, Leeds University),
Dr Naomi Moller (Open University) &
Dr Andreas Vossler (Open University)

Introduction

The aim of this final chapter of this book is twofold. We will look back at the journey so far and draw together the different strands and topics from the book. We will also look ahead and support you to establish your own unique relationship with research and motivate you to continue your research journey in the future. We have peppered the chapter with activities and pauses for reflection and we hope that you will take up their invitation, as doing so will help you to engage with the material and foster your self-identification as a researcher.

To start with, given that this is the final chapter of the book, it makes sense to revisit the starting point – reasons for being engaged with research, a topic introduced in Chapter 1 (see Activity 1.1 and the section on 'Reasons to engage with research'). It seems important to reiterate these reasons as the level of research engagement among counsellors and psychotherapists is still low (see the discussion on the 'research–practice' gap in Chapter 2 and McDonnell, Stratton, Butler & Cape, 2012), which is worrying given the tremendous importance of research in counselling and psychotherapy for the discipline as a whole (see Chapter 1).

Reasons to engage with research – revisited

> **PAUSE FOR REFLECTION**
>
> Look back at Activity 1.1 and the list you made of the reasons why it is important for trainees and practitioners to be informed about research or to do research themselves. Now that you have read the book, which of these reasons do you think are most important for you personally to become more actively involved in research in counselling and psychotherapy?

In setting the scene at the beginning of the book (Chapter 1), we presented you with arguments as to why research matters for the profession, and why trainees and practitioners should become actively involved in research in counselling and psychotherapy. These arguments were clustered in three thematic groups – moral, financial and professional. Let's have a second look at these and related arguments, this time grouped into reasons to be research *active*, and reasons to be research *aware*.

Reasons to be research active

This book is aimed at supporting and encouraging trainees of counselling and psychotherapy as well as established practitioners who have not yet engaged in research to undertake their own research. And, as we have seen, there are moral, financial and professional reasons to be research active. Doing research is:

- Critical for the survival (worst case) and the expansion (best case) of the profession – as discussed in Chapter 1 (financial argument), there is no question that funding of counselling and psychotherapy services is in part tied to the availability of research evidence for their effectiveness.
- Critical to ensure the continuing availability of a wide range of approaches to treatment. A wide range of treatments is important as research suggests that clients do better in therapy when they have some choice about the treatment approach (Swift, Callahan, Ivanovic & Kominiak, 2013) and that different clients benefit from different types of treatment (Cooper, 2008). However, many forms of practice that do not have a clear research base are at funding risk. An example of this comes from the British Association of Counselling and Psychotherapy, the biggest national professional body for counsellors. The BACP clearly state on their website (www.bacpresearchfoundation.org.uk/members_information.php) that concern over the side-lining of counselling as a treatment for depression led them to commission their own research in 2013 (Barkham, 2013).What caused them most concern? NICE guidelines that stated that anyone recommending counselling for those with persistent sub-threshold depression symptoms or mild to moderate depression must 'discuss with the person the uncertainty of the effectiveness of counselling ... in treating depression' (National Collaborating Centre for Mental Health, 2009, p. 23). However, just because empirical evidence does not exist *yet*, does not mean the therapy is not effective.
- Critical for practitioners since, as we have seen in Chapter 1 (professional argument), research provides us with a means by which we can each improve our own practice. This means research activity can contribute to both career development and the development of practitioner competencies – and, most importantly, better practice is of course also beneficial for clients. Research is also critical for employment prospects for practitioners, impacting the number of jobs as well as the type of jobs (e.g. jobs offered only in favoured approaches to therapy).

- Critical for funders – the politicians and commissioners of counselling and psychotherapy services, those whose job it is to advise where resources are directed, need knowledge produced by research in order to make the most effective funding and policy decisions, most especially at times when funding is tight.

Slightly less obviously, or at least to some, more contentiously, research also has a crucial role in the development of counselling and psychotherapy. We do not yet know enough about how psychotherapy works and the conditions in which it is of most value to clients (Cooper, 2008). In addition, research enables core theoretical concepts to be carefully evaluated. For example, there is substantial empirical evidence for the psychodynamic idea of transference, including research evidence for the importance of managing counter-transference reactions (e.g. see Hayes, Gelso & Hummel, 2011), but little for Freud's ideas of psychosexual stages.

Reasons to be research aware

For all the reasons mentioned above, we believe that counsellors and psychotherapists in general need to be doing (more) research. Yet this is not enough in itself. In addition to being research *active*, this book is arguing that practitioners in general also need to become more research *aware*. This is because the most active researcher is likely to be only engaged in doing research in a few areas and yet as a practitioner they may encounter a great range of presenting problems or types of client. This means that a narrow but in-depth research understanding in a particular area should be complemented by a broader research awareness.

However, and as outlined in Chapter 2, practitioners often prefer to rely on their own experience, and on supervision and consultation with others, and rarely in surveys cite research as a source of practice information. As Castonguay et al. (2010, p. 346) state, it can be assumed that 'the practice of many full-time psychotherapists is rarely or non-substantially influenced by research'. This lack of research awareness in the profession is problematic because it prevents practitioners from learning from systematic investigation by others, because it cuts practitioners off from potentially useful guidance about how best to work with particular presenting issues or clients, and because it allows therapists to continue doing as they have always done without considering if this is the best way to work. Becoming research aware is also important if a practitioner is to understand how to make arguments (e.g. within their service or at a national level), for thoughtful consideration of the research base in counselling and psychotherapy, e.g. to counter beliefs that only certain types of therapy are empirically supported. Finally, we also believe that a commitment to developing research awareness is an ethical issue. Core BACP ethical principles, such as *beneficence* (a commitment to the client's well-being), demand not ignoring a rigorous and peer-reviewed source of information on best practice (see Chapter 8, and Bond, 2010).

PAUSE FOR REFLECTION

You might have started reading this book feeling quite dubious about research in counselling and psychotherapy. You might have been reading this book mostly looking for support in doing a course-mandated piece of research. But here we are arguing that research engagement is a moral, ethical and professional issue for all counsellors and psychotherapists. What do you think? Are you convinced by the arguments of this and other chapters?

Comment

All of the authors of chapters in this book personally value research in counselling and psychotherapy. As such, the book is a bit of a manifesto to encourage you to get reading and doing research. But we also recognise that each practitioner will have their own values and preferences – about practice of course, but also about the importance they place on research. We want to encourage you to be a critical reader (see Chapter 4) of this book and identify your own views, not only about research in the field in general, but also about the types of research you most enjoy and value.

Evidence-based practice and practice-based evidence – a plea for a better balance

This book argues for the value of research in counselling and psychotherapy, and in this chapter we also argue more specifically for the value of a particular type of research, practice-based evidence (PBE). Chapter 1 summarised the evidence-based practice (EBP) versus the practice-based-evidence debate, as well as the arguments about randomised controlled trials (RCTs) and whether they should be considered (as currently) as the best form of evidence for therapy effectiveness. The political, social and therapeutic importance of this debate was underlined, and it was stated that neither paradigm alone is sufficient to build a robust knowledge base for the counselling and psychotherapy profession. However, in responding to the problems with the dominant EBP approach (see Information box 18.1), which is driven by the output of professional researchers, this chapter wants to go further and argue for a better balance between both movements. More emphasis is needed on PBE, which is often created by teams of counsellors and psychotherapists working in practice, in order to integrate research with practice (Barkham, Hardy & Mellor-Clark, 2010).

Information box 18.1 Responding to the problems with evidence-based practice – by Professor Peter Stratton

I would argue that a much broader perspective on what constitutes 'good' research is possible than that which is currently dominant. Current 'official' recommendations have the disadvantage that they can give an impression that only one paradigm of research is worth doing. And that paradigm, the randomised controlled trial, was developed for clearly diagnosed medical conditions for which there were two or more plausible treatments that could be administered in standard form. Not a situation that has much relevance for the everyday work of counsellors and psychotherapists (see discussion in Chapter 1).

Almost inevitably, a narrow definition of acceptable research has resulted in a narrow definition of forms of therapy that have so far been able to demonstrate their success within the 'gold standard'. At present, NICE guidance is overwhelmingly for varieties of cognitive-behavioural therapies. Sadly, it has been convenient for NICE guidance to be interpreted in rigid and restrictive ways, a process that is helped by only attending to the summary guidance that NICE provides. NICE itself says that it values a wide range of research approaches, stresses the importance of involving clients in the research and offers useful caveats about the limitations of evidence and the need for more research. Unfortunately, this wider perspective does not survive into the summary recommendations and, as NICE itself (National Collaborating Centre for Mental Health, 2012, p. 113) recognises, 'many people read only the recommendations'. In addition, some statements by NICE are designed to prevent any provision that is not specifically recommended. For example, therapists should warn every patient if they are using an approach that is not supported by evidence, and 'If evidence of effectiveness is either lacking or too weak for reasonable conclusions to be reached, the Guideline Development Group may recommend that particular interventions are used within the NHS only in the context of research' (National Collaborating Centre for Mental Health, 2012, p. 113). The current outcome of these pressures for simplicity and conformity is of a severe narrowing of the forms of research under consideration, and of the forms of therapy being made available in formats such as Improving Access to Psychological Therapies (IAPT). It is as if in the wish to find a universal answer to client needs, a 'one size fits all' provision has in fact become 'size 8 works for more people than any other size, so that is all we stock, and if it doesn't fit you, that is too bad'.

What we can take from this rather gloomy analysis is that those who call the shots need to be given good reasons before they will think differently. But it is easy for the research-minded experts who pronounce on what therapy the population needs to disregard practitioners when counselling and psychotherapy have a reputation for ignoring research. Especially when that

(Continued)

(Continued)

reputation is to some extent justified. We certainly need to make the case for the good research evidence that we already have, but it will not be enough for involvement with research to be left to a few research specialists. We need the great majority of practitioners to become research-informed as argued by Karam and Sprenkle (2010), and to begin contributing to practice-based evidence, starting with the readers of this handbook.

We are making an argument for a better balance between EBP and PBE because research created by practitioners, ideally in collaboration with their clients, is in our view more likely to have value for improving practice and to be informative about the factors that influence whether therapy, as it is actually conducted in real-world settings, will be effective. But the PBE argument is only as strong as the availability of research that is driven by practitioners. So our motivation is to do whatever we can to encourage our readers to extend their involvement in this type of research, and to value this research for its potential to directly feed into their practice.

Research is a many splendoured thing

We have been discussing the ways in which the context shapes which research is recognised and valorised. But let us not be colonised by current constrained thinking; there is in fact a glorious diversity of forms of useful research, and of valuable and effective ways of researching therapy. You will remember the potential sources of inspiration for research ideas, and the guidance through the process of finding a research question, which were provided in Chapter 3. And at the end of this book you will hopefully also be aware of the great variety of choices that are available regarding design, method and sample for research projects, as presented in Chapter 7, and the chapters on the different methodologies and methods for doing research (Chapter 6 and the chapters in Part III). But just in case you are still struggling to think of a way to contribute to the body of useful and valuable research in the field, here we present a few more ideas.

We could, for example, start from the entirely legitimate wish to know whether the achievements of different forms of counselling and psychotherapy justify the cost, a wish that is most clearly expressed by the move to 'payment by results' (see Chapter 10 and www.iapt.nhs.uk/pbr/). In the UK, both the Child and Adolescent Mental Health Services (CAMHS) Outcomes Research Consortium (CORC) and the Children and Young Persons component of the Improving Access to Psychotherapy programme (CYP-IAPT) are committed to measuring the outcomes of therapy. In the USA a parallel development is of 'value-based purchasing' (Jordan, VanLare & Conway, 2012). That is fine until

Table 18.1 *Four researchable aspects of counselling and psychotherapy*

	Examples of aspects that could be explored
Factors outside the therapy session	1. Sources of referral 2. *How cases are allocated* 3. Service drop-out rate 4. Aspects of organisation's therapists (e.g. gender, ethnicity, experience) 5. Aspects of organisation's clients (e.g. socio-economics, level of distress) 6. Therapist turnover in terms of how long they stay in the service 7. Client reports on overall satisfaction with the service
Factors inside the therapy session	1. Micro processes in therapy (e.g. number and length of silences) 2. Air time given to different types of theme or content 3. Use of particular techniques (e.g. Socratic questioning or interpretation) 4. *How a specific manualised therapy is implemented* 5. How therapists 'do' a therapeutic approach 6. How therapies are integrated with other provision (e.g. mindfulness) 7. Indications of relationship/alliance with the therapist 8. Client reports of satisfaction with their therapy
The client	1. *Diagnoses of mental illness* 2. Membership of a broad diagnostic group such as anxiety and depression 3. Client specification of goal of therapy 4. Additional complication (e.g. chronic physical condition) 5. Life course events (e.g. childhood maltreatment) 6. Significant current relationships or lack thereof 7. Education, economic or social circumstances 8. Age, gender, ethnicity, sexuality, socio-economic status, etc.
Therapy outcome	1. *Outcome related to a particular condition such as depression or anxiety* 2. Outcome related to a general symptom measure 3. Changes in objective measures (weight, drug use) 4. Changes in overall psychological functioning 5. Changes in well-being 6. Changes in relationships 7. Open-ended exploration of what client feels is/is not different following therapy

we start to say what results we are going to measure, which is where it begins to get much more complicated, as indicated in Table 18.1.

Table 18.1 delineates four broad areas that could be relevant to researching the effects of counselling and psychotherapy. For each area there is a very incomplete list of aspects that could be explored – some of these are very specific (e.g. changes in weight during therapy) and some are more general (e.g. the client's experience of therapy). You could use this chart to plot a research study. As outlined in Chapter 1, a randomised controlled trial specifies how cases should be allocated (randomly, and not, for example, by a case conference or multi-professional team meeting), and in RCTs the therapy for at least one group would typically be a well-defined form of therapy, normally as specified in a manual (e.g. CBT). Clients are selected into the RCT on the basis of having a clear diagnosis (e.g. a phobia), usually based on the *DSM 5* (APA, 2013). The outcome measure would be a proven quantitative measure of improvement for that condition (e.g. the Agoraphobia – Mobility Inventory). This combination is highlighted in Table 18.1 (in italics) by selecting one appropriate item from each section. However, endless alternative research designs can be mapped onto the chart.

Activity 18.1   Generating potential research ideas

If you have an idea for a research project you would like to see happening, you could try the exercise of mapping it onto the chart (Table 18.1). Another idea would be to generate a random four-digit number, use it to select an item from the four sections of the chart, and play with designing useful research for that sequence. Or take items in any of the sections that interest you and look at the connections that would suggest alternative research designs. For example, if you are interested in what difference the gender of the therapist might make, you are using a psychodynamic approach, and you are wondering about a difference in happiness and well-being, you could use the list of client aspects to think about what it might be interesting to explore – e.g. does the gender of the therapist make more difference in psychodynamic therapy focused on promoting client well-being when the client has a history of child maltreatment?

Comment

The intention of this activity is to push you to think about the endless opportunities and possibilities offered by research in counselling and psychotherapy. It can also be a source of inspiration when looking for a research question (see Activity 3.1: Realms of inspiration, in Chapter 3) or a tool to examine broad research ideas and whittle them down to researchable questions (similar to the 'looking through lenses' technique introduced in Chapter 3).

The research cycle

The thesis being argued in this chapter, and throughout the book, is that trainees and practitioners need to engage in research broadly (by reading it) and specifically (by doing it) because of the benefits this brings for individual clients and practitioners as well as for the practice of counselling and psychotherapy more broadly. This mutually beneficial relationship is depicted in Figure 18.1, which shows a Mobius strip, a 3-D shape that has a curious property. The image illustrates a desired interwoven and inseparable relationship between research and practice – feeding into each other in an endless loop.

Another way of thinking of this loop is by thinking about the stages for any research project. We start our research journeys typically from a grand vision

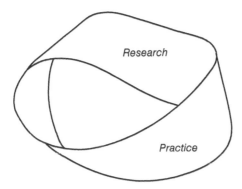

Figure 18.1 *Desired relationship between research and practice*

which must be progressively focused down on our objective; as you get into the research process, attention becomes more and more narrowed while you work to implement the methodology. However, as you emerge from the data gathering and analysis stages, it is time to widen the vision once again to make the best possible use of what you have created, and to consider how to bring it back to the wider world, as discussed in Chapter 16 which examined the process of dissemination.

Developing your own research identity

This aim of this chapter, and implicitly the whole book, is to encourage you to be a researcher – not just for the sake of one special project or so that you can gain your degree, but as part of your professional role. We hope, however, that by this point in the book you understand that being a researcher is something that comes pretty naturally to counsellors and psychotherapists, who are intrinsically motivated to understand their clients better and to want to work most effectively to help them. In addition to this natural curiosity, there is a strong correspondence between the skills of therapists and the skills of researchers, with many skills, values and qualities of counsellors and psychotherapists being transferable to the research arena (see Chapter 12; Finlay & Evans, 2009; Stratton & Hanks, 2008). Yet, just as each therapeutic relationship is unique, so too is it both desirable and necessary for each practitioner to formulate their own unique relationship with research.

If you are thinking about how to develop your own personal research identity, one place to start is to think about the way that you practise therapy and what approaches to doing research might or might not be compatible with that. For example, Chapter 6 reviewed different approaches to 'knowing' (epistemology) that have relevance for both therapy and research, and as Chapter 12 outlined, where you stand epistemologically will in turn predispose you to certain kinds of research methods. Of course, creating coherence between your approach to practice and your approach to research is not so easy, as documented in a paper by Peter Martin (Martin, 2005).

PAUSE FOR REFLECTION: ANALOGIES BETWEEN THERAPEUTIC AND RESEARCH RELATIONSHIPS

Think about your approach to working with clients. What do you prioritise and think is most important? How might this translate into how you might engage in research?

Comment

It can help to keep in mind what research has told us about what is most functional in the therapeutic relationship and then look for parallels in your relationship with research.

- There is a lot of empirical evidence that the therapeutic alliance is positively related to therapy outcome (e.g. Norcross, 2011). Would you say that your current alliance with research is positive? In what way? If it is not, perhaps it is time to start challenging this.
- Therapy is not 'done to' a passive client, and conducting a successful therapy changes the therapist. Think about the extent to which your relationship with research is reciprocal. Do you gain from research as a practitioner and does counselling and psychotherapy research gain from you?
- Research suggests that therapy should attend closely to cultural issues to build effective therapeutic relationships (Smith, Domenech Rodriguez & Bernal, 2011), avoid discrimination and capitalise on the psychological support that each different culture offers (Johannes & Erwin, 2004). Therapists must therefore cultivate a high level of respect for each culture they encounter, while avoiding creating distance by disparaging or exoticising it. If we think of research as a kind of culture, what does this mean? Are you respectful and tolerant of different types of research (culture)? Do you seek open communication across research culture barriers?
- As discussed in Chapter 1, one of the important factors that contributes to successful therapy outcome is a shared belief that the therapy will be effective (Snyder, Michael & Cheavens, 1999). Do you present yourself to your clients with a confidence that your work together will be effective? Could a greater knowledge of the research that supports aspects of your practice help with your level of confidence? Would your confidence have a stronger foundation if you drew on research findings wherever possible to improve your practice?

Another way to develop your own research identity is to think about aspects in your practice or training that could benefit from research and research findings. You could start by going back to the therapy–research connections mentioned above and consider how your own approach to therapy plays out. For example, in what ways does your therapy approach help you cultivate an alliance with the client? How does your approach to practice make use of events in the client's life? Then start thinking of research that you know about, research that would give you greater insight into these processes, or ways of enhancing them. The chances are that research already exists for some of these topics. How might you go about finding out more about this research?

Activity 18.2   Research in everyday life

This is an invitation to actively notice, over the next 24 hours, how much of your life is, in practice, impacted by research. Your choice of car, toothbrush, diet, is a product of your use of other people's research. Notice how many news and current affairs stories, web pages, newspapers, magazines, and blogs, derive their content and their energy from research.

Comment

We want to suggest that an engagement with research in every aspect of your life can feed into your stance towards research in psychotherapy and counselling. Or, more bluntly, why do you think it is that many therapists value research in so many aspects of their lives yet do not value it in their work?

Finally, in developing your own relationship with research it will be helpful to share your thoughts and experiences with other practitioners or trainees. Therapy with couples, groups and families (especially therapy with several families at the same time – Multifamily therapy, Asen, 2002) suggests that involving others with whom you have a relationship is highly effective in achieving active and lasting engagement, and can be more fun. Research into reflective adult learning (see Stratton, 2005) also stresses the importance of processing knowledge in conjunction with fellow learners. So, in line with suggestions in Chapter 4 and by the trainees in Chapter 17, we suggest that you engage with the contents of this chapter, wherever you can, with a friendly colleague. If you do so, there is the added bonus that you will be doing them a favour by helping them learn too. You could have a conversation in which you both revisit the ideas you had when reading the first two chapters and thinking about reasons to be more engaged with research. What, if anything, has changed in your attitudes as a result of reading this book? Or you could discuss situations where you noticed in your practice or training that a research finding or idea was, or could have been, helpful.

PAUSE FOR REFLECTION   PERSONAL RESEARCH OBJECTIVES

As a reader of this book, you want to engage with research. But what does that mean, specifically, for you? If you are going to increase your involvement with research, it is a good idea to be clear about what you hope to achieve. So take a few minutes to think about what your research objectives are for you right now? What about in a year?

Comment

Your objectives might be quite pragmatic, such as completing a piece of course work. Or they might be aspirational, such as making a difference to your client group. You could go back to Chapter 3 and check out the ideas and techniques about formulating a research question and use this to help you create your personal objectives in relation to research.

Making research part of your (professional) life

By this stage, we hope that you are well equipped to engage with research in the way that is most relevant for you. So let's take a bit of time to work on what that is. At the beginning of the book we provided you with ideas and examples of how research can be used to inform and enhance training and practice in counselling and psychotherapy (Chapter 2). Here is an additional set of suggestions to help you become excited about the prospect of becoming (more) involved with research. You may well already be some way down the list, but hopefully there is something here to take everybody to the next stage.

- Find an instrument to record the progress of your clients and use it to audit your practice (see Chapter 10 for more on how to select an instrument). Explore using the instrument clinically, because there is a strong case for clinical or therapeutic uses of outcome measures (Finn, 2009; Poston & Hanson, 2010). Also experiment with using the information to help you track if the therapy is drifting off course, since we have seen in Chapter 1 that there is evidence that counsellors and psychotherapists are often not able to predict the outcomes of therapy (see Lambert, 2010). You could use simple statistical methods (see Chapters 10 and 11) to explore how your clients (as a group) seem to be responding to counselling or therapy with you. You could also compare your data with those of colleagues and published sources (benchmarking, see Chapter 10).
- Transcribe one of your client sessions. It is amazing how much more you can see in a transcript of a session that you fail to notice at the time or while listening to or viewing a recording. And this is before you unleash the power of highly developed techniques like thematic analysis (see Chapter 13). You could also use session transcripts to begin to build the evidence for a pragmatic case study analysis (see Chapter 15).

- Discuss with colleagues whether it might be useful to research your own practice or training context. Explore the possibilities of doing this with a multidisciplinary staff group. This could include coherently gathering user perceptions of the service. You could also recruit service users to help you plan and design the research.
- Join or create a practitioner research network (PRN). UKCP has been putting significant resources into setting up PRNs so please check the website for current information and to gain ideas of what you might want to set up. See www.psychotherapy.org.uk/research_faculty.html.
- Join an existing group of researchers – contact a local university, or use the literature to identify interesting projects, and then make contact with the researchers and offer to become involved. This does not have to be local; one of Peter's groups includes colleagues in Tasmania.

Activity 18.3   The benefits of involvement in research

We have listed below different levels of involvement in research in counselling and psychotherapy. For each of these, consider the potential benefits for:

1. *your career*
2. *your practice (including, critically, benefit for your clients)*
3. *the broader counselling and psychotherapy profession*

As a second step, write down your own aspirations for each level of engagement. What might be a goal for you in each area?

- *Hearing about research in websites and social media*
- *Attending conferences and more generally talking with colleagues about research*
- *Reading about research in the broader therapy literature*
- *Reading research articles*
- *Using existing measures to audit your own therapy*
- *Offering your therapy material to a research project*
- *Joining or starting a practitioner research network*
- *Joining a research project*
- *Undertaking your own research project*
- *Utilising your expertise as a trainer*

The fact is that research can easily be seen as a luxury or, worse, a slightly threatening luxury, and so is easily pushed out by other pressures. We therefore want to invite you to make a concrete and realistic plan for how you will ensure that your work, and your life, receives the continuing benefit that involvement with research can confer. Concretely, what would you have to do less of if you were to devote one hour each week to research? Would what you give up be as valuable to your work, and as much fun, as the research hour? Of course not, so which hour is it going to be? Perhaps you could make a concrete plan of the space you will create each week to find out about research that could be useful for your practice, and create the opportunities to pursue your own research interests. This plan is an aspiration, so write it down and keep it visible. Put entries in your diary, reminders on your IT system, tell any colleague you have been working through this book with and ask them to remind you at intervals of your research ambitions.

Issues for training courses

We have been focused so far in this handbook on trainees and practitioners. However, it would be remiss of us not to address trainers also. Training courses are a context in which research should play a major role. But our experience as trainers is that coverage, and even encouragement of research, is extremely varied across training programmes. Weissman and Sanderson (2002) talk of a relative failure to incorporate research into training – either as a basis for what is taught, or as an inspiration that will carry past the end of the course so that practitioners will be committed to research.

As discussed in Chapter 1, the professional bodies that accredit counselling and psychotherapy training have responded to this issue by requiring trainees to engage in research and for courses to be research-informed. Despite this, there is still patchy engagement with this agenda, in part because many courses do not have any staff who are themselves research-informed. However, there are ways to foster research awareness and research engagement in training settings and here we make some recommendations, in addition to those already made in Chapter 2 (see Table 2.1).

PAUSE FOR REFLECTION

As you read the recommendations for training, think about your own training. Where does it not/has it not met these recommendations? Are there things you could do to make up the deficiencies?

1. The starting point must be that the research background of each aspect of training should be an intrinsic part of that training. For example, trainees should be required to undertake a search for relevant and useful research findings as they take on clients for supervised practice – e.g. examining the research on working effectively with depression with a person-centred approach if that is what they are about to be doing. Trainers also should routinely incorporate research critiques into the teaching

---

of theory, examining the research evidence for the approaches that they are teaching. Overall, the key focus should be a routine use of research findings so that the ethos becomes built into the thinking of students. Creating this type of research climate in a training institute can be aided by creating research discussion groups as part of training, and setting up staff–student research groups and in-house research conferences.

2. Training courses should include enough research training so that graduates can engage in discussions with managers, other professionals, clients and with each other without embarrassment. Making trainees conduct an independent original research project is one option for doing this, but another option for a course is to provide all students with opportunities for active participation in live research project(s) during training, so that the experience is of group research engagement. A group of students working together is one example of a practitioner research network, and they do not even have to be all on the same course.

3. All trainees should be required to routinely monitor their outcomes. Live supervision does not eliminate the need for this. As discussed in Chapter 1, there is considerable evidence that practitioners are not reliable judges of their own effectiveness ('self-assessment bias'; Walfish, McAlister, O'Donnell & Lambert, 2012) and supervision does not sufficiently compensate for this. Monitoring outcomes is not in itself research, but springs naturally from an approach to training that takes research seriously. The measures chosen are less important than the message that using well-researched instruments to gather clients' considered judgement of the effectiveness of therapy is good professional practice. There is a further advantage for training courses in that data on therapist effectiveness can be part of the evaluation of whether a trainee should be passed as qualified to practise independently. It is only a part because there are many complex considerations to include in this judgement. But deciding if a trainee is 'competent' as a counsellor or psychotherapist is one of the most difficult calls that a course has to make, so this extra information should outweigh the threat to the self-esteem of the supervisors or the trainees themselves.

4. Where it is possible for trainees to complete an independent research project, courses should build in an expectation of publication of what the research has created. Some courses require the reports to be presented in the form of a journal article. They will not be directly publishable in this form but they will be on the way to being more realistically written up. Doing them in this way also gives trainees an understanding of the 'how' and 'why' of writing for journals and so will help them make best use of the literature that they read.

5. It should not be acceptable to provide training only in quantitative or only in qualitative research methods. Each has such a major contribution to make that neither can be neglected. Courses must also help students to get past the idea that they cannot cope with arithmetic and therefore that qualitative research will be easier. Qualitative research, if done rigorously enough to be useful, is tough work and often harder to get through ethics committees who may be less familiar with this approach to research.

(Continued)

(Continued)

Comment on training recommendation #3

Andreas and Naomi as book editors wondered if this was potentially a controversial suggestion, so we (very unsystematically) asked our chapter authors, who are trainers or students, for their thoughts. Those who responded were mostly in favour, but we are aware that our sample might be skewed! Some of the responses were:

> I totally agree with this sentiment (and as the author points out, so does the evidence base!). I routinely use the Session Rating Scale (Scott Miller) and wish it had been a mandatory tool in training. *Harriet Smith, Counselling Psychology Doctoral Trainee*

> I think the suggestion is excellent. Probably our best students are already doing this, and include the information in their final piece of work. The ones that probably need to, don't, and I would like to see it as compulsory part of the assessment. *Julia McLeod, trainer*

> I personally agree that it would be a good idea if trainees monitored outcomes of their clients. With regard to whether it should be taken as a part of their evaluation, it is a complex issue (for instance, client characteristic, pressures on trainees, etc.), so it would need to be thought through very carefully. *Ladislav Timulak, trainer*

Conclusion – the end of the journey is the beginning of a new one

Hopefully this final chapter has both drawn together themes and ideas from the rest of the book as well as motivated you to build on what you have read here by becoming engaged with research and developing your own research identity. Research plays a key role for theory and practice in counselling and psychotherapy, and the profession needs practice-based researchers like you.

Throughout this book we have used the metaphor of a 'journey' for the research process and its different stages, as this reflects our understanding of research as a process and a reflexive and recursive activity full of opportunities for both personal and professional development. From this perspective, the journey never ends, as the findings and implications of one research process already contain questions and ideas for the start of the next research cycle, and so on. In the same way, we hope that the end of this book is the beginning of an exciting new journey into the world of research for you...

'We can't wait for the next piece of research!'

References

Aggs, C. & Bambling, M. (2010). Teaching mindfulness to psychotherapists in clinical practice: The Mindful Therapy Programme. *Counselling and Psychotherapy Research: Linking research with practice, 10(4),* 278–286.

Alderson, P. & Morrow, V. (2011). *Research with Children and Young People.* London: Sage.

APA (American Psychological Association) (2006). Evidence-based practice in psychology. *American Psychologist, 61,* 271–285.

APA (American Psychological Association) (2009). *Manual of the American Psychological Association* (6th edition). Washington, APA.

APA (American Psychiatric Association) (2013). *Diagnostic and statistical manual of mental disorders* (5th edition). Arlington, VA: American Psychiatric Publishing.

Asen, E. (2002). Multiple family therapy: An overview. *Journal of Family Therapy, 24,* 3–16.

Ashworth, P.D. (1993). Participant agreement in the justification of qualitative findings. *Journal of Phenomenological Psychology, 24,* 3–16.

Aveline, M. (2005). Clinical case studies: Their place in evidence-based practice. *Psychodynamic Practice, 11,* 133–152.

Aveyard, H. & Sharp, P. (2013). *A Beginner's Guide to Evidence-based Practice in Health and Social Care.* Maidenhead: Open University Press.

BACP (2009). *Accreditation of Training Courses* (5th edition). Lutterworth: British Association for Counselling and Psychotherapy.

Balderson, N. & Towell, T. (2003). The prevalence and predictors of psychological distress in men with prostate cancer who are seeking support. *British Journal of Health Psychology, 8(2),* 125–134.

Baldwin, S.A. & Imel, Z.E. (2013). Therapists effects: Findings and methods. In M.J. Lambert (Ed.), *Bergin and Garfield's Handbook of Psychotherapy and Behavior Change* (6th edition) (pp. 258–297). New York: Wiley.

Barker, C., Pistrang, N. & Elliott, R. (2002). *Research Methods in Clinical Psychology: An introduction for students and practitioners* (2nd edition). Chichester: Wiley.

Barker, M. (2013). *Mindful Counselling & Psychotherapy: Practising mindfully across approaches and issues*. London: Sage.

Barkham, M. (2013). Interview with Michael Barkham. *Therapy Today* (BACP magazine). Available at: www.therapytoday.net/article/show/3751/

Barkham, M. & Barker, M. (2010). Outcome research. In M. Barker, A. Vossler & D. Langdridge (Eds), *Understanding Counselling and Psychotherapy* (pp. 281–305). London: Sage.

Barkham, M., Hardy, G. & Mellor-Clark, J. (Eds) (2010). *Developing and Delivering Practice-based Evidence: A guide for the psychological therapies*. Chichester: Wiley-Blackwell.

Barkham, M., & Margison, F. (2007). Practice-based evidence as a complement to evidence-based practice: From dichotomy to chiasmus. In C. Freeman & M. Power (Eds), *Handbook of Evidence-Based Psychotherapies: A guide for research and practice* (pp. 443–476). Chichester: Wiley.

Barkham, M., & Mellor-Clark, J. (2000). Rigour and relevance: Practice-based evidence in the psychological therapies. In N. Rowland & S. Goss (Eds), *Evidence-based Counselling and Psychological Therapies* (pp. 127–144). London: Routledge.

Barkham, M. & Mellor-Clark, J. (2003). Bridging evidence-based practice and practice-based evidence: Developing a rigorous and relevant knowledge for the psychological therapies. *Clinical Psychology and Psychotherapy, 10*, 319–327.

Barney, L.J., Griffiths, K.M., Christensen, H. & Jorm, A.F. (2009). Exploring the nature of stigmatising beliefs about depression and help-seeking: Implications for reducing stigma. *BMC Public Health, 9(61)*. Available at: www.biomedcentral.com/1471-2458/9/61

Barr, W., Hodge, S., Leeven, M., Bowen L. & Knox, P. (2012). Emotional support and counselling for people with visual impairment: Quantitative findings from a mixed methods pilot study. *Counselling and Psychotherapy Research, 12(4)*, 294–302.

Beins, B.C. & Beins, A.M. (2012). *Effective Writing in Psychology: Papers, posters and presentations* (2nd edition). Chichester: Wiley-Blackwell.

BERA (2011). *Ethical Guidelines for Educational Research*. London: British Educational Research Association.

Bewick, B.M., Trusler, K., Mullin, T., Grant, S. & Mothersole, G. (2006). Routine outcome measurement completion rates of the CORE-OM in primary care psychological therapies and counselling. *Counselling and Psychotherapy Research, 6(1)*, 33–40.

Bishop, R.M. & Bieschke, K.J. (1998). Applying social cognitive theory to interest in research among psychology doctoral students. *Journal of Counseling Psychology, 45*, 182–188.

Bohart, A.C. & Greaves Wade, A. (2013). The client in psychotherapy. In M.J. Lambert (Ed.), *Bergin and Garfield's Handbook of Psychotherapy and Behavior Change* (6th edition) (pp. 219–257). New York: Wiley.

Bohart, A.C., Tallman, K.L., Byock, G. & Mackrill, T. (2011). The 'Research Jury' Method: The application of the jury trial model to evaluating the validity of descriptive and causal statements about psychotherapy process and outcome. *Pragmatic Case Studies in Psychotherapy, 7(1)*, 101–144.

Bond, T. (2004). *Ethical Guidelines for Researching Counselling and Psychotherapy*. Rugby: British Association for Counselling and Psychotherapy. Available at: www.bacp.co.uk/research/ethical_guidelines.php on 16/6/13.

Bond, T. (2010). *Standards and Ethics for Counselling in Action* (3rd edition). London: Sage.

Bower, P. (2003). Efficacy In evidence-based practice. *Clinical Psychology and Psychotherapy*, *10*, 328–336.

Bower, P. & Gilbody, S. (2010). The current view of evidence and evidence-based practice. In M. Barkham, G. Hardy & J. Mellor-Clark (Eds), *Developing and Delivering Practice-based Evidence: A guide for the psychological therapies* (pp. 3–20). Singapore: Wiley-Blackwell.

Boyatzis, R.E. (1998). *Transforming Qualitative Information: Thematic analysis and code development*. Thousand Oaks, CA: Sage.

Braud, W.G. & Anderson, R. (Eds) (1998). *Transpersonal Research Methods for the Social Sciences: Honoring human experience*. Thousand Oaks, CA: Sage.

Braun, V. & Clarke, V. (2006). Using thematic analysis in psychology. *Qualitative Research in Psychology*, *3(2)*, 77–101.

Braun, V. & Clarke, V. (2012). Thematic analysis. In H. Cooper (Ed.), *APA Handbook of Research Methods in Psychology: Vol. 2. Research designs* (pp. 57–91). Washington, DC: American Psychological Association.

Braun, V. & Clarke, V. (2013). *Successful Qualitative Research: A practical guide for beginners*. London: Sage.

British Psychological Society (2007). *Report of the Working Party on Conducting Research on the Internet: Guidelines for ethical practice in psychological research online*. Leicester: British Psychological Society. Available at: www.bps.org.uk/publications/policy-and-guidelines/research-guidelines-policy-documents/research-guidelines-poli.

British Psychological Society (2010). *Code of Human Research Ethics*. Leicester: British Psychological Society. www.bps.org.uk/sites/default/files/documents/code_of_human_research_ethics.pdf on 16/3/13.

Brotherson, M.J. (1994). Interactive focus group interviewing: A qualitative research method in early intervention. *Topics in Early Childhood Special Education, 14*, 101–118.

Buetow, S. (2010). Thematic analysis and its reconceptualization as 'saliency analysis'. *Journal of Health Service Resesearch & Policy, 15(2)*, 123–125.

Bulik, C.M., Berkman, N.D., Brownley, K.A., Sedway, J.A. & Lohr, K.N. (2007). Anorexia nervosa treatment: A systematic review of randomized controlled trials. *International Journal of Eating Disorders, 40*, 310–320.

Castonguay, L.G., Barkham, M., Lutz, W. & McAleavey, A. (2013). Practice-oriented research: Approaches and application. In M.J. Lambert (Ed.), *Bergin and Garfield's Handbook of Psychotherapy and Behavior Change* (6th edition) (pp. 85–133). New York: Wiley.

Castonguay, L.G., Nelson, D.L., Boutselis, M.A., Chiswick, N.A., Damer, D.D., Hemmelstein, N.A., Jackson, J.A., Morford, M., Ragusea, S.A., Roper, J.G., Spayd, C., Weiszer, T. & Borkovec, T.D. (2010). Psychotherapists, researchers, or both? A qualitative analysis of psychotherapists' experiences in a practice research network. *Psychotherapy Theory, Research, Practice, Training, 47(3)*, 345–354.

Cavanagh, K., Strauss, C., Cicconi, F., Griffiths, N., Wyper, A. & Jones, F. (2013). A randomised control trial of a brief online mindfulness-based intervention. *Behaviour, Research & Therapy, 51(9)*, 573–578.

CDC (1997). US Public Health Service Syphilis Study at Tuskegee. Atlanta, GA: Centers for Disease Control and Prevention. Available at: www.cdc.gov/tuskegee/clintonp.htm on 29/7/2013.

Charmaz, K. (2006). *Constructing Grounded Theory: A practical guide through qualitative analysis*. Thousand Oaks, CA: Sage.

Clough, P. & Nutbrown, C. (2012). *A Student's Guide to Methodology* (3rd edition). London: Sage.

Cohen, J. (1988). *Statistical Power Analysis for the Behavioral Sciences* (2nd edition). Hillsdale, NJ: Erlbaum.

Cohen, J. (1992). A power primer. *Psychological Bulletin, 112(1)*, 155–159.

Cook, J., Biyanova, T. & Coyne, J.C. (2009). Barriers to adoption of new treatments: An internet study of practicing community psychotherapists. *Administration and Policy in Mental Health and Mental Health Services Research, 36*, 83–90.

Cook, T.D. & Campbell, D.T. (1979). *Quasi-experimentation: Design and analysis issues for field settings*. Boston, MA: Houghton-Mifflin.

Cooper, M. (2007). Humanizing psychotherapy. *Journal of Contemporary Psychotherapy, 37*, 11–16.

Cooper, M. (2008). *Essential Research Findings in Counselling and Psychotherapy: The facts are friendly*. London: Sage.

Cooper, M. (2009). Counselling in UK secondary schools: A comprehensive review of audit and evaluation data. *Counselling and Psychotherapy Research, 9(3)*, 137–150.

Cooper, M. (2010). The challenge of counselling and psychotherapy research. *Counselling and Psychotherapy Research, 10*, 183–191.

Cooper, M. (2011). Meeting the demand for evidence-based practice. *Therapy Today, 22*, 10–16.

CORE System Group (2010). *Benchmarks for Primary Care Counselling Services: Outcome measure completion rates*. Available at: www.coreims.co.uk/site_downloads/PC%20 Benchmarks%20-%203%20-%20Completion%20-%20final.pdf. Last accessed 30/01/13.

Coyle, A. (2006). Discourse analysis. In G.M. Breakwell, S. Hammond & C. Fife-Schaw (Eds), *Research Methods in Psychology* (3rd edition) (pp. 366–387). London: Sage.

Cresswell, J.W. (1998). *Qualitative Inquiry and Research Design: Choosing among five traditions*. Thousand Oaks, CA: Sage.

Creswell, J.W. (2003). *Research Design: Qualitative, quantitative and mixed methods approaches* (2nd edition). London: Sage.

Creswell, J.W. (2012). *Qualitative Inquiry and Research Design: Choosing among five traditions* (3rd edition). Thousand Oaks, CA: Sage.

Cronbach, L.J. (1951). Coefficient alpha and the internal structure of tests. *Psychometrika, 16(3)*, 297–334.

Daniel, T. & McLeod, D. (2006). Weighing up the evidence: A qualitative analysis of how person-centred counsellors evaluate the effectiveness of their practice. *Counselling and Psychotherapy Research, 6(4)*, 244–249.

Davis, D., Corrin-Pendry, S. & Savill, M. (2008). A follow-up study of the long-term effects of counselling in a primary care counselling psychology service. *Counselling and Psychotherapy Research, 8(2)*, 80–84.

Deane, F.P., Spicer, J. & Todd, D.M. (1997). Validity of a simplified target complaints measure. *Assessment, 4*, 119–130.

Denzin, N.K. & Lincoln, Y.S. (Eds) (1994). *Handbook of Qualitative Research*. Thousand Oaks, CA: Sage.

DH (2007). *Improving Access to Psychological Therapies: Implementation plan. National guidelines for regional delivery.* London: Department of Health.

Drew, C.J. (1980). *Introduction to Designing and Conducting Research* (2nd edition). St Louis, MO: The C.V. Mosby Company.

Eells, T. (2010). The unfolding case formulation: The interplay of description and inference. *Pragmatic Case Studies in Psychotherapy, 6(4)*, 225–254.

Elliott, M. & Williams, D. (2002). The client experience of counselling and psychotherapy. *Counselling Psychology Review, 18*, 34–39.

Elliott, R. (2001). Hermeneutic single-case efficacy design: An overview. In K.J. Schneider, J. Bugental & J.F. Pierson (Eds), *The Handbook of Humanistic Psychology: Leading edges in theory, research and practice* (pp. 315–324). Thousand Oaks, CA: Sage.

Elliott, R. (2002). Hermeneutic single case efficacy design. *Psychotherapy Research, 12*, 1–20.

Elliott, R., Fischer, C.T. & Rennie, D.L. (1999). Evolving guidelines for publication of qualitative research in psychology and related fields. *British Journal of Clinical Psychology, 38*, 215–229.

Elliott, R., Fischer, C.T. & Rennie, D.L. (2000). Also against methodolatry: A reply to Reicher. *British Journal of Clinical Psychology, 39*, 7–10.

Elliott, R., Partyka, R., Wagner, J., Alperin, R., Dobrenski, R., Messer, S.B., Watson, J.C. & Castonguay, L.G. (2000). An adjudicated hermeneutic single case efficacy design study of experiential therapy for panic/phobia. *Psychotherapy Research, 19*, 543–557.

Elliott, R., Slatick, E. & Urman, M. (2001). Qualitative change process research on psychotherapy: Alternative strategies. In J. Frommer & D.L. Rennie (Eds), *Qualitative Psychotherapy Research: Methods and methodology* (pp. 69–111). Lengerich, Germany: Pabst Science.

Elliott, R. & Timulak, L. (2005). Descriptive and interpretive approaches to qualitative research. In J. Miles & P. Gilbert (Eds), *A Handbook of Research Methods in Clinical and Health Psychology* (pp. 147–159). Oxford: Oxford University Press.

Etherington, K. (2001). Research with ex-clients: A celebration and extension of the therapeutic process. *Counselling and Psychotherapy Research, 29(1)*, 5–19.

Evans, C., Margison, F. & Barkham, M. (1998). The contribution of reliable and clinically significant change methods to evidence-based mental health. *Evidence-Based Mental Health, 1*, 70–72.

Evans, C., Mellor-Clark, J., Margison, F., Barkham, M., Audin, K., Connell, J. & McGrath, G. (2000). CORE: Clinical Outcomes in Routine Evaluation. *Journal of Mental Health, 9*, 247–255.

Eysenck, H.J. (1957). The effects of psychotherapy: An evaluation. *Journal of Consulting Psychology, 16*, 319–324.

Fairfax, H. & Barfield, J. (2010). A group-based treatment for clients with obsessive compulsive disorder (OCD) in a secondary care mental health setting: Integrating new developments within cognitive behavioural interventions – an exploratory study. *Counselling and Psychotherapy Research, 10(3)*, 214–221.

Farrimond, H. (2012). *Doing Ethical Research.* Basingstoke: Palgrave Macmillan.

Feldman, D.B. & Silvia, P.J. (2010). *Public Speaking for Psychologists: A lighthearted guide to research presentations, job talks, and other opportunities to embarrass yourself.* Washington, DC: American Psychological Association.

Field, A. (2009). *Discovering Statistics Using SPSS* (3rd edition). London: Sage.

Field, A. (2013). *Discovering Statistics Using IBM SPSS Statistics* (4th edition). London: Sage.

Finlay, L. (2011). *Phenomenology for Therapists: Researching the lived world*. Chichester: Wiley.

Finlay, L. (2014). Embodying research. *Person-Centered and Experiential Psychotherapies, 13,* 4–18.

Finlay, L. & Ballinger, C. (Eds) (2006). *Qualitative Research for Allied Health Professionals: Challenging choices*. Chichester: Wiley.

Finlay, L. & Evans, K. (Eds) (2009). *Relational-centred Research for Psychotherapists: Exploring meanings and experience*. Chichester: Wiley.

Finlay, L. & Gough, B. (Eds) (2003). *Reflexivity: A practical guide for researchers in health and social science*. Oxford: Blackwell.

Finn, S. (2009). *Therapeutic Assessment: Using psychological testing to help clients change*. London: Routledge Mental Health.

Fishman, D.B. (1999). *The Case for a Pragmatic Psychology*. New York: New York Universities Press.

Flavin-Hall, D.K. (2013). *How Can I Overcome My Fear of Public Speaking*. Mayo Clinic Website, www.mayoclinic.com/health/fear-of-public-speaking/AN01979. Accessed on 28/02/13.

Flyvbjerg, B. (2006). Five misunderstandings about case-study research. *Qualitative Inquiry, 12,* 219–245.

Gelso, C.J. (2006). On the making of a scientist-practitioner: A theory of research training in professional psychology. *Training and Education in Professional Psychology, 1,* 3–16.

Girden, E.R. & Kabacoff, R.I. (2010). *Evaluating Research Articles from Start to Finish* (3rd edition). Thousand Oaks, CA: Sage.

Glaser, B.G. & Strauss, A. (1967). *The Discovery of Grounded Theory: Strategies for qualitative research*. Chicago, IL: Aldine.

Gomm, R., Needham, G. & Bullman, A. (2000). *Evaluating Research in Health and Social Care*. London: Sage.

Grimes, D. & Schulz, K. (2002). An overview of clinical research: The lay of the land. *Lancet, 359,* 57–61.

Guba, E.G. & Lincoln, Y.S. (1994). Competing paradigms in qualitative research. In N.K. Denzin & Y.S. Lincoln (Eds), *Handbook of Qualitative Research* (pp. 105–117). London: Sage.

Guest, G., MacQueen, K.M. & Namey, E.E. (2012). *Applied Thematic Analysis*. Thousand Oaks, CA: Sage.

Gurman, A.S. (1977). The patient's perception of the therapeutic relationship. *Effective Psychotherapy: A Handbook of Research* (pp. 503–543). Michigan: Pergamon Press.

Haley, D. (2012). *Pharmageddon*. Berkeley, CA: University of California Press.

Halling, S. (2002). Making phenomenology accessible to a wider audience. *Journal of Phenomenological Psychology, 33(1),* 19–38.

Halling, S., Leifer, M. & Rowe, J.O. (2006). Emergence of the dialogal approach: Forgiving another. In C.T. Fischer (Ed.), *Qualitative Research Methods for Psychologists: Introduction through empirical examples* (pp. 247–278). New York: Academic Press.

Hanley, T., Lennie, C. & West, W. (2013). *Introducing Counselling and Psychotherapy Research*. London: Sage.

Hart, C. (2000). *Doing a Literature Review: Releasing the social science research imagination.* London: Sage.

Hatcher, R.L. & Gillaspy, J.A. (2006). Development and validation of a revised short form of the Working Alliance Inventory. *Psychotherapy Research, 16*, 12–25.

Hayes, J.A., Gelso, C.J. & Hummel, M.S. (2011). Managing counter-transference. In J.C. Norcross (Ed.), *Psychotherapy Relationships that Work* (pp. 239–259). New York: Oxford University Press.

Henwood, K. & Pidgeon, N. (1994). Beyond the qualitative paradigm: Introducing diversity within qualitative psychology. *Journal of Community and Applied Social Psychology, 4*, 225–238.

Heppner, P.P., Wampold, B.E. & Kivlighan, D.M., Jr (2008). *Research Design in Counselling* (3rd edition). Belmont, CA: Thomson Brooks/Cole.

Hieftje, K. (2012). The role of social networking sites in the memorialization of college students. In C. Sofka, I.N. Cupitt & K.R. Gilbert (Eds), *Dying, Death and Grief in an Online Universe* (pp. 31–46). New York: Springer.

Hill, C.E. & Knox, S. (2013). Training and supervision in psychotherapy. In M.J. Lambert (Ed.), *Bergin and Garfield's Handbook of Psychotherapy and Behavior Change* (6th edition) (pp. 775–811). New York: Wiley.

Holaday, M., Smith, D.A. & Sherry, A. (2000). Sentence completion tests: A review of the literature and results of a survey of members of the society for personality assessment. *Journal of Personality Assessment, 74*, 371–383.

Iphofen, R. (2009). *Ethical Decision-making in Social Research.* Basingstoke: Palgrave Macmillan.

Israel, M. & Hay, I. (2006). *Research Ethics for Social Scientists.* London: Sage.

Jackson, J.L., Chui, H.T. & Hill, C.E. (2011). The modification of consensual qualitative research for case study research: An introduction to CQR-C. In C.E. Hill (Ed.), *Consensual Qualitative Research: A practical resource for investigating social science phenomena* (pp. 822–844). Washington, DC: American Psychological Association.

Jacobson, N.S. & Truax, P. (1991). Clinical significance: A statistical approach to defining meaningful change in psychotherapy research. *Journal of Consulting and Clinical Psychology, 59(1)*, 12–19.

Joffe, H. (2011). Thematic analysis. In D. Harper & A.R. Thompson (Eds), *Qualitative Methods in Mental Health and Psychotherapy: A guide for students and practitioners* (pp. 209–223). Chichester: Wiley.

Johannes, C.K. & Erwin, P.G. (2004). Developing multicultural competence: Perspectives on theory and practice. *Counselling Psychology Quarterly, 17(3)*, 329–338.

Johnson, K. & Scott, D. (1997). Confessional tales: An exploration of the self and other in two ethnographies. *The Australian Journal of Social Research, 4(1)*, 27–48.

Jones, J.H. (1993). *Bad Blood: The Tuskegee syphilis experiment.* New York: Free Press.

Jordan M., VanLare, A.B. & Conway, P.H. (2012). Value-based purchasing: National programs to move from volume to value. *New England Journal of Medicine, 367*, 292–295.

Karam, E.A. & Sprenkle, D.H. (2010). The research informed clinician: A guide to training the next-generation. *Journal of Marital and Family Therapy, 36(3)*, 307–319.

Kasket, E. (2012). Continuing bonds in the age of social networking: Facebook as a modern-day medium. *Bereavement Care, 31(2)*, 62–69.

Kasket, E. & Gil-Rodriguez, E. (2011). The identity crisis in trainee counselling psychology research. *Counselling Psychology Review, 26(4)*, 20–30.

Kasper, L.B., Hill, C.E. & Kivlighan, D.E. (2008). Therapist immediacy in brief psychotherapy: Case study 1. *Psychotherapy: Theory, Research, Practice and Training, 45*, 281–297. Available at: www.safranlab.net/uploads/7/6/4/6/7646935/kasper__hill_immediacy_2008.pdf.

Kazdin, A.E. (2003). *Research Design in Clinical Psychology* (4th edition). Boston, MA: Allyn and Bacon.

Keel, P.K. & Brown, T.A. (2010). Update on course and outcome in eating disorders. *International Journal of Eating Disorders, 43*, 195–204.

King, N. & Horrocks, C. (2010). *Interviews in Qualitative Research.* London: Sage.

Kirsten, L.T., Grenyer, B.F.S., Wagner, R. & Manicavasagar, V. (2008). Impact of separation anxiety on psychotherapy outcomes for adults with anxiety disorders. *Counselling and Psychotherapy Research, 8(1)*, 36–42.

Kroenke, K., Spitzer, R.L. & Williams, J.B. (2001). The PHQ-9: Validity of a brief depression severity measure. *Journal of General Internal Medicine, 16(9)*, 606.

Kuenzli, F. (2009). Turning away from difficult problems with gentle solutions: Therapy with a teenager battling with anger. *The International Gestalt Journal, 32*, 138–164. Available at: www.reflexivepractices.com.

Kvale, S. (1996). *Interviews: An introduction to qualitative research interviewing.* Thousand Oaks, CA: Sage.

Kvale, S. (2008). *Doing interviews.* London: Sage.

Lambert, M.J. (1992). Psychotherapy outcome research: Implications for integrative and eclectic therapists. In J.C. Norcross & M.R. Goldfried (Eds), *Handbook of Psychotherapy Integration* (pp. 94–129). New York: Basic Books.

Lambert, M.J. (2010). *Prevention of Treatment Failure: The use of measuring, monitoring & feedback in clinical practice.* Washington, DC: APA Press.

Lambert, M.J., & Ogles, B.M. (2004). The efficacy and effectiveness of psychotherapy. In M.J. Lambert (Ed.), *Bergin and Garfield's handbook of psychotherapy and behavior change* (5th edition) (pp. 139–193). New York: Wiley.

Layard, R. (2006). *The Depression Report: A new deal for depression and anxiety disorders.* London: London School of Economics, The Centre for Economic Performance's Mental Health Policy Group.

Lepper, G. & Riding, N. (2006). *Researching the Psychotherapy Process: A practical guide to transcript-based methods.* Basingstoke: Palgrave Macmillan.

Levy, J.A., Glass, C.R., Arnkoff, D.B., Gersheffski, J.J. & Elkin, I. (1996). Clients' perceptions of treatment for depression. 2. Problematic or hindering aspects. *Psychotherapy Research, 6*, 249–262.

Lincoln, Y.S. & Guba, E.A. (1985). *Naturalistic Inquiry.* Beverly Hills, CA: Sage.

Llewelyn, S. (1988). Psychological therapy as viewed by clients and therapists. *British Journal of Clinical Psychology, 27*, 223–238.

Locke, L.F., Silverman, S.J. & Spirduso, W.W. (2010). *Reading and Understanding Research.* (3rd edition). Thousand Oaks, CA: Sage.

Luborsky, L. & Crits-Christoph, P. (1998). *Understanding Transference.* New York: Basic Books.

Luca, M. (2012). Therapeutic activities and psychological interventions by cognitive behavioural and psychodynamic therapists working with medically unexplained symptoms: A qualitative study. *Counselling and Psychotherapy Research, 12(2)*, 118–127.

Marek, P.J., Christopher, A.N. & Koenig, C.S. (2001). *Guidelines for Preparing Posters Using PowerPoint™ Presentation Software.* Davidson, NC: The Office of Teaching Resources in

Psychology. Retrieved 29 October 2013 from http://teachpsych.org/resources/Documents/otrp/resources/marek01.pdf.

Martin, P. (2005). Sturdy roots for the graceful eucalyptus: The parallel process of integrating counselling around a client's needs and aligning research paradigms with methodology. *Counselling Psychology Quarterly, 18(3)*, 207–213.

Mason, M. (2010). Sample size and saturation in PhD studies using qualitative interviews. *Qualitative Social Research, 11(3)*, 1–19.

Matthews, S.H. (2005). Crafting qualitative research articles on marriages and families. *Journal of Marriage and Family, 67(4)*, 799–808.

McCrone, P., Knapp, M., Proudfoot, J., Ryden, C., Cavanagh, K., Shapiro, D.A., Ilson, S., Gray, J.A., Goldberg, D., Mann, A., Marks, I., Everitt, B. & Tylee, A. (2004). Cost-effectiveness of computerised cognitive-behavioural therapy for anxiety and depression in primary care: Randomised controlled trial. *British Journal of Psychiatry, 185*, 55–62.

McDonnell, L., Stratton, P., Butler, C. & Cape, N. (2012). Developing research-informed practitioners: An organisational perspective. *Counselling and Psychotherapy Research, 12*, 167–177.

McFarlane, B. (2009). *Researching with Integrity: The ethics of academic enquiry*. Abingdon: Routledge.

McLeod, J. (1999). *Practitioner Research in Counselling*. London: Sage.

McLeod, J. (2001). *Qualitative Research in Counselling and Psychotherapy*. London: Sage.

McLeod, J. (2003). *Doing Counselling Research* (2nd edition). London: Sage.

McLeod, J. (2010a). Process research: Using qualitative methods to explore therapeutic practice around issues of fear and sadness. In M. Barker, A. Vossler & D. Langdridge (Eds), *Understanding Counselling and Psychotherapy* (pp. 307–326). London: Sage.

McLeod, J. (2010b). *Case Study Research in Counselling and Psychotherapy*. London: Sage.

McLeod, J. (2011). *Qualitative Research in Counselling and Psychotherapy* (2nd edition). London: Sage.

McLeod, J. (2012). Engagement in research self-rating scale. Paper presented at the BACP Research Conference in Edinburgh, UK, 11–12 May.

McLeod, J. (2013). *An Introduction to Research in Counselling and Psychotherapy*. London: Sage.

McLeod, J. & Cooper, M. (2011). A protocol for systematic case study research in pluralistic counselling and psychotherapy. *Counselling Psychology Review, 26*, 47–58.

McLeod, J., Elliott, R. & Wheeler, S. (2010). *Developing and Enhancing Research Capacity in Counselling and Psychotherapy: A research training manual*. Leicester: British Association for Counselling and Psychotherapy.

McLeod, J. & McLeod, J. (2011). *Counselling Skills: A practical guide for counsellors and helping professionals* (2nd edition). Maidenhead: Open University Press.

Medical Research Council (2012). *Good Research Practice: Principles and Guidelines*. Swindon: Medical Research Council.

Mellor-Clark, J., Connell, J., Barkham, M. & Cummins, P. (2001). Counselling outcomes in primary health care: A CORE system data profile. *European Journal of Psychotherapy, Counselling and Health, 4*, 65–86.

Midgley, N. (2006). The 'inseperable bond between cure and research': Clinical case study as a method of psychoanalytic inquiry. *Journal of Child Psychotherapy, 32*, 122–147.

Midgley, N. (2012). The therapist's perspective on participation in research: Learning from experience. *Counselling and Psychotherapy Research, 12,* 165–166.

Miller, R.B. (2011). Real Clinical Trials (RCT) – Panels of psychological inquiry for transforming anecdotal data into clinical facts and validated judgments: Introduction to a pilot test with the case of 'Anna'. *Pragmatic Case Studies in Psychotherapy, 7(1),* 6–36.

Moller, N.P. & Rance, N. (2013). The good, the bad and the uncertainty: Trainees' perceptions of the personal development group. *Counselling and Psychotherapy Research, 13,* 282–289.

Moller, N.P., Timms, J. & Alilovic, K. (2009). Risky business or safety net? Trainee perceptions of personal therapy: A qualitative thematic analysis. *European Journal of Psychotherapy and Counselling, 11(4),* 369–384.

Monahan, B.J. (2010). Non-adherence to group therapy in a community drug and alcohol unit: A thematic analysis. Unpublished Masters dissertation, Auckland University of Technology, http://aut.researchgateway.ac.nz/handle/10292/1163.

Moodley, R. (2001). (Re)Searching for a client in two different worlds: Mind the research practice gap. *Counselling and Psychotherapy Research, 1(1),* 18–23.

Moran, P. (2011). Bridging the gap between research and practice in counselling and psychotherapy training: Learning from trainees. *Counselling and Psychotherapy Research, 11,* 171–178.

Morley, S. (2007). Single case methodology in psychological therapy. In S.J.E. Lindsay & G.E. Powell (Eds), *A Handbook of Clinical Adult Psychology* (3rd edition) (pp. 822–844). London: Brunner Routledge.

Morrow, S.L. (2005). Quality and trustworthiness in qualitative research in counseling psychology. *Journal of Counseling Psychology, 52,* 250–260.

Morrow-Bradley, C. & Elliott, R. (1986). Utilization of psychotherapy research by practicing psychotherapists. *American Psychologist,* Special Issue: *Psychotherapy Research, 41,* 188–197.

Munder, T., Gerger, H., Trelle, S. & Barth, J. (2011). Testing the allegiance bias hypothesis: A meta-analysis. *Psychotherapy Research, 21(6),* 670–684.

Nathan, P.E., Stuart, S.P. & Dolan, S.L. (2000). Research on psychotherapy efficacy and effectiveness: Between Scylla and Charybdis? *Psychological Bulletin, 126,* 964–981.

National Collaborating Centre for Mental Health (2009). *Depression in adults: The treatment and management of depression in adults.* Clinical Guideline 90. London: National Institute for Health and Clinical Excellence.

National Collaborating Centre for Mental Health (2011). *Service User Experience in Adult Mental Health: Improving the experience of care for people using adult NHS mental health services.* Clinical Guideline 136. London: National Institute for Health and Clinical Excellence.

National Collaborating Centre for Mental Health (2012). *Guidelines Manual Consultation.* London: National Institute for Health and Clinical Excellence.

Norcross, J.C. (Ed.) (2002). *Psychotherapy Relationships that Work: Therapist contributions and responsiveness to patients.* New York: Oxford University Press.

Norcross, J.C. (Ed.) (2011). *Psychotherapy Relationships that Work: Therapist contributions and responsiveness to patients* (2nd edition). New York: Oxford University Press.

Nyman, S.R., Dibb, B., Victor, C.R. & Gosney, M.A. (2012). Emotional well-being and adjustment to vision loss in later life: A meta-synthesis of qualitative studies. *Disability & Rehabilitation, 34(12)*, 971–981.

Ogilvie, A.J., Abreu, I. & Safran, J.D. (2005). What findings do psychotherapy researchers use in their own practice? A survey of the Society for Psychotherapy Research. *The New School Psychology Bulletin, 3*, 17–34.

Oliver, P. (2010). *The Student's Guide to Research Ethics* (2nd edition). Maidenhead: Open University Press.

Onwuegbuzie, A.J. & Wilson, V.A. (2003). Statistics anxiety: Nature, etiology, anteced-ents, effects, and treatments – a comprehensive review of the literature. *Teaching in Higher Education, 8(2)*, 195–209.

Pagoto, S.L., Spring, B., Coups, E.J., Mulvaney, S., Coutu, M. & Ozakinci, G. (2007). Barriers and facilitators of evidence-based practice perceived by behavioural science health professionals. *Journal of Clinical Psychology, 63*, 695–705.

Palmer, D. & Ward, K. (2007). 'Lost': Listening to the voices and mental health needs of forced migrants in London. *Medicine, Conflict and Survival, 23(3)*, 198–212.

Papanastasiou, E.C. (2005). Factor structure of the attitudes toward research scale. *Statistics Education Research Journal, 4(1)*, 16–26.

Pass, E.R. (2012). Combining expressive writing with an affect- and attachment-focused psychotherapeutic approach in the treatment of a single-incident trauma survivor: The case of 'Grace'. *Pragmatic Case Studies in Psychotherapy, 8(2)*, 60–112. Available at: http://pcsp.libraries.rutgers.edu.

Paulson, B.L., Everall, R.D. Stuart, J. (2001). Client perceptions of hindering experiences in counselling. *Counselling and Psychotherapy Research, 1(1)*, 53–61.

Perl, K.G. & Kahn, M.W. (1983). Psychology graduate students' attitudes toward research: A national survey. *Teaching of Psychology, 10*, 139–143.

Perren, S. (2010). *How to Write a Research Proposal*. BACP Information Sheet R9. Lutterworth: British Association for Counselling and Psychotherapy.

Ponterotto, J. (2005). Qualitative research in counseling psychology: A primer on research paradigms and philosophy of science. *Journal of Counseling Psychology, 52*, 126–136.

Poston, J.M. & Hanson, W.E. (2010). Meta-analysis of psychological assessment as a therapeutic intervention. *Psychological Assessment, 22*, 203–212.

Punch, K.F. (2006). *Developing Effective Research Proposals* (2nd edition). London: Sage.

Quality Assurance Agency (2008). *The Framework for Higher Education Qualifications in England, Wales and Northern Ireland*. Gloucester: Quality Assurance Agency.

Råbu, M., Halvorsen, M.S. & Haavind, H. (2011). Early relationship struggles: A case study of alliance formation and reparation. *Counselling and Psychotherapy Research, 11*, 23–33.

Rance, N.M., Moller, N.P. & Clarke, V. (2012). 'Eating disorders are not about food, they're about life': Client perspectives on anorexia nervosa treatment. Manuscript under review.

Rance, N.M., Moller, N.P. & Douglas, B.A. (2010). Eating disorder counsellors with eating disorder histories: A story of being 'normal'. *Eating Disorders, 18(5)*, 377–392.

Rawlins, M.D. (2008). De testimonio: On the evidence for decisions about the use of therapeutic interventions. The Harveian Oration of 2008, Royal College of Physicans. Reprinted in *The Lancet* (2008), *372*, 2152–2161.

Reeves, A. (2010). *Counselling Suicidal Clients*. London: Sage.

Reeves, A. & Seber, P. (2010). *Working with Suicidal Clients*. BACP Information Sheet P7. Lutterworth: British Association for Counselling and Psychotherapy.

Reeves, A., Shears, J. & Wheeler, S. (2010). *Tight Ropes and Safety Nets: Counselling suicidal clients*. Training DVD, University of Leicester.

Reicher, S. (2000). Against methodolatry: Some comments on Elliott, Fischer and Rennie. *British Journal of Clinical Psychology, 39*, 1–6.

Rennie, D. (1994). Human science and counselling psychology: Closing the gap between research and practice. *Counselling Psychology Quarterly, 7(3)*, 235–250.

Rhodes, J. & Smith, J.A. (2010). 'The top of my head came off': An interpretative phenomenological analysis of the experience of depression. *Counselling Psychology Quarterly, 23(4)*, 399–409.

Ridley, D. (2008). *The Literature Review: A step-by-step guide for students*. London: Sage.

Riessman, C.K. (2007). *Narrative Methods for the Human Sciences*. Thousand Oaks, CA: Sage.

Riley, W.T., Schumann, M.F., Forman-Hoffman, V.L., Mihm, P., Applegate, B.W. & Asif, O. (2007). Responses of practicing psychologists to a website developed to promote empirically supported treatments. *Professional Psychology: Research and Practice, 38*, 44–53.

Robinson, S. (2011). Did five sessions of CBT help Linda? Unpublished MSc dissertation, University of Wales, Newport.

Rogers, A., Maidman, J. & House, R. (2011). The bad faith of evidence-based practice: Beyond counsels of despair. *Therapy Today, 22*, 26–29.

Rogers, C.R. (1951). *Client-centred Therapy*. Boston, MA: Houghton-Mifflin.

Rogers, C.R. (1961). *On Becoming a Person*. Boston, MA: Houghton-Mifflin.

Rogers, C.R. (1978). *Carl Rogers on Personal Power: Inner strength and its Revolutionary Impact*. London: Constable.

Rogers, C.R. (1980). *A Way of Being*. Boston, MA: Houghton-Mifflin.

Rosenhan, D.L. (1973). On being sane in insane places. *Science, 179*, 250–258.

Rowan, J. (2001). Counselling psychology and research. *Counselling Psychology Review, 16*, 7–8.

Royal National Institute of Blind People. (2012). *Sight Loss UK, 2012: The latest evidence*. London: Royal National Institute of Blind People.

Royalty, G.M., Gelso, C.J., Mallinckrodt, B. & Garrett, K.D. (1986). The environment and the student in counseling psychology: Does the research training environment influence graduate students' attitudes toward research? *The Counseling Psychologist, 14*, 9–30.

Sandelowski, M. (1994). Notes on transcription. *Research in Nursing & Health, 17*, 311–314.

Sanders, P. & Wilkins, P. (2010). *First Steps in Practitioner Research: A guide to understanding and doing research in counselling and health and social care*. Ross-on-Wye: PCCS Books.

Schielke, H.J., Fishman, J.L., Osatuke, K. & Stiles, W.B. (2009). Creative consensus on interpretations of qualitative data: The Ward method. *Psychotherapy Research, 19*, 558–565.

Schmitt Freire, E. (2006). Randomized controlled clinical trial in psychotherapy research: An epistemological controversy. *Journal of Humanistic Psychology, 46*, 323–335.

Shadish, W.R., Cook, T.D. & Campbell, D.T. (2002). *Experimental and Quasi-experimental Design for Generalized Causal Inference*. Boston, MA: Houghton-Mifflin.

Silver, C. & Fielding, N. (2008). Using computer packages in qualitative research. In C. Willig & W. Stainton Rogers (Eds), *The Sage Handbook of Qualitative Research in Psychology* (pp. 334–351). Los Angeles: Sage.

Skinner, A.E.G. & Latchford, G. (2006). Attitudes to counselling via the internet. A comparison between in-person counselling clients and Internet support group users. *Counselling and Psychotherapy Research, 6(3)*, 158–163.

Smith, J.A. (Ed.) (2008). *Qualitative Psychology: A practical guide to research methods*. London: Sage.

Smith, J.A., Flowers, P. & Larkin, M. (2009). *Interpretative Phenomenological Analysis: Theory, method and research*. London: Sage.

Smith, T.B., Domenech Rodriguez, M.M. & Bernal, G. (2011). Culture. In J.C. Nocross (Ed.), *Psychotherapy Relationships that Work: Evidence-based responsiveness* (2nd edition) (pp. 316–335). Oxford: Oxford University Press.

Snyder, C.R., Michael, S.T. & Cheavens, J.S. (1999). Hope as a foundation of common factors, placebos, and expectancies. In M. Hubble, B.L. Duncan & S.D. Miller (Eds), *The Heart and Soul of Change: What works in therapy* (pp. 179–200). Washington, DC: American Psychological Association.

Sofka, C., Cupitt, I.N. & Gilbert, K.R. (2012). *Dying, Death and Grief in an Online Universe*. New York: Springer.

Söllner, W., DeVries, A., Steixner, E., Lukas, P., Sprinzl, G., Rumpold, G. & Maislinger, S. (2001). How successful are oncologists in identifying patient distress, perceived social support, and need for psychosocial counselling? *British Journal of Cancer, 84(2)*, 179–185.

Speedy, J. (with Margie, Fay, Jack, Pauline & Jermaine Jones) (2005). Failing to come to terms with things: A multi-storied conversation about poststructuralist ideas and narrative practices in response to some of life's failures. *Counselling and Psychotherapy Research, 5(1)*, 65–73.

Spitzer, R.L., Kroenke, K., Williams, J.B. & Lowe, B. (2006). A brief measure for assessing generalized anxiety disorder: The GAD-7. *Archives of International Medicine, 166(10)*, 1092–1097.

Stephen, S. & Elliott, R. (2011). Developing the adjudicated case study method. *Pragmatic Case Studies in Psychotherapy, 7(1)*, 230–224.

Stephen, S., Elliott, R. & Macleod, R. (2011). Person-centred therapy with a client experiencing social anxiety difficulties: A hermeneutic single case efficacy design. *Counselling and Psychotherapy Research, 11*, 55–66.

Stewart, R.E. & Chambless, D.L. (2010). Interesting practitioners in training in empirically supported treatments: Research reviews versus case studies. *Journal of Clinical Psychology, 66*, 73–95.

Stewart, R.E., Stirman, S.W. & Chambless, D.L. (2012). A qualitative investigation of practicing psychologists' attitudes toward research-informed practice: Implications for dissemination strategies. *Professional Psychology: Research and Practice, 43*, 100–109.

Stiles, W.B. (2007). Theory-building case studies of counselling and psychotherapy. *Counselling and Psychotherapy Research, 7*, 122–127.

Stiles, W.B., Barkham, M., Mellor-Clark, J. & Connell, J. (2008). Effectiveness of cognitive-behavioural, person-centred, and psychodynamic therapies in UK primary-care routine practice: Replication in a larger sample. *Psychological Medicine, 38,* 677–688.

Stinckens, N., Elliott, R. & Leijssen, M. (2009). Bridging the gap between therapy research and practice in a person-centered/experiential therapy training program: The Leuven Systematic Case Study Protocol. *Person-centered and Experiential Psychotherapies,* 8, 143–162.

Stone, C. & Elliott, R. (2011). Clients' experience of research within a research clinic setting. *Counselling Psychology Review, 26,* 71–86.

Storr, M. (2011). Against RCTs. *Therapy Today, 22.*

Stratton, P. (2005). A model to coordinate understanding of active autonomous learning. *Journal of Family Therapy, 27(3),* 217–236.

Stratton, P. (2007). Dialogical construction of the selves of trainees as competent researchers. *Journal of Family Therapy, 29,* 342–345.

Stratton, P. & Hanks, H. (2008). From therapeutic skills to research competence: Making use of common ground. *Human Systems, 19,* 153–171.

Strauss, A. & Corbin, J. (1998). *Basics of Qualitative Research: Grounded theory procedures and techniques* (2nd edition). Thousand Oaks, CA: Sage.

Strupp, H.H. (1980). Success and failure in time-limited psychotherapy. A systematic comparison of two cases: Comparison 1. *Archives of General Psychiatry, 37,* 595–603.

Surgenor, L.J., Maguire, S. & Beumont, P.J.V. (2004). Drop-out from inpatient treatment for anorexia nervosa: Can risk factors be identified at point of admission? *European Eating Disorders Review, 12,* 94–100.

Swift, J.K., Callahan, J.L., Ivanovic, M. & Kominiak, N. (2013). Further examination of the psychotherapy preference effect: A meta-regression analysis. *Journal of Psychotherapy Integration, 23(2),* 134–145.

Thériault, A. & Gazzola, N. (2006). What are the sources of feelings of incompetence in experienced therapists? *Counselling Psychology Quarterly, 19(4),* 313–330.

Thériault, A. & Gazzola, N. (2008). Feelings of incompetence among experienced therapists: A substantive theory. *European Journal of Qualitative Research in Psychotherapy, 4,* 19–29.

Thomas, M. & Smith, A. (2007). An evaluation of counselling and rehabilitation courses for Chronic Fatigue Syndrome. *Counselling and Psychotherapy Research: Linking Research with Practice, 7(3),* 164–171.

Thurin, J.M., Thurin, M. & Midgley, N. (2012). Does participation in research lead to changes in attitudes among clinicians? Report on a survey of those involved in a French practice research network. *Counselling and Psychotherapy Research, 12(3),* 187–193.

Thurston, M., Thurston, A. & McLeod, J. (2012). Counselling for sight loss: Using hermeneutic single case efficacy design methods to explore outcome and common factors. *Counselling Psychology Review, 27,* 56–70.

Timulak, L. (2008a). Significant events in psychotherapy: An update of research findings. Paper presented at the ScotCon/Scottish SPR Seminars, Glasgow.

Timulak, L. (2008b). *Research in Psychotherapy and Counselling.* London: Sage.

Tischler, V., Rademeyer, A. & Vostanis, P. (2007). Mothers experiencing homelessness: Mental health, support and social care needs. *Health & Social Care in the Community, 15(3),* 246–253.

Tracey, A., McElearney, A., Adamson, G. & Shevlin, M. (2009). Practitioners' views and experiences of participating in a school counseling evaluation study. *Counselling and Psychotherapy Research, 9,* 193–203.

Tracy, S.J. (2010). Qualitative quality: Eight 'big-tent' criteria for excellent qualitative research. *Qualitative Inquiry, 16(10),* 837–851.

Twigg, E. (2012). *A Study of Excellence: Use of the CORE system in My Sister's Place counselling service,* CORE IMS Occasional Paper. Rugby: CORE IMS Ltd.

Tryon, G.S., Blackwell, S.C. & Hammel, E.F. (2007). A meta-analytic examination of client–therapist perspectives and the working alliance. *Psychotherapy Research, 17,* 629–642.

UKCP (2012). Standards of Education and Training. UKCP SETs (Psychotherapy with Adults), Minimum Core Criteria. London: United Kingdom Council for Psychotherapy.

UKRIO (2009). *Code of Practice for Research.* Falmer: UK Research Integrity Office.

Unsworth, G., Cowie, H. & Green, A. (2012). Therapists' and clients' perceptions of routine outcome measurement in the NHS: A qualitative study. *Counselling and Psychotherapy Research, 12,* 71–80.

Vossler, A. (2004). The participation of children and adolescents in family counselling: The German experience. *Counselling and Psychotherapy Research, 4,* 54–61.

Walfish, S., McAlister, B., O'Donnell, P. & Lambert, M.J. (2012). An investigation of self-assessment bias in mental health providers. *Psychological Reports, 110,* 639–644.

Wallier, J., Vibert, S., Berthoz, S., Huas, C., Hubert, T. & Godart, M. (2009). Dropout from inpatient treatment for anorexia nervosa. *International Journal of Eating Disorders, 42,* 636–647.

Walsh, D. & Downe, S. (2005). Meta-synthesis method for qualitative research: A literature review. *Journal of Advanced Nursing, 50(2),* 204–211.

Weissman, M.M. & Sanderson, W.C. (2002). Problems and promises in modern psychotherapy: The need for increased training in evidence-based treatments. In B. Hamburg (Ed.), *Modern Psychiatry: Challenges in educating health professionals to meet new needs* (pp. 132–160). New York: Josiah Macy Foundation.

Wertz, F.J., Charmaz, K., McMullen, L.M., Josselson, R., Anderson, R. & McSpadden, E. (2011). *Five Ways of Doing Qualitative Analysis: Phenomenological psychology, grounded theory, discourse analysis, narrative research, and intuitive inquiry.* New York: Guilford Press.

Westen, D., Novotny, C.M. & Thompson-Brenner, H. (2004). The empirical status of empirically supported psychotherapies: Assumptions, findings, and reporting in controlled clinical trials. *Psychological Bulletin, 130,* 631–663.

Wetherell, M., Taylor, S. & Yates, S. (Eds) (2001). *Discourse as Data: A guide for analysis.* London: Sage.

Wheeler, S. & Elliott, R. (2008). What do counsellors and psychotherapists need to know about research? *Counselling and Psychotherapy Research, 8,* 133–135.

White, P. (2009). *Developing Research Questions: A guide for social scientists.* Basingstoke: Palgrave Macmillan.

Widdowson, M. (2012a). Perceptions of psychotherapy trainees of psychotherapy research. *Counselling and Psychotherapy Research, 13,* 176–186.

Widdowson, M. (2012b). TA treatment of depression: A hermeneutic single-case efficacy design study – 'Peter'. *International Journal of Transactional Analysis Research, 3,* 3–13. Also available at: www.ijtar.org.

Wilkinson, S. (1988). The role of reflexivity in feminist psychology. *Women's Studies International Forum, 11*, 493–502.

Wilkinson, S. (1998). Focus group methodology: A review. *International Journal of Social Research Methodology, 1*, 181–203.

Willig, C. (2008). *Introducing Qualitative Research in Psychology* (2nd edition). Maidenhead: Open University Press.

Yardley, L. (2008). Demonstrating validity in qualitative psychology. In J.A. Smith (Ed.), *Qualitative Psychology: A practical guide to research methods* (pp. 235–251). London: Sage.

Index